Student Study Guide

for use with

Traditions and Encounters
A Global Perspective on the Past
Volume II
From 1500 to the Present

Third Edition

Jerry H. Bentley
University of Hawai`i

Herbert F. Ziegler
University of Hawai`i

Updated and Revised for the Third Edition by
Kenneth E. Koons
Virginia Military Institute

Boston   Burr Ridge, IL   Dubuque, IA   Madison, WI   New York   San Francisco   St. Louis
Bangkok   Bogotá   Caracas   Kuala Lumpur   Lisbon   London   Madrid   Mexico City
Milan   Montreal   New Delhi   Santiago   Seoul   Singapore   Sydney   Taipei   Toronto

Student Study Guide for use with
TRADITIONS AND ENCOUNTERS: A GLOBAL PERSPECTIVE ON THE PAST: VOLUME II: FROM 1500 TO THE PRESENT
Jerry H. Bentley, Herbert F. Ziegler

1 2 3 4 5 6 7 8 9 0 BKM/BKM 0 9 8 7 6 5

ISBN 0-07-301395-1

www.mhhe.com

CONTENTS

INTRODUCTION

This study guide has been designed to help students improve their understanding of the world history textbook, *Traditions and Encounters: A Global Perspective on the Past,* 3rd Edition (Volume II: From 1500 to the Present), by Jerry H. Bentley and Herbert F. Ziegler. The intention of this volume is to promote student learning through a variety of formats that address different learning styles and strategies. People learn differently, and students are encouraged to make this study guide work for them.

CHAPTER INTRODUCTION

This section provides an introduction to the major themes and events in each chapter. Connections are emphasized within chapters and also to material from previous chapters. Students might find it useful to read this introduction before reading the chapter in the textbook in order to have a framework for approaching the text.

CHAPTER OUTLINE

The chapter outline follows the structure of the textbook closely, although not in as much detail. The outline can be useful in reviewing the chapter and also for clarifying a section that may have been difficult to understand. It should be understood, however, that the outline is a simplification and cannot be a substitute for the full text. Space has been provided for students to take notes as they read.

IDENTIFICATION: PEOPLE

The significant players in each chapter are listed here, and space has been provided to note the significant accomplishments of each. To do this efficiently, students should wait until completing the chapter before deciding what is most important about each figure. Notes should include the country of origin, dates, and significance to world history. Here is a sample:

> *Tokugawa Ieyasu:* Seventeenth-century Japanese shogun (military governor) who ended a period of civil war, unified Japan, and established a military dynasty that lasted until 1867.

IDENTIFICATION: TERMS/CONCEPTS

Likewise, the major terms and concepts for each chapter are listed with space for definitions. Students should be able to explain in their own words what each term means and why it is important to world history. Terms that involve difficult religious or political concepts or terms that appear in several chapters have been defined in the glossary at the end of the textbook. These terms are indicated with an asterisk (*). Here is a sample definition:

> *Indulgences:* The practice by the Catholic church of reducing time in purgatory (after death) in exchange for a donation to the Church; by the sixteenth century, subject to widespread abuse and the spark of the Protestant Reformation.

STUDY QUESTIONS AND INQUIRY QUESTIONS

These questions are offered to help frame students' reading of the text. There are two kinds of questions here: study questions ask for recall and comprehension of information, while inquiry questions ask for interpretation and application of new learning. Inquiry questions could easily become the subject of further research and discussion.

STUDENT QUIZ

A practice quiz is provided to help students review the details in each chapter. Students would do well to read the chapter first, take notes on the people, terms, and study questions, and then take the student quiz to test for overall comprehension. These are multiple-choice quizzes, with the answers provided in the back of the study guide.

MATCHING

This review activity targets the people, groups, places, or terms presented in the chapter. Again, students should first read the chapter carefully and then try the matching activity. Answers are provided.

SEQUENCING

Students are given four to seven related events and asked to put them in chronological order. These are not random and isolated incidents, but rather connected events. This exercise helps students recognize that global events are often related. Answers are provided.

QUOTATIONS

A series of quotes relevant to the chapter content are presented in this section. Students should be able to identify either the speaker or the point of view and explain the significance of the passage. Some quotes are taken directly from the text, while others reflect perspectives from the textbook and should be clear from the content. Answers are given in the back of the study guide.

MAP EXERCISES

These exercises ask students to work with visual displays of information. In some cases, students are asked to label outline maps in the study guide as an aid to learning. In other exercises, they are asked to interpret geographic information from maps in the textbook. At times other sorts of exercises, like graphing population trends, are included in this section.

CONNECTIONS

A pair—of people, concepts, or events—is suggested, and students must try to establish a historic connection. In some instances the connection is direct and causal, but in others it may be subtler. Students can use these pairs to test their own comprehension.

FILMS

Ours is a highly visual culture, and it often helps to see history enacted in order to understand how it has unfolded in human terms. To this end, a list of feature films has been provided to help students see world history as they read about it. Unfortunately, this section is uneven: there are far more films made about recent events and about Western history. Some films suggested here are excellent, and others are more entertainment than history. All the films can be purchased in the United States, but some of the foreign films may be more difficult to rent.

CHAPTER 23
TRANSOCEANIC ENCOUNTERS
AND GLOBAL CONNECTIONS

INTRODUCTION

Before 1500, there was considerable cross-cultural interaction between Europe and Asia and, to a lesser extent, with sub-Saharan Africa. With the voyages of discovery of the fifteenth century, these contacts accelerated and became global in reach. Russian adventurers built an empire that stretched across Eurasia, and they began to explore in the Pacific Ocean basin. Meanwhile, the Chinese and the Ottomans ventured into and explored the Indian Ocean basin. The impact of European contact on the previously isolated societies of the Americas and the Pacific islands was profound and devastating and will be discussed in detail in Chapter 25. This chapter considers the motives and methods of European trade and exploration between the fifteenth and the eighteenth centuries. Some common themes of this era include

- Mixed motives. European explorers acted from a complex mix of greed, daring, and missionary zeal. Christian princes, such as Prince Henry of Portugal, and Ferdinand and Isabel of Spain, underwrote voyages to expand Christianity. Equally compelling were the profits to be made in the spice trade, especially if Arab intermediaries could be eliminated.

- New technologies used in navigation. From Arab traders, the Portuguese borrowed the astrolabe and the cross staff and used these tools to determine their north/south position. Other new technologies included the magnetic compass, more flexible combinations of sails, improved shipbuilding, cannons, and more accurate navigational charts.

- Adventure. Curiosity and a sense of adventure also drew Europeans out into the world. Between 1500 and 1800, European mariners charted the oceans, seas, and coasts of the entire globe. Important geographic questions were resolved: the circumference of the earth, the quest for a northwest passage across North America, and the patterns of winds and currents.

- The Columbian exchange. Contact with European diseases was a demographic catastrophe for the populations of the Americas and the Pacific islands, who usually suffered 80 percent to 90 percent mortality within the first generation. The cross-cultural exchange was more beneficial for Europeans, who gained significant new food crops.

OUTLINE

I. The European reconnaissance of the world's oceans

    A. Motives for exploration

        1. Resource-poor Portugal searched for fresh resources

            a) From the thirteenth to the fifteenth century they ventured into the Atlantic

            b) Established sugar plantations in the Atlantic islands

2. The lure of direct trade without Muslim intermediaries

    a) Asian spice trade

    b) African gold, ivory, and slaves

3. Missionary efforts of European Christians

    a) New Testament urged Christians to spread the faith throughout the world

    b) Crusades and holy wars against Muslims in early centuries

    c) *Reconquista* of Spain inspired Iberian crusaders

4. Various motives combined and reinforced each other

B. The technology of exploration enabled European mariners to travel offshore

  1. Sternpost rudder and two types of sails enabled ships to advance against wind

  2. Navigational instruments

    a) Magnetic compass

    b) Astrolabe (and cross and back staffs)

  3. Knowledge of winds and currents enabled Europeans to travel reliably

    a) Trade winds north and south of the equator

    b) Regular monsoons in Indian Ocean basin

    c) The *volta do mar*

C. Voyages of exploration: from the Mediterranean to the Atlantic

  1. Prince Henry of Portugal encouraged exploration of west Africa

    a) Portuguese conquered Ceuta in north Africa in 1415

    b) Soon after, established trading posts at Sao Jorge da Mina, west Africa

    c) Dias rounded the Cape of Good Hope and entered the Indian Ocean, 1488

  2. Vasco da Gama of Portugal

    a) Crossed Indian Ocean; reached India, 1497; brought back huge profit

    b) Portuguese merchants built a trading post at Calicut, 1500

  3. Christopher Columbus, Genoese mariner

    a) Proposed sailing to Asian markets by a western route

    b) Sponsored by Catholic kings of Spain; sailed to Bahamas in 1492

  4. Columbus's voyage enabled other mariners to link eastern and western hemispheres

D. Voyages of exploration: from the Atlantic to the Pacific

  1. Ferdinand Magellan, Portuguese navigator, in service of Spain

    a) Crossed both the Atlantic and Pacific Oceans 1519–1522

    b) One ship out of five completed the circumnavigation of the world

    c) Magellan died in conflict in a Philippine island on the way home

2. Exploration of the Pacific took three centuries to complete

    a) Trade route between the Philippines and Mexico, by Spanish merchants

    b) English mariners searched for a northwest passage from Europe to Asia

3. American and Pacific explorations

    a) Vitus Bering led two maritime expeditions across Asia to the Pacific Ocean

    b) Other Russian explorers pushed farther into Alaska and west Canada

4. Captain James Cook (1728–1779), British explorer

    a) Led three expeditions to the Pacific, the Arctic, Australia; died in Hawai`i

    b) By late eighteenth century, Europeans had reasonably accurate geographical knowledge of the world

II. Trade and conflict in early modern Asia

  A. Trading-post empires

    1. Portuguese built more than fifty trading posts between west Africa and east Asia

    2. Afonso d'Alboquerque, sixteenth-century Portuguese commander in Indian Ocean

       a) Seized Hormuz in 1508, Goa in 1510, and Melaka in 1511

       b) Forced all merchant ships to purchase safe-conduct passes

       c) Portuguese hegemony grew weak by the late sixteenth century

    3. English and Dutch established parallel trading posts in Asian coasts

       a) English in India, the Dutch at Cape Town and Indonesia

       b) Sailed faster, cheaper, and more powerful ships than Portuguese

       c) Created an efficient commercial organization—the joint-stock company

    4. Formation of powerful, profitable joint-stock companies

       a) The English East India Company, founded in 1600

       b) The United East India Company (VOC), Dutch company founded in 1602

       c) Both were private enterprises, enjoyed government support, little oversight

  B. European conquests in southeast Asia

    1. Spanish conquest of the Philippines led by Legazpi, 1565

    2. Manila, the bustling port city, became the Spanish capital

       a) Spanish and Filipino residents massacred Chinese merchants by thousands

       b) Christianity throughout the archipelago

       c) Muslim resistance on southern island of Mindanao

    3. Conquest of Java by the Dutch

       a) Began with VOC trading city of Batavia in 1619

       b) Policy: secure VOC monopoly over spice production and trade

       c) Enormous monopoly profit led to prosperity of Netherlands, seventeenth century

  C. The Russian empire in Asia

    1. By late eighteenth century Russia controlled Volga River to Caspian Sea

       a) Georgia: Orthodox Christians; absorbed into Russian empire, 1783

       b) Armenia and Azerbaijan also annexed

    2. Siberia less hospitable, but rich in resources, especially furs

       a) Conquest began in 1581 when cossacks crossed the Ural Mountains

       b) Local peoples forced to pay tribute in furs at Russian forts

    3. Native peoples of Siberia lived by hunting, fishing, or herding reindeer

       a) Some groups welcomed Russian trade

       b) Yakut people resisted and were brutally crushed; 70 percent of population killed

       c) Smallpox reduced more than half of total Siberian population

       d) Few Siberians converted to Christianity

    4. By 1763 population of Siberia doubled with addition of trappers, soldiers, serfs

  D. Commercial rivalries and the Seven Years' War

    1. Global competition and conflict

       a) Dutch forces expelled most Portuguese merchants from southeast Asia

       b) Conflict between English and French merchants over control of Indian cotton and tea from Ceylon, early eighteenth century

       c) Competition in the Americas among English, French, and Spanish forces

    2. The Seven Years' War (1756–1763)

       a) In Europe: British and Prussia against France, Austria, and Russia

       b) In India: fighting between British and French forces, each with local allies

       c) In the Caribbean: Spanish and French united to limit British expansion

       d) In North America: fights between British and French forces

    3. Outcome: British hegemony

       a) British gained control of India, Canada, Florida

       b) In Europe, Prussian armies held off massive armies of the enemies

       c) War paved the way for the British empire in the nineteenth century

III. Global exchanges

  A. The Columbian exchange

    1. Biological exchanges between Old and New Worlds

       a) Columbian exchange—global diffusion of plants, food crops, animals, human populations, and disease pathogens after Columbus's voyages

      b)   Permanently altered the earth's environment

  2. Epidemic diseases—smallpox, measles, diphtheria, whooping cough, and influenza—led to staggering population losses

      a)   Smallpox reduced Aztec population by 95 percent in one century after 1519

      b)   Contagious diseases had same horrifying effects in the Pacific islands

      c)   Between 1500 and 1800, one hundred million people died of imported diseases

  3. New foods and domestic animals

      a)   Wheat, horses, cattle, sheep, goats, and chickens went to Americas

      b)   American crops included maize, potatoes, beans, tomatoes, peppers, peanuts

      c)   Growth of world population: from 425 million in 1500 to 900 million in 1800

  4. Migration of human populations

      a)   Enslaved Africans were largest group of migrants from 1500 to 1800

      b)   Sizable migration from Europe to the Americas

      c)   Nineteenth century, European migration to South Africa, Australia, and Pacific islands

B. The origins of global trade

  1. Transoceanic trade: European merchants created a genuinely global trading system of supply and demand, linking the ports of the world

  2. The Manila galleons

      a)   Sleek, fast, heavily armed ships that sailed between Manila and Mexico

  3. Environmental effects of global trade

      a)   Animals, especially fur-bearers, heavily exploited as commodities

      b)   Global trade in furs, skins, and other animal products burgeoned

      c)   Global consumption led many species to extinction or brink of extinction

IDENTIFICATION: PEOPLE

What is the contribution of each of the following individuals to world history? Identification should include answers to the questions *who, what, where, when, how,* and *why is this person important?*

Prince Henry

Vasco da Gama

Christopher Columbus

Ferdinand Magellan

Vitus Bering

James Cook

Afonso d'Alboquerque

IDENTIFICATION: TERMS/CONCEPTS

State in your own words what each of the following terms means and why it is significant to a study of world history. (Terms with an asterisk are defined in the glossary.)

*Reconquista**

Cross staff*

*Volta do mar**

Seven Years' War

Columbian Exchange

Galleons

Joint-stock companies*

English East India Company*

VOC

STUDY QUESTIONS

1. What specific motives prompted European overseas voyages? Of all these motives, which do you think took precedence?

2. What new knowledge and technologies enabled fifteenth-century mariners to make long overseas voyages? Where did much of this new technology originate?

3. What was Columbus's goal in setting forth across the Atlantic in 1492? Was his voyage successful?

4. What was the significance of Magellan's voyage of 1519–1522? What were the some of the challenges for explorers of the Pacific Ocean?

5. What factors contributed to the dramatic economic growth and the ensuing population growth of Russia in the eighteenth century?

6. What were some of the striking aspects of the battle for Hormuz, as recounted by Afonso d'Alboquerque (page 614 in the textbook)? What was the strategic importance of Hormuz?

7. How were the English and Dutch trading companies organized and administered? How were these companies able to establish themselves in Asia?

8. Compare the Spanish conquest of the Philippines with the Dutch conquest of Indonesia. What kind of colony emerged in each case?

9. What factors led to the Seven Years' War in the eighteenth century? What was the outcome, globally, of that conflict?

10. What were some of the positive aspects of the Columbian exchange? What were some of the destructive aspects of this exchange? Give some specific examples.

11. Overall, what was the demographic impact (demography concerns the health and size of populations) of European contact with the New World?

INQUIRY QUESTIONS

1. Why was Portugal able to take an early lead in the exploration of the Indian Ocean? How did such a tiny country gain supremacy over the trade in that region? When and how did it lose that supremacy?

2. What were some of the new trade goods entering the world markets in the sixteenth century? How would European demand for these products affect overseas trade and colonization?

STUDENT QUIZ

1. Major motivations for European exploration of the world's oceans included all of the following *except*
   a. the search for raw materials and mineral resources.
   b. the search for new lands to settle and cultivate.
   c. population pressures in Europe.
   d. the desire to trade directly with Asian markets.
   e. the urge to extend Christianity beyond Europe.

2. Portuguese sailors were able to tack against the prevailing winds by using
   a. a combination of square and lateen sails.
   b. a sternpost rudder.
   c. a magnetic compass.
   d. an astrolabe.
   e. a sextant.

3. European and Arab mariners in the fifteenth century determined latitude by measuring the angle of the sun or pole star above the horizon with
   a. a magnetic compass.
   b. a telescope.
   c. an astrolabe or cross staff.
   d. a mechanical clock.
   e. none of the above.

4. By the mid-fifteenth century Portuguese mariners used a strategy called the *volta do mar* that
   a. enabled them to sail directly into the wind.
   b. enabled them to measure their location north and south of the equator with accuracy.
   c. allowed them to avoid the use of sails for extended periods of time.
   d. enabled them to sail with westerly winds rather than force their way against trade winds.
   e. allowed them to sneak up on their enemies unannounced.

5. The sea route to the Indian Ocean discovered by Vasco da Gama offered European merchants
   a. a chance to trade with Muslim intermediaries.
   b. a chance to buy goods directly from Indian merchants.
   c. quicker access to the slave trade of west Africa.
   d. proof that the earth was round.
   e. none of the above.

6. Christopher Columbus believed that by sailing west 2,500 nautical miles he would
   a. reach the Canary Islands and initiate a spice trade with the natives.
   b. find a direct and profitable route to Japan.
   c. discover a new continent and lost city of gold.
   d. find a quick passage around Africa.
   e. none of the above.

7. By 1800 European exploration of the Pacific Ocean resulted in all of the following *except*
   a. the discovery of a northwest passage from Europe to Asia.
   b. the first complete circumnavigation of the world.
   c. mapping of Australia, New Zealand, and the islands of the South Pacific.
   d. exploration of the coast of Alaska and the waters of the Arctic Ocean.
   e. European colonization of the Philippines.

8. Portuguese mariners succeeded in building a trading-post empire early in the sixteenth century for all of the following reasons *except*
   a. the ruthless policies of naval commander Afonso d'Alboquerque.
   b. the head start that Portugal enjoyed over other European powers in the exploration of the Indian Ocean.
   c. the use of heavy artillery to overpower other craft and onshore sights.
   d. the Portuguese control of strategic ports such as Hormuz and Melaka.
   e. the superiority of the Portuguese navy to English and Dutch forces.

9. The English East India Company and the VOC were privately owned companies that enjoyed all of the following advantages *except*
   a. funds to outfit ships and hire crews.
   b. commodities and money for trade.
   c. direct government supervision.
   d. the potential for tremendous profits.
   e. heavily armed ships to back up their demands.

10. Spanish forces were able to conquer the Philippines because of the
    a. assistance of China and India.
    b. lack of a centralized, powerful state to organize resistance.
    c. unhappiness of many of the Philippine people with Muslim rule.
    d. desire of the island chiefdoms to enter into a treaty with the Spanish.
    e. eagerness of many islanders to convert to Christianity.

11. The Dutch in Indonesia concentrated their efforts on
    a. establishing settler colonies.
    b. establishing a Dutch Reform mission to counter the Catholic presence in the Philippines.
    c. building a plantation society on the island of Java.
    d. dominating the spice trade through the Sundra Strait.
    e. all of the above.

12. Which trading post is incorrectly paired with a European power?
    a. Goa and Portugal
    b. Manila and Spain
    c. Hormuz and England
    d. Batavia and the Netherlands
    e. Cape Town and the Netherlands

13. Which of the following was *not* a significant presence in the Indian Ocean by the mid-eighteenth century?
    a. Britain
    b. France
    c. the Netherlands
    d. Portugal
    e. Russia

14. As a result of the Seven Years' War, Britain gained all the following *except*
    a. the French colonies in Canada.
    b. the French trading posts in India.
    c. Spanish Florida.
    d. Cape Town from the Dutch.
    e. Britain gained all of the above.

15. In spite of the isolation and harsh climate, Russians ventured over the Urals into Siberia in search of
    a. trade routes to China.
    b. access to the Pacific.
    c. gold and silver.
    d. furs.
    e. timber.

16. In the New World, the Columbian exchange generally resulted in
    a. the introduction of infectious diseases.
    b. the staggering loss of indigenous populations.
    c. the introduction of domesticated animals such as cattle and horses.
    d. the introduction of food crops such as wheat.
    e. all of the above.

17. Smallpox, influenza, and measles spread rapidly in the Americas because of
    a. the densely populated urban centers.
    b. poor hygiene and contaminated water.
    c. lack of previous exposure that would build natural immunity.
    d. lack of access to immunizations.
    e. all of the above.

18. In Eurasia, new American food crops translated into
    a. overall improvements in diet and nutrition.
    b. steady population growth in the sixteenth and seventeenth centuries.
    c. more varied cuisine.
    d. better forage for livestock.
    e. all of the above.

19. By 1750, all of the following regions were linked by trade and commerce *except*
    a. Australia.
    b. Brazil.
    c. India.
    d. Indonesia.
    e. South Africa.

20. Which region is incorrectly paired with a primary trade good?
    a. Brazil and sugar
    b. South Africa and wheat
    c. India and cotton
    d. Japan and spices
    c. Peru and silver

21. The Manila galleons were noted for
    a. carrying large cargoes between Mexico and the Philippines.
    b. supporting imperial communication since they were small and swift.
    c. dominating the trans-Atlantic slave trade.
    d. defeating the Portuguese in southeast Asia.
    e. all of the above.

MATCHING

Match these figures or groups with the statements that follow.

A. Vasco da Gama
B. Bartolomeu Dias
C. the Yakut
D. Prince Henry
E. King Fernando of Aragon

F. James Cook
G. Christopher Columbus
H. Ferdinand Magellan
I. Afonso d'Alboquerque
J. Vitus Bering

1. ___ English mariner who explored much of the Pacific Ocean while seeking a northwest passage across North America

2. ___ Portuguese mariner who sailed around Cape of Good Hope, sailed up the east coast of Africa, and reached India

3. ___ Iberian monarch who set up navigation schools and hired cartographers to create up-to-date maps

4. ___ Danish navigator hired by Russian officials to explore the north Pacific and determine whether Asia and North America were joined

5. ___ Portuguese who first rounded the Cape of Good Hope and reached the Indian Ocean

6. ___ Spanish mariner who crossed the Pacific Ocean and died in the Philippines, but whose ships succeeded in circling the globe

7. ___ Iberian monarch who sponsored a daring trans-Atlantic voyage in 1492

8. ___ Native inhabitants of Siberia who resisted Russian rule and were brutally suppressed

9. ___ Genoese mariner who miscalculated the distance from Europe west to Asia and stumbled on an unknown landmass

10. ___ Portuguese admiral who seized in rapid succession, Hormuz, Goa, and Melaka

SEQUENCING

Place the following clusters of events in chronological order. Consider carefully how one event leads to another, and try to determine the internal logic of each sequence.

A.

_____ Bartolomeu Dias reaches the Cape of Good Hope.

_____ A Portuguese fleet sacks the Swahili city-states.

_____ Prince Henry of Portugal gathers the best cartographers and mariners of Europe in his tiny kingdom.

_____ The Portuguese conquer Melaka.

_____ Vasco da Gama sails up the east coast of Africa and crosses the Indian Ocean.

B.

_____ The Portuguese overseas empire proves fragile and difficult to defend.

_____ Soon after its founding in the fourteenth century, Melaka becomes a powerful Muslim city-state by controlling the trade and traffic through the Strait of Melaka.

_____ Mercenaries and merchant ships in the employ of the Dutch East India Company seize Melaka.

_____ Arab traders bring Islam to southeast Asia soon after the life of the Prophet; by the eleventh century, it has become a prominent force in the region.

_____ From their base at Goa, a Portuguese fleet under Commander d'Alboquerque seizes Melaka and kills all resident Arab merchants.

QUOTATIONS

For each of the following quotes, identify the speaker, if known, or the point of view. What is the significance of each passage?

1. "But it seemed to me that they were a people very poor in everything. All of them go as naked as their mothers bore them. . . . They do not carry arms nor are they acquainted with them, because I showed them swords and they took them by the edge and through ignorance cut themselves. . . . I believe that they would become Christians very easily, for it seemed to me that they had no religion. . . . They are very gentle and do not know what evil is; nor do they kill others, nor steal. . . . And they are credulous and aware that there is a God in heaven and convinced that we come from the heavens; and they say very quickly any prayer that we tell them to say. . . . Your Highnesses ought to resolve to make them Christians."

2. "He ordered a broadside to be fired. The bombardiers took aim so that with the first two shots they fired they sent two large ships which were in front of them, with all their men, to the bottom—one being the prince of Cambay's ship. . . . Manuel Telez, after having caused great

slaughter upon some vessels, . . . ran into a large vessel that lay close to him and killed a part of the men in it, while the rest of the crew threw themselves into the sea, and those who were heavily armed went down at once."

MAP EXERCISES

1. The *volta do mar* was used to help Iberian mariners sail to and from the Caribbean Sea. Use the information about winds and currents on Map 23.1 (pages 602–603 in the textbook) to explain how this was done. Where else would this information have been useful?

2. Using the information on Map 23.1, determine the best route and, if possible, the best season for travel to and from each of the following:

   - Portugal to Brazil
   - Goa to Mozambique
   - England to the Bahamas
   - England to Hawai`i
   - Mexico to Manila

3. List all the places charted by James Cook in his three voyages to the Pacific Ocean (see Map 23.3, pages 610–611). Then try to list all the significant geographic facts that Cook either discovered or confirmed. You can start your list with "The ice pack of Antarctica."

4. On the outline map of Asia below, locate and label the following trading cities. Indicate by color or symbol the European country that held each city (see Map 23.4, page 615).
   Batavia, Bombay, Calicut, Calcutta, Colombo, Goa, Hormuz, Macau, Madras, Manila, Melaka, Nagasaki
   Which European power appears to have had the strongest presence in India by 1700? Which appears to have had the strongest presence in southeast Asia?

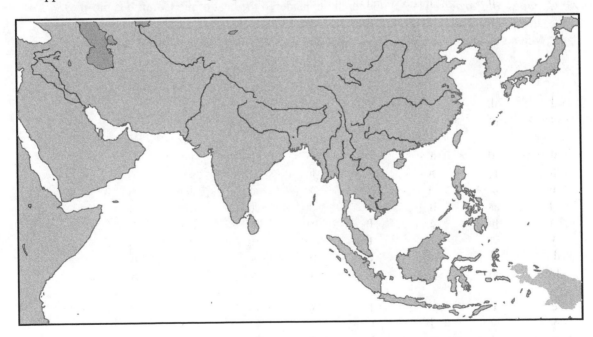

5. Create a chart of the Columbian exchange. Divide the chart between the Americas and Eurasia. List for each region the significant plants, food crops, domestic animals, and disease pathogens contributed by each region. (Some additional research would provide more details for this chart.)

CONNECTIONS

In fifty words or less, explain the relationship between each of the following pairs. How does one lead to or foster the other? Be specific in your response.

- *reconquista* and Columbus's voyage
- the cross staff and the settlement of Cape Town
- corn-and-potatoes and global migrations
- spice trade and missionaries
- smallpox and population growth

FILMS

Squanto: A Warrior's Tale (1994). Shows the tragic consequences of European and Native American contact in New England; the hero is seized by English explorers and converted to Christianity. He returns to find his village destroyed by epidemic. Ends with the Pilgrim settlement.

Last of the Mohicans (1992). The hero, Hawkeye, an American settler raised by the Mohican Indians, is forced to serve as a guide for British troops on the New York frontier during the Seven Years' War. Vivid battle scenes of eighteenth-century hand-to-hand combat. With Daniel Day-Lewis.

1492: Conquest of Paradise (1992). Generally considered the best of the Columbus bio-pics. Directed by Ridley Scott and starring Gerard Depardieu as Columbus and Sigourney Weaver as Queen Isabella. Visually stunning, historically reasonably accurate.

CHAPTER 24
THE TRANSFORMATION OF EUROPE

<u>INTRODUCTION</u>

This chapter presents the dramatic transformation of Europe between 1500 and 1800 from a subregion of Eurasia to a dynamic global powerhouse. The expansion of European powers overseas is addressed in Chapters 22 and 23. Here we will consider some of the internal changes that enabled the nations of western Europe, in particular, to assume such preeminence. This transformation occurred simultaneously and on multiple levels. Also, this chapter considers state-building and social and economic change in Russia under Peter I and Catherine II.

- Religious transformation. The Protestant Reformation, launched by Martin Luther in 1517 in Germany, successfully challenged the monopoly of the Roman Catholic church on western Christendom. The printing press, recently introduced to Europe from China, advanced the ideas and texts of the Reformation throughout Europe.

- Political transformation. Powerful nation-states evolved with the resources and institutions to advance national interests abroad. At the same time, two models for political order emerged, represented by the absolutist monarchies of France and Spain and the constitutional monarchies of England and the Netherlands.

- Economic transformation. The emergence of capitalism is evident in changes to the structures of banking, finance, and manufacturing. Adam Smith advocated a free market economy, with prices and wages determined through competition.

- Intellectual transformation. New technologies and new scientific discoveries of the sixteenth and seventeenth centuries fueled debate about the nature of the universe and called into question the authority of the Church in such matters. This discussion eventually led to the Enlightenment of the eighteenth century, an intellectual movement that raised important questions about the nature of humanity, religion, and political authority.

<u>OUTLINE</u>

I.   The fragmentation of western Christendom

   A. The Protestant Reformation

      1. Martin Luther (1483–1546) attacked the sale of indulgences, 1517

         a) Attacked corruption in the Roman Catholic church; called for reform

         b) His argument was reproduced with printing presses and widely read

         c) Enthusiastic popular response from lay Christians, princes, and many cities

         d) By mid-sixteenth century, half the German people adopted Lutheran Christianity

      2. Reform spread outside Germany

         a) Protestant movements popular in Swiss cities, Low Countries

  b) English Reformation sparked by King Henry VIII's desire for divorce

 3. John Calvin, French convert to Protestantism

  a) Organized model Protestant community in Geneva in the 1530s

  b) Calvinist missionaries were successful in Scotland, Low Countries, also in France and England

B. The Catholic Reformation

 1. The Council of Trent, 1545–1563, directed reform of Roman Catholic church

 2. The Society of Jesus (Jesuits) founded 1540 by Ignatius Loyola

  a) High standards in education

  b) Became effective advisors and missionaries worldwide

C. Witch-hunts and religious wars

 1. Witch-hunts in Europe

  a) Theories and fears of witches intensified in the sixteenth century

  b) Religious conflicts of Reformation fed hysteria about witches and devil worship

  c) About sixty thousand executed, 95 percent of them women

 2. Religious wars between Protestants and Catholics throughout the sixteenth century

  a) Civil war in France for thirty-six years (1562–1598)

  b) War between Catholic Spain and Protestant England, 1588

  c) Protestant provinces of the Netherlands revolted against rule of Catholic Spain

 3. The Thirty Years' War (1618–1648), the most destructive European war up to WWI

  a) Began as a local conflict in Bohemia; eventually involved most of Europe

  b) Devastated the Holy Roman Empire (lost one-third population)

II. The consolidation of sovereign states

A. The attempted revival of empire

 1. Charles V (reigned 1519–1556), Holy Roman emperor

  a) Inherited a vast empire of far-flung holdings

  b) Unable to establish a unified state

  c) Pressures from France and Ottomans halted expansion of the empire

B. The new monarchs of England, France, and Spain

 1. Enhanced state treasuries by direct taxes, fines, and fees

  a) State power enlarged and more centralized

  b) Standing armies in France and Spain

  c) Reformation increased royal power and gave access to wealth of the Church

 2. The Spanish Inquisition, Catholic court of inquiry, founded 1478

a) Intended to discover secret Muslims and Jews

b) Used by Spanish monarchy to detect Protestant heresy and political dissidents

C. Constitutional states

1. Constitutional states of England and the Netherlands: political experiments in which states harnessed popular support to magnify state power

a) Characterized by limited powers, individual rights, and representative institutions

b) Constitutional monarchy in England evolved out of a bitter civil war, 1642–1649

c) In the Netherlands, representative government emerged after a long struggle for independence

d) In both states, constitutional government enabled merchants to flourish

2. The English Civil War

a) Tensions between kings and parliament over taxation and religion

b) Kings tried to institute new taxes without parliamentary approval

c) Religion: Anglican kings vs. Calvinists (Puritans)

d) Civil War ensued; Charles I beheaded

3. Glorious Revolution (1688–1689)

a) Restoration of monarchy in 1660 after period of Puritan dictatorship

b) Continuing conflict between kings and parliament resulted in deposition of King James II; William and Mary assume throne

c) New arrangement: kings rule in cooperation with Parliament

4. The Dutch Republic

a) King Philip II of Spain controlled the Netherlands

b) Philip, a devout Catholic, suppressed Calvinism there, provoking rebellion

c) In 1581, organization of the United Provinces as a Dutch Republic

D. Absolute monarchies

1. Based on the theory of the divine right of kings

2. Cardinal Richelieu, French chief minister 1624–1642, crushed power of nobles

3. The Sun King of France, Louis XIV (reigned 1643–1715)

a) Model of royal absolutism: the court at Versailles

b) Large standing army kept order

c) Promoted economic development: roads, canals, industry and exports

4. Absolutism in Russia

a) By 1600, Russian a vast Eurasian empire

b) Romanov Dynasty (1613–1917) greatly centralized government

    c) Peter I (reigned 1682–1725) transformed Russia using western European models

    d) Fascinated with technology, Peter imposed program of rapid modernization

        (1) Russian industries to incorporate the most advanced science and technology

        (2) Russians sent abroad to study

        (3) Peter himself traveled to Europe to study government, military, and industry

    e) Military reform: to build powerful, modern army

        (1) Offered better pay and modern weapons to peasants

        (2) Aristocratic officers ordered to study mathematics and geometry

        (3) Built navy for expansion into Baltic and northern seas

    f) Bureaucratic reform: to facilitate collection of taxes and improve administrative efficiency

    g) Social reforms challenged established customs and provoked protest

        (1) Ordered subjects to wear western clothing

        (2) Ordered men to shave beards

    h) St. Petersburg built by Peter in 1703

        (1) New capital on the Baltic Sea

        (2) Headquarters for Russian navy, administrative center for government

    i) Catherine II (reigned 1762–1795) continued administrative reforms

        (1) Divided empire into fifty administrative provinces

        (2) Promoted economic development

        (3) Worked to improve conditions among peasants and to eliminate cruel punishments

    j) Pugachev's Rebellion in Caucasus (1773–1774): the end of Catherine's reforms

        (1) Adventurers, exiles, peasants, and serfs, led by Yemelian Pugachev

        (2) Killed thousands of nobles, officials, and priests; crushed by imperial army

        (3) Pugachev's rebellion soured Catherine on reform; afterwards she focused on preserving autocratic rule rather than promoting change based on western European models

5. The partitioning of Poland (three partitions, 1772–1797)

    a) A weak Poland partitioned out of existence by Austria, Prussia, and Russia

    b) Lesson: European states needed strong, effective government in order to survive

E. The European states system

1. The Peace of Westphalia (1648) ended the Thirty Years' War

a) Laid foundation for system of independent sovereign states

b) Abandoned notion of religious unity

c) Did not end war between European states

2. The balance of power

a) No ruler wanted to see another state dominate

b) Diplomacy based on shifting alliances in national interests

3. Military development costly and competitive

a) New armaments (cannons and small arms) and new military tactics

b) Other empires—China, India, and the Islamic states—did not keep pace

III. Early capitalist society

A. Population growth and urbanization

1. Population growth

a) American food crops improved Europeans' nutrition and diets

b) Increased resistance to epidemic diseases after the mid-seventeenth century

c) European population increased from 81 million in 1500 to 180 million in 1800

2. Urbanization

a) Rapid growth of major cities, for example, Paris from 130,000 in 1550 to 500,000 in 1650

b) Cities increasingly important as administrative and commercial centers

B. Early capitalism and protoindustrialization

1. The nature of capitalism

a) Private parties sought to take advantage of free market conditions

b) Economic decisions by private parties, not by governments or nobility

c) Forces of supply and demand determined price

2. Supply and demand

a) Merchants built efficient transportation and communication networks

b) New institutions and services: banks, insurance, stock exchanges

3. Joint-stock companies like EEIC and VOC organized commerce on a new scale

4. Capitalism actively supported by governments, especially in England and Netherlands

a) Protected rights of private property, upheld contracts, settled disputes

b) Chartered joint-stock companies and authorized these to explore, conquer, and colonize distant lands

5. The putting-out system, or protoindustrialization, of seventeenth and eighteenth centuries

a) Entrepreneurs bypassed guilds, moved production to countryside

b) Rural labor cheap, cloth production highly profitable

C. Social change in early modern Europe

1. Early capitalism altered rural society: improved material standards, increased financial independence of rural workers

2. Serfdom in Russia

a) Law code of 1649 placed serfs under strict control of noble landlords

b) Serfs were not slaves but could be sold as private property

c) A caste-like social order that restricted occupational and geographic mobility

d) Capitalism flourished in western Europe because of serfdom in eastern Europe

3. Profits and ethics

a) Medieval theologians considered profit making to be selfish and sinful

b) Adam Smith: society would prosper as individuals pursued their own interests

c) Capitalism generated deep social strains also: bandits, muggers, witch-hunting

4. The nuclear family strengthened by capitalism

a) Families more independent economically, socially, and emotionally

b) Love between men and women, parents and children became more important

IV. Science and enlightenment

A. The reconception of the universe

1. The Ptolemaic universe: A motionless earth surrounded by nine spheres

a) Could not account for observable movement of the planets

b) Compatible with Christian conception of creation

2. The Copernican universe

a) Nicolaus Copernicus suggested that the sun was the center of the universe, 1543

b) Implied that the earth was just another planet

B. The Scientific Revolution

1. Galileo Galilei (1564–1642)

a) Johannes Kepler (1571–1630) demonstrated planetary orbits to be elliptical

b) With a telescope, Galileo saw sunspots, moons of Jupiter, mountains of the moon

      c) Galileo's theory of velocity of falling bodies anticipated the modern law of inertia

  2. Isaac Newton (1642–1727)

      a) Published *Mathematical Principles of Natural Philosophy* in 1686

      b) Offered mathematical explanations of laws that govern movements of bodies

      c) Newton's work symbolized the scientific revolution—direct observation and mathematical reasoning

C. The Enlightenment

  1. Science and society

      a) Enlightenment thinkers sought natural laws that governed human society in the same way that Newton's laws governed the universe

      b) John Locke attacked divine-right theories of government, advocated constitutional government; sovereignty resides in people, not state or rulers

      c) Adam Smith: laws of supply and demand determine price

      d) Montesquieu: used political science to argue for political liberty

      e) Center of Enlightenment was France where philosophes debated issues of day

  2. Voltaire (1694–1778)

      a) French philosophe, champion of religious liberty and individual freedom

      b) Prolific writer; wrote some seventy volumes in life, often bitter satire

  3. Deism popular among thinkers of Enlightenment, including Voltaire

      a) Accepted the existence of a god but denied supernatural teachings of Christianity

      b) God the watchmaker ordered the universe according to rational and natural laws

  4. The theory of progress—the ideology of the philosophes

  5. Impact of Enlightenment

      a) Weakened the influence of organized religion

      b) Encouraged secular values based on reason rather than revelation

      c) Subjected society to rational analysis, promoted progress and prosperity

IDENTIFICATION: PEOPLE

What is the contribution of each of the following individuals to world history? Identification should include answers to the questions *who, what, where, when, how,* and *why is this person important?*

Martin Luther

John Calvin

Ignatius Loyola

Henry VIII

Charles V

Charles I

James II

Philip II

Richelieu

Louis XIV

Peter I (the Great)

Catherine II (the Great)

Yemelian Pugachev

Nicolaus Copernicus

Galileo Galilei

Isaac Newton

John Locke

Adam Smith

Voltaire

IDENTIFICATION: TERMS/CONCEPTS

State in your own words what each of the following terms means and why it is significant to a study of world history. (Terms with an asterisk are defined in the glossary.)

Indulgences

95 Theses

Protestant Reformation*

Catholic Reformation*

Jesuits

Thirty Years' War

Spanish Inquisition*

Glorious Revolution

Absolutism*

Divine right of kings

Versailles*

Capitalism*

Putting-out system*

Enlightenment*

Philosophes

Deism*

STUDY QUESTIONS

1. What theological concerns prompted Martin Luther's challenge of the authority of the Catholic church? What specific reforms did he advocate?

2. What were the circumstances of the English Reformation?

3. By the end of the sixteenth century, which European countries had become Protestant and which had remained Catholic?

4. What are some the reasons suggested for the widespread persecution of suspected witches in the sixteenth and seventeenth centuries?

5. Why was Charles V, despite such vast holdings, unable to establish a durable empire? What forces worked against such an empire in the sixteenth century?

6. How did European monarchs increase their power in the early modern era? What are some of the common characteristics of the new monarchs?

7. What is the fundamental difference between absolute monarchy and a constitutional government?

8. What factors encouraged the evolution of a constitutional government in England and the Netherlands?

9. How did Louis XIV maintain control over the nobles of France? What were some of the structures of absolutism during his reign?

10. What aspects of European culture did Peter I seek to graft onto Russian society? What aspects did he reject?

11. What factors led to the dramatic population growth of Europe between 1500 and 1700?

12. What are the characteristics of capitalism in the early modern age? What financial innovations supported the growth of capitalism in Europe?

13. What are some of the social changes that resulted from the growth of capitalism? What groups would have been most threatened by or resistant to these changes?

14. Three great minds collaborated to shatter the ancient Ptolemaic view of the universe. Note the contributions of Copernicus, Kepler, and Galileo. Who do you think made the most significant contribution? Who took the greatest risk?

15. In what ways can it be said that "Isaac Newton symbolized the scientific revolution"? What was his role in the Enlightenment?

16. What were the principal concerns of the philosophes of the Enlightenment? What solution did they propose?

INQUIRY QUESTIONS

1. To what extent did Martin Luther create the Protestant Reformation? Or was he simply the right man at the right time?

2. How does the Enlightenment alter perceptions toward the natural world? Toward religion?

3. Consider the passage in the textbook from Adam Smith's *Wealth of Nations*. How does capitalism benefit society, according to Smith? What role does Smith envision for the state in the national economy?

STUDENT QUIZ

1. Martin Luther's criticism of the Roman Catholic church was greatly aided by
    a. the printing press.
    b. the enthusiastic support of clergy in the Catholic church.
    c. local newspapers.
    d. active guilds and artisans.
    e. all of the above.

2. Martin Luther's work had an enthusiastic popular support because
    a. he attacked the sale of indulgences that the poor could not afford.
    b. many Christians shared his concern about the corruption of the Church.
    c. many German princes saw this as a way to break away from the Church.
    d. he supported the translation of the Bible from Latin into the vernacular languages.
    e. all of the above.

3. What political motivations encouraged the spread of Protestantism?
   a. Protestantism provided people an opportunity to overthrow monarchies.
   b. Protestantism encouraged people to claim their individual rights.
   c. Protestantism encouraged militarism in European nations.
   d. Protestantism provided monarchs an opportunity to break away from the political domination of Rome.
   e. All of the above.

4. In response to the challenges raised by the Protestant Reformation, the Catholic church
   a. launched a military campaign against the German states.
   b. abandoned its monasteries in Germany.
   c. abandoned the practice of selling indulgences.
   d. summoned a council to clarify doctrine and strengthen its spiritual commitment.
   e. all of the above.

5. What was the principal work of the Society of Jesus (the Jesuits)?
   a. to expose witches and heretics
   b. to be disciplined, educated representatives of the Church throughout the world
   c. to be soldiers for Jesus in the battle against the Protestants
   d. to direct the Court of the Inquisition on behalf of the pope
   e. to raise money for the Church by selling indulgences

6. One reason for the hysterical witch-hunts of the sixteenth century was that
   a. the conflicts of the Reformation contributed to a climate of suspicion and violence.
   b. unusual natural phenomena suggested supernatural causes.
   c. desperate people turned to magic to try to improve their lives.
   d. new texts claimed scientific evidence of witchcraft.
   e. all of the above.

7. The Thirty Years' War began when
   a. the pope tried to force his subjects to return to the Catholic church.
   b. Elizabeth I attempted to force Protestantism on Spain.
   c. Charles V attempted to imprison Martin Luther.
   d. the Holy Roman emperor tried to force his Bohemian subjects to return to Catholicism.
   e. Louis XIV invaded the Low Countries.

8. Who benefited most from the religious controversy generated by the Reformation?
   a. the people, because they had religious freedom
   b. the peasants, because they were able to leave the estates and move in to the cities
   c. centralizing monarchs, because they gained more independent authority
   d. the Catholic church, because it gained more committed supporters
   e. the Islamic empires, because Europe was divided and weakened

9. Which of the following was *not* part of Charles V's holdings?
   a. Austria
   b. England
   c. the Netherlands
   d. Hungary
   e. Spain

10. Charles V was unable to forge a united empire for all of the following reasons *except:*
    a. the Lutheran challenge sapped much of his attention.
    b. French kings undermined his efforts and allied themselves with his enemies.
    c. there was no central administration to the empire; each state was governed separately.
    d. his empire was geographically fragmented.
    e. he alienated the pope for failing to crush Luther.

11. The new monarchs were characterized by all of the following *except*
    a. large centrally administered bureaucracies.
    b. standing professional armies.
    c. increased state revenues through taxes.
    d. enhanced power at the expense of the nobles.
    e. a commitment to individual liberty.

12. The Spanish Inquisition relied on religious justifications to advance what political ends?
    a. increasing the revenues for the Spanish crown
    b. raising a vast army for Spain
    c. discouraging the Spanish nobles from adopting Protestantism
    d. crushing a suspected Muslim rebellion
    e. none of the above

13. Seventeenth-century constitutional monarchies are characterized by all of the following *except*
    a. representational institutions such as Parliament.
    b. a system of shared authority.
    c. state support for maritime trade and international commerce.
    d. recognition of individual rights.
    e. the election of the monarch by the merchant class.

14. According to the divine-right theory of government,
    a. power and authority are based on a contract between the sovereign and his citizens.
    b. the king derives his authority from God alone and is not accountable to his subjects.
    c. the king has a divine mandate to serve his people well; if he violates that trust then he can be overthrown.
    d. the people and the state exist only to enrich the sovereign.
    e. God is the real sovereign and the Church represents His authority in earthly matters.

15. Louis XIV managed to control the nobles of France and their activities by
    a. crushing the most powerful nobles in a civil war early in his reign.
    b. heavily taxing the nobles' estates so they could no longer fund private armies.
    c. requiring the nobility to live at Versailles where he could distract them and keep an eye on them.
    d. appointing hundreds of new nobles from the merchant class, who were loyal to him.
    e. all of the above.

16. The reforms of Peter I included all of the following *except*
    a. offering better pay for peasants who served for life as professional soldiers.
    b. forcing his subjects to adopt western European fashions.
    c. forming a council of nobles to advise him on how best to improve the lives of serfs.
    d. building the city of St. Petersburg to serve as a base of naval operations.
    e. providing extensive training and modern weapons to soldiers.

17. The Peace of Westphalia, which ended of the Thirty Years' War, ensured that
    a. Germany remained fragmented.
    b. the nations of Europe would no longer go to war over religion.
    c. each nation was permitted to direct its own internal affairs.
    d. the balance of power was the new principle of European diplomacy.
    e. all of the above.

18. The population of Europe grew dramatically in the seventeenth century because of
    a. improved nutrition with new American food crops.
    b. new agricultural technology, which increased output.
    c. the development of the first immunizations for smallpox and plague.
    d. improved public health and sanitation.
    e. all of the above.

19. New institutions that supported early capitalism included all of the following *except*
    a. banks and lending institutions.
    b. craft guilds.
    c. stock exchanges.
    d. joint-stock companies.
    e. insurance companies.

20. The putting-out system was profitable for all of the following groups *except* the
    a. entrepreneurs who moved cloth production into the countryside.
    b. rural workers who did the spinning and weaving.
    c. consumers who bought the finished cloth.
    d. merchant and traders who shipped woolen cloth outside the country.
    e. guild members who specialized in specific elements of cloth production such as weaving or dyeing.

21. Which individual is incorrectly paired with a scientific discovery?
    a. Newton and the principle of gravity
    b. Kepler and the planetary orbits
    c. Galileo and the principle of inertia
    d. Copernicus and the sun-centered model of the universe
    e. Ptolemy and the moons of Jupiter

22. Galileo's discoveries would not have been possible without
    a. the telescope.
    b. the printing press.
    c. the astrolabe.
    d. the development of calculus.
    e. all of the above.

23. Isaac Newton's work seemed to suggest that
    a. the solar system was only one of many thousand such systems in an infinite universe.
    b. the stars and planets were part of a unified system, governed by the same natural laws.
    c. God was indifferent to the prayers and concerns of humanity.
    d. it was possible to mathematically prove the existence of God.
    e. time and space were relative, not absolute constructs.

MATCHING

Match these figures with the statements that follow.

A. Martin Luther
B. John Calvin
C. Catherine II
D. Henry VIII
E. Charles V
F. Louis XIV

G. Nicolaus Copernicus
H. Galileo Galilei
I. Isaac Newton
J. Adam Smith
K. Peter I
L. Voltaire

1. ___ In order to divorce his queen, he severed ties between England and the Catholic church.

2. ___ This Sun King of France was the model of an absolute monarch.

3. ___ With a telescope, he demonstrated that the moon and the planets were made of matter and confirmed that the planets revolved around the sun.

4. ___ This Polish mathematician theorized that, if the sun were placed at the center of the heavens, the orbits of the earth and the planets appeared more orderly.

5. ___ Ruler of a vast and scattered continental kingdom, he was never able to unify his holdings into a single kingdom.

6. ___ Ruler noted for his forceful efforts to modernize Russia.

7. ___ This Scottish economist argued that self-interested capitalism was ultimately the best for society as a whole.

8. ___ An English mathematician, his laws concerning gravitation and universal motion provided the rational explanation for the solar system.

9. ___ This Protestant leader, with his strict doctrines of reformed Christianity, strongly influenced the Reformation in Switzerland, France, the Netherlands, and Scotland.

10. ___ French satirist and social critic, his attacks on the state and the Catholic church typified the spirit of the Enlightenment.

11. ___ Russian ruler who flirted with progressive reforms but grew increasingly repressive.

12. ___ This German monk attacked the Catholic sale of indulgences and launched the Reformation.

SEQUENCING

Place the following clusters of events in chronological order. Consider carefully how one event leads to another, and try to determine the internal logic of each sequence.

A.

_____ Brought before the emperor, Luther refuses to recant, saying, "Here I stand. I can do no other."

_____ The Catholic Church expands the sale of indulgences in order to finance a massive renovation of St. Peter's basilica in Rome.

_____ The German states are divided: roughly half remain loyal to the Catholic Church, the rest become Lutheran.

_____ In his *95 Theses,* Martin Luther raises a challenge to the Church leadership, questioning the authority of the pope to issue indulgences.

B.

_____ Kepler demonstrates the elliptical orbits of the planets.

_____ Copernicus postulates that the sun might actually be at the center of the universe, a theory that explains apparent inconsistencies in the planetary orbits.

_____ The Ptolemaic view of the universe holds that the earth is at the center of creation and the heavens revolve around it in crystal spheres.

_____ Newton explains how the system works with his law of universal gravitation.

QUOTATIONS

For each of the following quotes, identify the speaker, if known, or the point of view. What is the significance of each passage?

1. "I cannot and will not recant anything, for it is neither safe nor right to act against one's conscience. Here I stand. I can do no other. God help me."

2. *"Écrasez l'infame!"* (Crush the damn thing!)

3. *"L'etat c'est moi."* (I am the state.)

4. "Every individual is continually exerting himself to find out the most advantageous employment for whatever capital he can command. It is his own advantage, indeed, and not that of the society, which he has in view. . . . By pursuing his own interest he frequently promotes that of the society more effectually than when he really intends to promote it."

MAP EXERCISES

1. Use the outline maps provided to illustrate the religious transformation of Europe over the course of the sixteenth century. On the first map, for the year 1500, identify the Catholic, Orthodox, and Muslim regions with different colors. The second map, for the year 1600, will introduce a new group, the Protestants. Choose a single color (say, blue) to represent Protestantism, but use different shades or hatchings to indicate the various Protestant sects—Lutherans, Calvinists, and Anglicans. From this latter map, can you identify regions where there are likely to be religious conflicts?

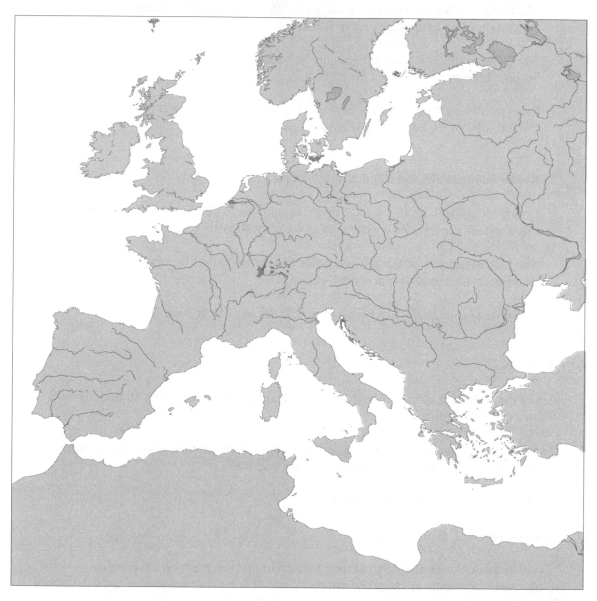

Map 1: 1500

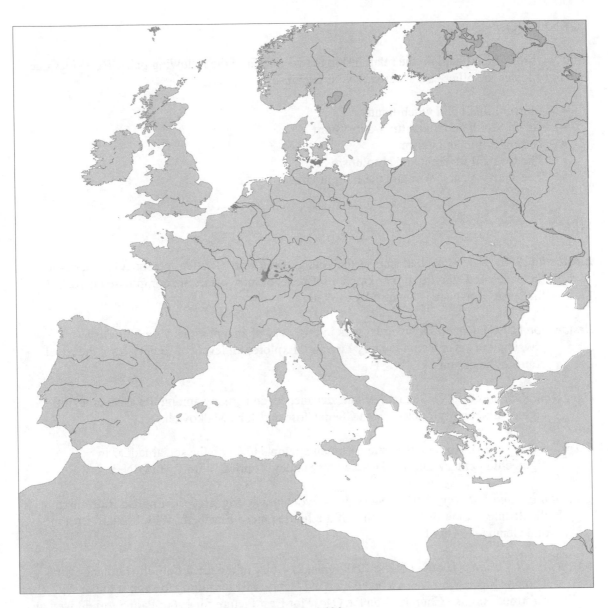

Map 2: 1600

2. Compare the political boundaries of Europe before and after the Thirty Years' War (pages 638 and 647 in the textbook). What new states do you see? How have the boundaries of Europe shifted? (And how are the borders different from those on the modern map of Europe?)

<u>CONNECTIONS</u>

In fifty words or less, explain the relationship between each of the following pairs. How does one lead to or foster the other? Be specific in your response.

- Martin Luther and witch-hunts
- Adam Smith and the putting-out system
- Isaac Newton and deism
- The Council of Trent and absolutism
- The Thirty Years' War and the Enlightenment

<u>FILMS</u>

Elizabeth (1998). Cate Blanchett stars as the young queen who sacrifices personal happiness for the peace and stability of her kingdom. Events of many years are compressed here, but the spirit of the age is beautifully evoked.

Restoration (1994). Robert Downey Jr. stars in this story of an ambitious young English physician in seventeenth-century England. Explores all levels of society from the royal court to the prisons.

Dangerous Liaisons (1989). Sexual intrigue, decadence, and cruelty among the aristocracy of eighteenth-century France. With Glenn Close and John Malkovich.

Barry Lyndon (1975). An opportunistic Irishman attempts to climb the social ladder in eighteenth-century Europe. Directed by Stanley Kubrick. With Ryan O'Neal.

Anne of the Thousand Days (1969). Story of the woman who triggered the English Reformation, the ill-fated Anne Boleyn, mother of the future Queen Elizabeth. With Richard Burton and Genevieve Bujold.

A Man for All Seasons (1966—not the 1988 remake). Story of the great Catholic humanist Sir Thomas More, who was executed by King Henry VIII for failing to submit to the reformed English Church. Won the Oscar for Best Picture for 1966; Paul Scofield won an Oscar for the title role.

CHAPTER 25
NEW WORLDS: THE AMERICAS AND OCEANIA

INTRODUCTION

This chapter traces the devastating impact of European exploration and conquest on the societies in the Americas and on the Pacific islands. Those societies, described in detail in Chapter 21, succumbed quickly under the combined pressures of European diseases and superior technology. By 1700, most of the western hemisphere had been claimed by western powers. Colonial societies were shaped by a number of considerations:

- Conquests of the Aztec empire by Cortés and the Inca empire by Pizarro were swift and brutal. The Spanish empire brought the Indian empires of Mexico and Peru under royal authority, represented by the viceroy, and a small class of white landowners. Indigenous peoples were impressed into service in mines and on plantations.

- In Brazil, the Portuguese established a plantation society based on sugar mills (*engenhos*). After the native population died off, African slaves were imported and forced to labor under brutal conditions.

- The earliest British and French colonies in North America centered on the fur trade and subsistence farming. Plantations in Virginia and the Carolinas were originally worked by indentured servants from Europe, but by the late seventeenth century, planters found African slaves to be a better investment.

- Catholic missions in Spanish and Portuguese colonies actively sought the conversion of native peoples. In North America, there were fewer contacts and more native resistance to conversion.

OUTLINE

I. Colliding worlds

   A. The Spanish Caribbean

      1. Indigenous peoples were the Taino

         a) Lived in small villages under authority of chiefs

         b) Showed little resistance to European visitors

      2. Columbus built the fort of Santo Domingo, capital of the Spanish Caribbean

         a) Taino were conscripted to mine gold

         b) *Encomiendas:* land grants to Spanish settlers with total control over local people

         c) Brutal abuses plus smallpox brought decline of Taino populations

   B. The conquest of Mexico and Peru

      1. Hernan Cortés

         a) Aztec and Inca societies wealthier, more complex than Caribbean societies

b) With 450 men, Cortés conquered the Aztec empire, 1519–1521

c) Tribal resentment against the Mexica helped Cortés

d) Epidemic disease (smallpox) also aided Spanish efforts

2. Francisco Pizarro

a) Led a small band of men and toppled the Inca empire, 1532–1533

b) Internal problems and smallpox aided Pizarro's efforts

c) By 1540 Spanish forces controlled all the former Inca empire

C. Iberian empires in the Americas

1. Spanish colonial administration formalized by 1570

a) Administrative centers in Mexico and Peru governed by viceroys

b) Viceroys reviewed by *audiencias,* courts appointed by the king

c) Viceroys had sweeping powers within jurisdictions

2. Portuguese Brazil: given to Portugal by Treaty of Tordesillas

a) Portuguese king granted Brazil to nobles, with a governor to oversee

b) Sugar plantations by mid-sixteenth century

3. Colonial American society

a) European-style society in cities, indigenous culture persisted in rural areas

b) More exploitation of New World than settlement

c) Still, many Iberian migrants settled in the Americas, 1500–1800

D. Settler colonies in North America

1. Foundation of colonies on east coast, exploration of west coast

a) France and England came seeking fur, fish, trade routes in the early seventeenth century

b) Settlements suffered isolation, food shortages

2. Colonial government different from Iberian colonies

a) North American colonies controlled by private investors with little royal backing

b) Royal authority and royal governors, but also institutions of self-government

3. Relations with indigenous peoples

a) Settlers' farms interrupted the migrations of indigenous peoples

b) Settlers seized lands, then justified it with treaties

c) Natives retaliated with raids on farms and villages

d) Attacks on European communities brought reprisals from settlers

e) Between 1500 and 1800, native population of North America dropped 90 percent

II. Colonial society in the Americas

A. The formation of multicultural societies

1. In Spanish and Portuguese settlements, *mestizo* societies emerged

   a) Peoples of varied ancestry lived together under European rule

   b) *Mestizo:* the children of Spanish and Portuguese men and native women

   c) Society of Brazil more thoroughly mixed: *mestizos, mulattoes, zambos*

2. Typically the social (and racial) hierarchy in Iberian colonies was as follows:

   a) Whites (*peninsulares* and *criollos*) owned the land and held the power

   b) Mixed races (*mestizos* and *zambos*) performed much of the manual labor

   c) Africans and natives were at the bottom

3. North American societies

   a) Greater gender balance among settlers allowed marriage within their own groups

   b) Relationships of French traders and native women generated some *métis*

   c) English disdainful of interracial marriages

   d) Cultural borrowing: plants, crops, deerskin clothes

B. Mining and agriculture in the Spanish empire

1. Silver more plentiful than gold, the basis of Spanish New World wealth

   a) *Conquistadores* melted Aztec and Inca gold artifacts into ingots

   b) Two major sites of silver mining: Zacatecas (Mexico) and Potosi (Peru)

   c) For labor at Potosi, Spanish authorities relied on *mita* system in which each village required to send one-seventh of male population to work for four months

   d) Under *mita* system, wages low, work harsh, death rate high

2. The global significance of silver

   a) One-fifth of all silver mined went to royal Spanish treasury (the *quinto*)

   b) Paid for Spanish military and bureaucracy

   c) Passed on to European and then to Asian markets for luxury trade goods

3. Large private estates, or haciendas, were the basis of Spanish-American production

   a) Produced foodstuffs for local production

   b) Abusive *encomienda* system replaced by the *repartimiento* system

   c) *Repartimiento* system replaced by debt peonage by the mid-seventeenth century

4. Resistance to Spanish rule by indigenous people

   a) Various forms of resistance: rebellion, indolence, retreat

   b) Pueblo revolt in northern Mexico (1680)

   c) Tupac Amaru rebellion in Peru (1780)

        d) Difficult for natives to register complaints: Poma de Ayala's attempt

C. Sugar and slavery in Portuguese Brazil

    1. The Portuguese empire in Brazil dependent on sugar production

        a) Colonial Brazilian life revolved around the sugar mill, or *engenho*

        b) *Engenho* combined agricultural and industrial enterprises

        c) Sugar planters became the landed nobility

    2. Growth of slavery in Brazil

        a) Native peoples of Brazil were not cultivators; they resisted farm labor

        b) Smallpox and measles reduced indigenous population

        c) Imported African slaves for cane and sugar production after 1530

        d) High death rate and low birth rate fed constant demand for more slaves

        e) Roughly, every ton of sugar cost one human life

D. Fur traders and settlers in North America

    1. The fur trade was very profitable

    2. Native peoples trapped for and traded with Europeans

    3. Impact of the fur trade

        a) Environmental impact

        b) Conflicts among natives competing for resources

    4. European settler-cultivators posed more serious threat to native societies

        a) Cultivation of cash crops—tobacco, rice, indigo, and later, cotton

        b) Indentured labor flocked to North America in the seventeenth and eighteenth centuries

    5. African slaves replaced indentured servants in the late seventeenth century

        a) Slave labor not yet prominent in North America (lack of labor-intensive crops)

        b) New England merchants participated in slave trade, distillation of rum

E. Christianity and native religions in the Americas

    1. Spanish missionaries introduced Catholicism

        a) Mission schools and churches established

        b) Some missionaries recorded the languages and traditions of native peoples

        c) Native religions survived but the Catholic church attracted many converts

    2. In 1531, the Virgin of Guadalupe became a national symbol

    3. French and English missions less successful

        a) North American populations not settled or captive

        b) English colonists had little interest in converting indigenous peoples

c) French missionaries worked actively, but met only modest success

III. Europeans in the Pacific

    A. Australia and the larger world

        1. Dutch mariners explored west Australia in the seventeenth century

            a) No spices, no farmland

            b) Australia held little interest until the eighteenth century

        2. British captain James Cook explored east Australia in 1770

            a) In 1788, England established first settlement in Australia as a penal colony

            b) Free settlers outnumbered convicted criminal migrants after 1830s

    B. The Pacific islands and the larger world

        1. Spanish voyages in the Pacific after Magellan

            a) Regular voyages from Acapulco to Manila on the trade winds

            b) Spanish mariners visited Pacific islands; some interest in Guam and the Marianas

            c) Indigenous Chamorro population resisted but decimated by smallpox

        2. Impact on Pacific islanders of regular visitors and trade

            a) Occasional misunderstandings and skirmishes

            b) Whalers were regular visitors after the eighteenth century

            c) Missionaries, merchants, and planters followed

IDENTIFICATION: PEOPLE

What is the contribution of each of the following individuals to world history? Identification should include answers to the questions *who, what, where, when, how,* and *why is this person important?*

Hernán Cortés

Motecuzoma II

Francisco Pizarro

Atahualpa

Cabeza de Vaca

James Cook

IDENTIFICATION: TERMS/CONCEPTS

State in your own words what each of the following terms means and why it is significant to a study of world history. (Terms with an asterisk are defined in the glossary.)

*Mestizo**

Mita

*Encomienda**

Taino*

*Conquistadores**

Treaty of Tordesillas

Tupac Amaru rebellion

*Engenho**

Indentured labor*

Aboriginal Australians

STUDY QUESTIONS

1. What became of the Taino people of the Caribbean?

2. Consider the impact of the *encomienda* system of land distribution on the future of Spanish America.

3. How did Pizarro conquer the Inca empire with 180 men?

4. What kinds of communities were established in the New World colonies of Portugal and Spain? How were they organized? How were they governed?

5. Compare the French and English settlements of North America. What kind of settlers came to each? How did these colonies differ from the Iberian colonies farther south?

6. Describe the typical relations between French and English settlers and the Native Americans.

7. What determined the social hierarchy in the Iberian colonies? Who tended to have wealth and power?

8. What was the basis of the economy of the Spanish empire? Who profited most from this?

9. Explain how sugar production came to dictate so much of colonial Brazilian life.

10. What became the basis of the economy and settlement in the North American colonies of France and England?

11. When and how did slavery come to North America? How did the arrival of slavery impact the societies that emerged there?

12. What was distinctive about the European exploration and settlement of Australia?

INQUIRY QUESTIONS

1. How was such a small Spanish force able to bring down the Aztec empire? What specific advantages did the Spanish enjoy? In what ways were the Aztecs vulnerable?

2. Compare the treatment of indigenous peoples by the Spanish in Mexico, the Portuguese in Brazil, and the French and British in North America.

3. One of the rationales for overseas colonization was the need to bring primitive peoples to Christianity. How successful were the colonists in these efforts?

STUDENT QUIZ

1. What was Doña Marina's role in the Spanish conquest of the Aztecs?
    a. She unwittingly infected many of her people with smallpox.
    b. She betrayed the secret entrance to Tenochtitlan.
    c. She bore Cortés a child, who would bring unity between both peoples.
    d. She could speak several native languages and served as an interpreter.
    e. She was the first Catholic convert.

2. The first indigenous people that the Spanish empire dispossessed of their lands and forced into labor were the
    a. Aztecs.
    b. Incas.
    c. Iroquois.
    d. Maya.
    e. Tainos.

3. The labor system that compelled Indians to work in Spanish mines and fields in exchange for protection and Christian conversion was known as
    a. the *encomienda* system.
    b. the hacienda.
    c. slavery.
    d. indentured servitude.
    e. the *repartimiento* system.

4. Which of the following was *not* a significant factor in Cortés's defeat of the Aztec empire?
   a. superior Spanish technology, especially swords, muskets, cannons, and horses
   b. a devastating smallpox epidemic
   c. the inadequate defenses of Tenochtitlan
   d. the resentment of many indigenous peoples to Aztec rule
   e. All of the above *were* factors.

5. In colonial governments, the power of the Spanish viceroy was kept in check by the authority of the
   a. Catholic church.
   b. audiencias.
   c. colonial legislature.
   d. Spanish crown.
   e. colonial militias.

6. How did Portugal gain an empire in Brazil?
   a. Portuguese mariners were first to explore the Amazon basin.
   b. The Treaty of Tordesillas, designed to divide the Atlantic between Spain and Portugal, unintentionally granted Brazil to Portugal.
   c. Initially, the Spanish had no interest in South America.
   d. The Indians of Brazil successfully resisted Spanish invaders.
   e. None of the above.

7. The English settlements in North America grew slowly at first because
   a. of the large, densely populated Indian communities that dominated the coast.
   b. the first English settlements did not prepare sufficient food crops.
   c. the colonies did not produce commodities that Europeans were eager to buy.
   d. the English government did not support or protect the colonies.
   e. all of the above.

8. One significant difference in the administration of English colonies compared to their Spanish counterparts was
   a. the Spanish crown was less actively involved in the government of their colonies.
   b. English governors were elected directly by the colonists, while Spanish viceroys were appointed by the crown.
   c. Spanish colonies had powerful local assemblies, while the English did not.
   d. English colonies were often financed by private investors, who retained control over colonial affairs.
   e. the Church played a greater role in the administration of Spanish colonies.

9. How did European settlers in North America legally justify seizing lands from native North American peoples?
   a. The settlers negotiated treaties.
   b. Because the Indians were not Christian, they had no right to the land.
   c. Because the Indians were hunters and gatherers rather than farmers, their claims to the land were not considered valid.
   d. The settlers established squatters' rights on unoccupied lands.
   e. By defeating the Indians in battle, the English and French claimed the land as a spoil of war.

10. A *mestizo* is a person
   a. born in Spain who immigrated to the New World.
   b. of Spanish descent born in the New World.
   c. of mixed Spanish and Indian descent.
   d. of mixed African and Indian descent.
   e. of mixed Spanish and African descent.

11. *Criollos* differed from *peninsulares* only in that
   a. they were born in the western hemisphere, not the eastern hemisphere.
   b. their mothers were part Indian.
   c. they had no land and were economically dependent.
   d. they had not yet been baptized in the Catholic church.
   e. they were indentured servants while *peninsulares* were free.

12. The most valuable commodity for the Spanish in the Americas was
   a. minerals like silver and gold.
   b. sugar and rum.
   c. tobacco.
   d. furs.
   e. timber.

13. How did the mining industries of the Americas stimulate global economic growth?
   a. Mining increased the demand for labor, sparking the growth of an Indian middle class.
   b. Mineral ores from Mexico provided the raw materials for European manufacturing.
   c. The sale of slaves to the mines by the Portuguese resulted in the Portuguese spending their wealth throughout Europe and Africa.
   d. The Spanish *quinto* circulated throughout European and Asian markets.
   e. All of the above.

14. Which of the following is *not* true of the *mita* system?
   a. It was used by the Spanish at Potosi.
   b. It had been used by the Inca.
   c. It was a form of slavery in that workers were not paid.
   d. It led to high rates of death among workers.
   e. It affected a large portion of the indigenous population.

15. The labor system that dominated on haciendas of Spanish America was
   a. indentured servitude.
   b. slavery.
   c. the *mita* system.
   d. the *encomienda* system.
   e. wage labor.

16. Why did the production of sugar differ from that of other agricultural commodities of the western hemisphere?
   a. Sugar production was particularly hard on the environment.
   b. Sugarcane required extensive processing to turn it into a profitable export.
   c. African slaves were the only ones who knew how to grow sugarcane.
   d. Sugar was extremely profitable with very little investment.
   e. It was only possible to grow in Brazil, and it had an extremely short growing season.

17. Which of the following was *not* a typical result of the North American fur trade?
    a. intense competition and even warfare between indigenous peoples for European trade
    b. intense competition between French, Dutch, and English fur traders
    c. the decimation of the beaver population in North America
    d. hostile relations between European traders and Native American trappers
    e. the introduction of European manufactured goods to indigenous peoples

18. Indentured servants who worked off their contracts in the colonies often
    a. returned disappointed to Europe.
    b. hoped to become wealthy plantation-owners.
    c. hoped to become active in the politics of the colonies.
    d. hoped to become independent artisans or planters.
    e. remained in debt for many years.

19. Why were the indigenous peoples of Mesoamerica and South America more likely to accept Christianity than the peoples of North America were?
    a. Mesoamerican and South American Indians found many similarities between their religions and Catholicism.
    b. North American Indians were more geographically scattered and thus harder for missionaries to reach.
    c. Catholic missionaries in Spanish America were more tolerant of native cultures than were the Protestant missionaries in North America.
    d. Catholic rule in the New World was more generous and enlightened than the English or the French rule.
    e. None of the above.

20. The first explorers to Australia were not interested in settlement because
    a. the first explorers were driven away by hostile aborigines.
    b. the first explorers could not sail across the Great Barrier Reef.
    c. the land appeared too densely forested to settle easily.
    d. it was too far from European markets.
    e. the first explorers explored only the barren western coast of Australia.

MATCHING

Match these figures with the statements that follow.

A. Hernán Cortés
B. Motecuzoma
C. Francisco Pizarro
D. Taino
E. *Mestizos*
F. *Conquistadores*

G. Viceroy
H. James Cook
I. Cabez de Vaca
J. Doña Marina
K. *Peninsulares*
L. Atahualpa

1. ___ The original inhabitants of the Caribbean Islands.

2. ___ Mixed-race descendants of European and Indian parents.

3. ___ Spanish conqueror of the Inca peoples.

4. ___ Spanish conqueror of the Aztec peoples.

5. ___ The last Aztec emperor.

6. ___ The last Inca emperor.

7. ___ Provided both intelligence and translating services to the Spanish conquerors.

8. ___ Failed to complete the northwest passage but charted most of the Pacific Ocean in the process.

9. ___ Spanish soldiers who came to the Americas seeking gold and glory.

10. ___ Distinction claimed by those who lived in the Americas but were born in Iberia.

11. ___ Title of the Spanish king's representative in the Americas.

12. ___ A European who explored Florida and the southeast of North America.

SEQUENCING

Place the following clusters of events in chronological order. Consider carefully how one event leads to another, and try to determine the internal logic of each sequence.

A.

_____ English Puritan settlement of Massachusetts

_____ Portuguese settlement of Brazil

_____ English settlement of Jamestown, Virginia

_____ Spanish settlement of Mexico

_____ Spanish settlement of Hispaniola

B.

_____ Native resistance is brutally crushed by the superior Spanish weapons.

_____ Columbus finds Hispaniola densely populated by the Tainos.

_____ African slaves are imported to perform manual labor.

_____ The Taino are forced to work in Spanish mines and on plantations.

_____ Smallpox and measles devastate the indigenous population of the Caribbean, which dwindles to a few thousand by the mid-sixteenth century.

For each of the following quotes, identify the speaker, if known, or the point of view. What is the significance of each passage?

1. "Especially did it cause [Motecuzoma] to faint away when he heard how the gun, at [the Spaniards'] command, discharged the shot. . . . And when [the shot] struck a mountain, it was as if it were destroyed, dissolved. And a tree was pulverized; it was as if someone blew it away."

2. "We no sooner landed [on the beach], than a trade was set on foot for hogs and sweet potatoes, which the people gave us in exchange for nails and pieces of iron, formed into something like chisels. . . . As soon as everything was settled, I took a walk up the Valley. . . . Our guide proclaimed our approach and every one whom we met fell on their faces and remained in that position till we passed. This, as I afterwards understood, is done to their great chiefs."

3. "Therefore, for the sake of peace and concord [between] the King of Portugal and the King and Queen of Spain, they and their representatives agreed that a boundary or straight line be drawn north and south, from pole to pole, on the [Atlantic Ocean], at a distance of three hundred and seventy leagues west of the Cape Verde Islands. . . . And all lands, found or yet to be discovered, on the eastern side of [that boundary] shall belong to the King of Portugal and his successors. And all other lands, found or yet to be discovered, on the western side of [that boundary] shall belong to King and Queen of Spain and to their successors."

4. "I obey, but I do not enforce."

5. "There were never Englishmen left in a foreign Country in such misery as we were in this new discovered *Virginia*. . . . Our food was but a small can of Barley sodden in water, to five men a day. Our drink cold water taken out of the River; which was, at a [high tide], very salt; at a low tide, full of slime and filth: which was the destruction of many of our men."

6. "We Spanish suffer from a disease of the heart which can only be cured with gold."

MAP EXERCISES

1. On the map of the New World below, clearly label each of the following colonies and indicate whether claimed by the Dutch, English, French, Portuguese, or Spanish: Brazil, Cuba, Florida, Guiana, Hispaniola, Jamaica, Jamestown, Louisiana, Massachusetts (Boston), New Castille, New Granada, New Spain, Quebec, Rio de la Plata. By 1700, which European power appears to have the strongest claim to South America? To North America? (See Map 25.1, page 672 in the textbook).

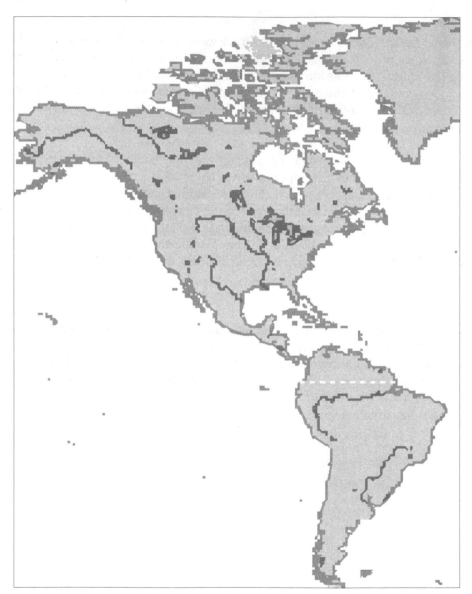

2. On a map of North America, indicate the various European territorial claims just before and just after the Seven Years' War of 1756–1763 (discussed in Chapter 23). How had the balance of power in North America shifted by 1763?

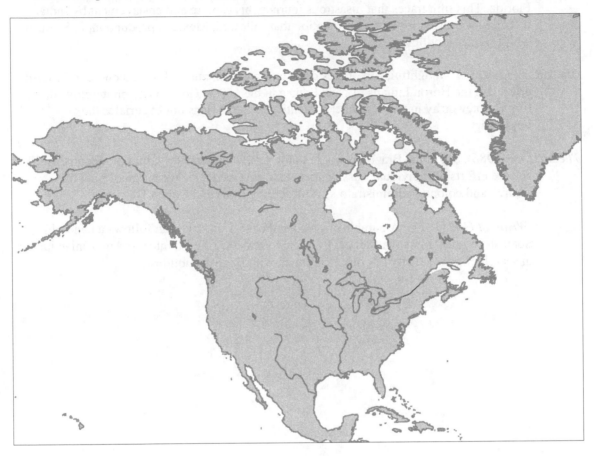

CONNECTIONS

In fifty words or less, explain the relationship between each of the following pairs. How does one lead to or foster the other? Be specific in your response.

- Colombian exchange and tobacco plantations
- *Encomienda* system and African slave trade
- Smallpox and indentured servants
- Joint-stock companies and colonial legislatures

FILMS

Cabeza de Vaca (1992). In 1527, the Spanish conquistador Cabeza de Vaca led an expedition into Florida. This film traces that disastrous journey, his capture and enslavement by Indians in Texas, and the spiritual transformation that followed. Mexican production, in Spanish with English subtitles.

Black Robe (1991). A thoughtful, sometimes devastating examination of the encounter of a Jesuit priest and the Huron Indians of New France in the 1600s. Gorgeously photographed, this film is noteworthy in that it neither romanticizes the Indians nor excoriates the missionary.

The Mission (1986). Set in the Brazilian jungle in the seventeenth century, this film contrasts the sincere efforts of individual missionaries with the greed and corruption of both the Church and colonial administrators. With Jeremy Irons and Robert De Niro.

Aguirre, Wrath of God (1971). A parable of greed and obsession, this film follows a band of Spanish conquistadors who set off from the mountains of Peru into the Amazonian jungle in search of a fabled city of gold. In German with English subtitles.

CHAPTER 26
AFRICA AND THE ATLANTIC WORLD

INTRODUCTION

For thousands of years, sub-Saharan Africa was a remote and isolated region, cut off from much of the outside world by vast oceans and the Sahara Desert. In the eighth century Muslim caravans reached west Africa, and in the tenth century Arab merchant ships began trading with the Swahili city-states of east Africa (see Chapter 19). These contacts were, for the most part, mutually beneficial to both African rulers and Muslim merchants. Traders sought gold, ivory, exotic foods such as kola nuts, and slaves. Africans, in turn, gained horses, salt, and other manufactured goods and were also introduced to the religion, law, and culture of Islam. Several African societies, such as the Songhay, the Kongo, and the Ndongo, shifted from band level units to larger, more formal kingdoms.

This political evolution was disrupted after the fifteenth century, when Portuguese mariners reached the west coast of Africa. Direct European contact brought rapid and dramatic changes, which profoundly affected all sub-Saharan societies. Some dimensions of that change are

- Political upheaval. In the Kongo, for example, the Portuguese undermined the authority of the king and even assassinated uncooperative rulers.

- Outright conquest and settlement. Kongo, Ndongo, and south Africa became European settlements that had Africans as the servant class. The Swahili city-states were seized and forced to pay tribute.

- Intertribal warfare. Portuguese slave traders encouraged African slavers to make raids on their neighbors and to resist their own rulers. Coastal Dahomey profited from the slave trade, while inland peoples suffered.

- Economic exploitation. Indigenous economies were corrupted by the trade, exchanging slaves for manufactured goods such as guns and rum.

- Social disruption. Sixteen million, able-bodied young Africans were enslaved between 1600 and 1800, two-thirds of them men. This disruption seriously impacted village and family life, especially in west Africa.

OUTLINE

I. African politics and societies in early modern times

    A. The states of west Africa and east Africa

        1. The Songhay empire was the dominant power of west Africa, replacing Mali

            a) Expansion under Songhay emperor Sunni Ali after 1464

            b) Elaborate administrative apparatus, powerful army, and imperial navy

            c) Muslim emperors ruled prosperous land, engaged in trans-Saharan trade

2. Fall of Songhay to Moroccan army in 1591

    a) Revolts of subject peoples brought the empire down

    b) A series of small, regional kingdoms and city-states emerged

3. Decline of Swahili city-states in east Africa

    a) Vasco da Gama forced the ruler of Kilwa to pay tribute, 1502

    b) Massive Portuguese naval fleet subdued all the Swahili cities, 1505

    c) Trade disrupted; Swahili declined

B. The kingdoms of central Africa and south Africa

1. Kongo, powerful kingdom of central Africa after fourteenth century

    a) Established diplomatic and commercial relations with Portugal, 1482

    b) Kings of Kongo converted to Christianity sixteenth century; King Afonso

2. Slave raiding in Kongo

    a) Portuguese traded textiles, weapons, and advisors for Kongolese gold, silver, ivory, and slaves

    b) Slave trade undermined authority of kings of Kongo

    c) Deteriorated relations led to war in 1665; Kongo king decapitated

3. Kingdom of Ndongo (modern Angola) attracted Portuguese slave traders

    a) Queen Nzinga led spirited resistance to Portuguese, 1623–1663

    b) Nzinga able to block Portuguese advances but not expel them entirely

    c) By end of the seventeenth century, Ndongo was the Portuguese colony of Angola

4. Southern Africa dominated by regional kingdoms, for example, Great Zimbabwe

5. Europeans in south Africa after the fifteenth century

    a) First Portuguese, then Dutch mariners landed at Cape of Good Hope

    b) Dutch mariners built a trading post at Cape Town, 1652

    c) Increasing Dutch colonists by 1700, drove away native Khoikhoi

    d) South Africa became a prosperous European colony in later centuries

C. Islam and Christianity in early modern Africa

1. Islam popular in west Africa states and Swahili city-states of east Africa

    a) Islamic university and 180 religious schools in Timbuktu in Mali

    b) Blended Islam with indigenous beliefs and customs, a syncretic Islam

    c) The Fulani, west African tribe, observed strict form of Islam, eighteenth and nineteenth centuries

2. Christianity reached sub-Saharan Africa through Portuguese merchants

    a) Also blended with traditional beliefs

b) Antonian movement of Kongo, a syncretic cult, addressed to St. Anthony

c) Charismatic Antonian leader, Doña Beatriz, executed for heresy, 1706

D. Social change in early modern Africa

1. Kinship and clans remained unchanged at the local level

2. American food crops, for example, manioc, maize, peanuts, introduced after the sixteenth century

3. Population growth in sub-Sahara: 35 million in 1500 to 60 million in 1800

II. The Atlantic slave trade

A. Foundations of the slave trade

1. Slavery common in traditional Africa

a) Slaves typically war captives, criminals, or outcasts

b) Most slaves worked as cultivators, some as administrators or soldiers

c) With all land held in common, slaves were a measure of power and wealth

d) Slaves often assimilated into their masters' kinship groups, even earned freedom

2. The Islamic slave trade well established throughout Africa

a) Ten million slaves may have been shipped out of Africa by Islamic slave trade between eighth and eighteenth centuries

b) Muslim slave merchants sometimes raided villages to capture individuals then forced into servitude

c) Europeans used these existing networks and expanded the slave trade

B. Human cargoes

1. The early slave trade on the Atlantic started by Portuguese in 1441

a) By 1460 about five hundred slaves a year shipped to Portugal and Spain

b) By fifteenth century African slaves shipped to sugar plantations on Atlantic islands

c) Portuguese planters imported slaves to Brazil, 1530s

d) Spanish settlers shipped African slaves to the Caribbean, Mexico, Peru, and Central America, 1510s and 1520s

e) English colonists brought slaves to North America early seventeenth century

2. Triangular trade: all three legs of voyage profitable

a) European goods traded for African slaves

b) Slaves traded in the Caribbean for sugar or molasses

c) American produce traded in Europe

3. At every stage the slave trade was brutal

a) Individuals captured in violent raids

b) Forced to march to the coast for transport

c) The dreaded middle passage, where between 25 percent and 50 percent died

C. The impact of the slave trade in Africa

1. Volume of the Atlantic slave trade increased dramatically after 1600

a) At height—end of the eighteenth century—about one hundred thousand shipped per year

b) Altogether about twelve million brought to Americas, another four million died en route

2. Profound impact on African societies

a) Impact uneven: some societies spared, some societies profited

b) Distorted African sex ratios, since two-thirds of exported slaves were males

c) Encouraged polygamy and forced women to take on men's duties

3. Politically disruptive

a) Introduced firearms; fostered conflict and violence between peoples

b) Dahomey, on the "slave coast," grew powerful as a slave-raiding state

III. The African diaspora

A. Plantation societies

1. Cash crops introduced to fertile lands of Caribbean early fifteenth century

a) First Hispaniola, then Brazil and Mexico

b) Important cash crops: sugar, tobacco, rice, indigo, cotton, coffee

c) Plantations dependent on slave labor

2. Plantations racially divided: one hundred or more slaves with a few white supervisors

a) High death rates in the Caribbean and Brazil; continued importation of slaves

b) Only about 5 percent of slaves to North America, where slave families more common

3. Resistance to slavery widespread, though dangerous

a) Slow work, sabotage, and escape

b) Slave revolts were rare and were brutally suppressed by plantation owners

c) 1793: slaves in French colony of Saint-Domingue revolted, abolished slavery, and established the free state of Haiti

B. The making of African-American cultural traditions

1. African and Creole languages

a) Slaves from many tribes; lacked a common language

      b) Developed creole languages, blending several African languages with the language of the slaveholder

  2. African-American religions also combined elements from different cultures

      a) African-American Christianity was a distinctive syncretic practice

      b) African rituals and beliefs: ritual drumming, animal sacrifice, magic, and sorcery

  3. Other African-American cultural traditions: hybrid cuisine, weaving, pottery

C. The end of the slave trade and the abolition of slavery

  1. New voices and ideas against slavery

      a) American and French revolutions encouraged ideals of freedom and equality

      b) Olaudah Equiano was a freed slave whose autobiography became a best-seller

  2. Slavery became increasingly costly

      a) Slave revolts made slavery expensive and dangerous

      b) Decline of sugar price and rising costs of slaves in the late eighteenth century

      c) Manufacturing industries were more profitable; Africa became a market

  3. End of the slave trade

      a) Most European states abolished the slave trade in the early nineteenth century

      b) British naval squadrons helped to stop the trade

      c) The abolition of slavery followed slowly: 1833 in British colonies, 1848 in French colonies, 1865 in the United States, 1888 in Brazil

IDENTIFICATION: PEOPLE

What is the contribution of each of the following individuals to world history? Identification should include answers to the questions *who, what, where, when, how,* and *why is this person important?*

Thomas Peters

Sunni Ali

Afonso I

Nzinga

Doña Beatriz

Olaudah Equiano

IDENTIFICATION: TERMS/CONCEPTS

State in your own words what each of the following terms means and why it is significant to a study of world history. (Terms with an asterisk are defined in the glossary.)

Songhay

Ndongo (Angola)*

Fulani*

Antonianism*

Triangular trade*

Middle passage

Maroons*

STUDY QUESTIONS

1. Compare the decline of Songhay with the decline of the Swahili city-states of east Africa.

2. How was the kingdom of Kongo transformed by its contacts with the Portuguese?

3. What were the objectives of Dutch colonists in South Africa? What kind of colony did they establish? Compare these objectives to the Portuguese objectives in colonizing Angola.

4. In what ways did Islam adapt to the customs and traditions of sub-Saharan Africa? Consider Songhay as an example. Where had strict Islam taken root by the end of the seventeenth century?

5. Besides religion, what other changes came to sub-Saharan Africa as a result of increased contact with the outside world?

6. Compare the institution of slavery within traditional African society with slavery as practiced in Europe and the New World.

7. What was the impact of the trans-Atlantic slave trade on the societies of west Africa? Consider social, political, and demographic effects.

8. Compare the experience of slaves in the Caribbean, in Brazil, and in North America.

9. What are some of the enduring elements of African-American culture? What elements of a culture can survive the ordeal and disruption of slavery?

10. What factors ultimately led to the abolition of the slave trade and ultimately to the abolition of slavery itself?

1. Did any African states or kingdoms benefit from their contacts with European traders? Who would be the likely beneficiaries? Who would suffer the most?

2. State the arguments for and against slavery in American colonies in strictly *economic* terms. Can you suggest a more economical alternative to slave labor? (This question, of course, ignores the moral debate over slavery.)

3. Why was it so difficult for slaves to revolt once they reached the New World? What were some of the obstacles to a successful revolt?

STUDENT QUIZ

1. Sunni Ali's administration of the Songhay was strengthened by
    a. a system of provincial governors.
    b. an effective chain of military command.
    c. an imperial navy to patrol the Niger River.
    d. the profitable trans-Saharan traffic.
    e. all of the above.

2. Which of the following was *not* conquered or defeated by the Portuguese?
    a. Angola
    b. Kilwa
    c. Kongo
    d. Songhay
    e. Zimbabwe

3. Although relations between Portugal and the Kongo were initially friendly, the Kongo was ultimately destroyed because
    a. the royal family resisted the efforts of Catholic missionaries.
    b. the Kongo had no trade goods of any value to the Europeans.
    c. King Afonso converted to Islam.
    d. Portuguese slave traders undermined the authority of the kings.
    e. all of the above.

4. Queen Nzinga resisted the Portuguese conquest of Angola by
    a. marriage to Dutch aristocracy.
    b. mobilizing military resistance to the Portuguese.
    c. entering into a trading alliance with Portugal.
    d. forging a military alliance with neighboring Kongo.
    e. none of the above.

5. The indigenous religions of sub-Saharan African were essentially
    a. polytheistic, recognizing numerous local gods as well as a single creator god.
    b. monotheistic, worshipping a supreme creator.
    c. messianic, worshipping a personal savior.
    d. universal, affirming that all religions are essentially the same.
    e. syncretic, taking the best from a variety of religions.

6. An example of a syncretic cult combining elements of Christianity and African beliefs is
   a. the Antonian movement.
   b. the Coptic church.
   c. the Fulani movement.
   d. King Afonso.
   e. all of the above.

7. One significant difference between the Portuguese settlement of Angola and the Dutch settlement of Cape Town was that
   a. the Dutch had better relations with the local Africans.
   b. the Portuguese had better relations with the local Africans.
   c. the Portuguese came to Angola as traders while in South Africa the Dutch settled on the land as farmers.
   d. the Portuguese sent farmers to Angola, while the Dutch came to South Africa primarily as merchants and traders.
   e. the Khoikhoi resisted Dutch colonization, while the people of Angola accepted Portuguese rule without resistance.

8. In spite of the ravages of the slave trade, the population of Africa actually increased in the eighteenth century due to
   a. European settlement of Africa.
   b. resettlement of Asian workers in parts of Africa.
   c. the introduction of new staple foods from the Americas.
   d. improved health and life expectancy.
   e. the cessation of intertribal warfare in Africa.

9. Factors in the decline of slavery included all of the following *except*
   a. the anti-slavery movement.
   b. the frequency of slave revolts.
   c. the declining profitability of slaves.
   d. the realization that wage labor in factories was cheaper than slave labor on plantations.
   e. all of the above.

10. All of the following are characteristics of slavery in Africa *except*
   a. slaves in Africa had opportunities to earn their freedom.
   b. slaves in Africa were the primary source of wealth and power.
   c. slaves in Africa were frequently assimilated into their owners' kinship groups.
   d. slaves in Africa had certain civil rights and could appeal to the law for justice.
   e. occasionally slaves worked as soldiers or as advisors.

11. The Portuguese slave trade began in the mid-fifteenth century with Portuguese raiders capturing African men and selling them in Europe. How had this trade changed by the mid-sixteenth century?
   a. Portuguese raiders captured slaves and sold them in the Americas.
   b. Portuguese raiders captured slaves and sold them to British merchants.
   c. The Portuguese no longer participated in the slave trade.
   d. Portuguese merchants bought slaves from African raiders and sold them to Europe and the Americas.
   e. The Portuguese bought slaves from Dutch raiders and sold them in the Americas.

12. Which of the following could *not* be a leg of the triangular trans-Atlantic trade?
    a. African slaves delivered to the Americas
    b. Barbados rum sold to England
    c. Mexican silver delivered to Manila
    d. manufactured goods sold to Africans
    e. Barbados rum sold to North America

13. African slaves were in demand for the New World because
    a. so many Native Americans died from imported diseases.
    b. native peoples frequently escaped into the hinterlands.
    c. sugar plantations in the Caribbean required considerable labor.
    d. Spanish and Portuguese conquerors disdained manual labor.
    e. all of the above.

14. The middle passage of the slave trade was
    a. the forced march of slaves through central Africa from their homelands.
    b. the holding pens where African captives were held before sale to plantation owners.
    c. the ship voyage across the Atlantic in the cargo decks.
    d. the public auction of slaves in the Caribbean.
    e. none of the above.

15. Olaudah Equiano's experience contributed to the abolishment of slavery because he
    a. served as a legal representative for slaves in the United States.
    b. established the underground railroad.
    c. returned to Africa as a Christian missionary.
    d. exposed the horrors of slavery, particularly the middle passage, to a European audience.
    e. all of the above.

16. Slavery's impact on Africa
    a. fell most heavily on the societies of west Africa.
    b. was limited to the eastern shores of Africa.
    c. was felt on the entire continent.
    d. was barely noticeable by the end of the eighteenth century due to demographic growth.
    e. was offset by the advances that came with European trade.

17. Most African slaves went to
    a. the tropical and subtropical plantations of the Americas.
    b. tobacco plantations on Chesapeake Bay.
    c. rice and sugar plantations in the southern United States.
    d. the silver mines of Mexico and Peru.
    e. work as domestic servants in upper-class homes throughout the New World.

18. On the plantations of the Caribbean and Brazil, slaves
    a. thrived because climate and diet were similar to Africa.
    b. suffered heavy losses due to tropical diseases and brutal conditions.
    c. quickly intermarried with the indigenous populations.
    d. formed families and re-created kinship ties similar to those in Africa.
    e. none of the above.

19. Maroons were
   a. slaves who had intermarried with Indians.
   b. the descendants of slaves and white slave-owners.
   c. the revolutionary force that led the Haitian rebellion.
   d. slaves who ran away and formed their own communities in remote areas.
   e. slaves who collaborated with their owners and gained power within the plantation system.

20. African culture in the Americas included all of the following *except*
   a. distinctive language and dialect.
   b. syncretic African-American religions.
   c. traditional kinship ties.
   d. distinctive foods and cuisine.
   e. distinctive handicrafts.

MATCHING

Match these groups or individuals with the statements that follow.

   A. Fulani   F. Thomas Peters
   B. Dutch   G. Olaudah Equiano
   C. Portugal   H. Doña Beatriz
   D. Sunni Ali   I. Antonians
   E. Nzinga   J. Afonso I

1. ___ Sixteenth-century king of the Kongo, a devout Catholic, who tried to convert all his subjects to Christianity.

2. ___ Songhay ruler who conquered Ghana and Mali and established a powerful central African empire in the fifteenth century.

3. ___ Defiant Ndongo queen who resisted Portuguese intrusions into her kingdom for forty years.

4. ___ Freed slave whose account of capture and life under slavery helped fuel the European abolitionist movement.

5. ___ European power that dominated the trans-Atlantic slave trade in the sixteenth century.

6. ___ Europeans who came to Africa more as settlers than as raiders and traders.

7. ___ A charismatic religious prophet who advocated an Africanized form of Christianity.

8. ___ Islamic purists who sought to establish strict Islamic states in central Africa.

9. ___ West African leader, a former slave, who helped establish the free colony of Sierra Leone as a haven for free blacks.

10. ___ A syncretic African-Christian cult that believed Jesus was a black man and the Kongo was the true Holy Land.

SEQUENCING

Place the following clusters of events in chronological order. Consider carefully how one event leads to another, and try to determine the internal logic of each sequence.

A.

_____ Dutch settlers

_____ Bantu cultivators

_____ Islamic traders

_____ Portuguese raiders and traders

B.

_____ Portuguese traders introduce the first African slaves to Virginia.

_____ Slaves are imported to sugar plantations in the Caribbean after the Taino Indians die off.

_____ African slaves are taken from west Africa to work on Atlantic island plantations.

_____ Importation of slaves to the North American colonies remains small, but those slaves are more likely to form families and raise children.

_____ Portuguese mariners reach west Africa, seize a dozen men, and sell them in Europe.

C.

_____ Inspired in part by the ideals of the Enlightenment, westerners begin to question the morality of slavery.

_____ In the 1880s, Cuba and Brazil are the last states in the New World to abolish slavery.

_____ Gradually the nations of Europe outlaw the slave trade and begin policing the Atlantic to stop the human traffic.

_____ Most Europeans accept the rationale that slavery is consistent with Christian values.

_____ Olaudah Equiano describes the horrors of the slave trade and middle passage from an African perspective.

<u>QUOTATIONS</u>

For each of the following quotes, identify the speaker, if known, or the point of view. What is the significance of each passage?

1. "Morever, Sir, in our Kingdoms there is another great inconvenience which is of little service to God, and this is that many of our people, keenly desirous as they are of the wares and things of your Kingdoms, which are brought here by your people, and in order to satisfy their voracious appetite, sieze many of our people, freed and exempt men, and very often it happens that they kidnap even noblemen and the sons of noblemen, and our relatives, and take them to be sold to the white men who are in our Kingdoms."

2. "I was not long suffered to indulge my grief; I was soon put down under the decks, and there I received such a salutation in my nostrils as I had never experienced in my life: so that with the loathsomeness of the stench and crying together, I became so sick and low that I was not able to eat, nor had I the least desire to taste anything. I now wished for the last friend, death, to relieve me; but . . . on my refusing to eat, one of them held me fast by the hands and laid me across I think the windlass and tied my feet while the other flogged me severely."

MAP EXERCISES

1. Locate all the following on an outline map (see Map 26.1, page 698 in the textbook).
   Bodies of water: Atlantic Ocean; Indian Ocean; Mediterranean Sea; Nile, Niger, Congo, Zambezi rivers
   States: Netherlands, Portugal, Spain, Sierra Leone, Dahomey, Kongo, Ndongo, Mozambique
   Cities: Cape Town, Kilwa, Gao, Great Zimbabwe, Timbuktu

2. Create a poster that graphically represents the triangular trans-Atlantic trade of the seventeenth and eighteenth centuries. Include a map of the Atlantic regions, icons, and colors to represent the items traded and the countries that profited from this trade (see Map 26.2, page 709).

CONNECTIONS

In fifty words or less, explain the relationship between each of the following pairs. How does one lead to or foster the other? Be specific in your response.

- Olaudah Equiano and the Enlightenment
- Capitalism and the middle passage
- Doña Beatriz and Nzinga

FILMS

Amistad (1997). Based on the story of a slave ship, the *Amistad,* that was taken over by the slaves in 1838 and later seized by the United States government. Although these events fall beyond the scope of this chapter, the film gives a powerful description of the slave trade and the middle passage.

Sankofa (1996). Through the mystery of time travel, a modern African-American model journeys from the ruins of a west African slave fortress to a French Louisiana sugar plantation in the eighteenth century. In spite of the fanciful pretext, a realistic account of plantation slavery in Louisiana and the Caribbean.

Quilombo (1984). Acclaimed Brazilian film about a community of escaped slaves hiding in the Amazonian jungle in the sixteenth century. A realistic portrait of the brutality of slavery and the courage of resistance in colonial Brazil. In Portuguese with English subtitles.

Roots (1977). The entire ten-hour miniseries is extraordinary, but the first episode is most relevant to this chapter. Alex Haley's family saga begins with the kidnapping of Kunta Kinte from his village in west Africa in the 1700s and his experiences as a slave in the American colonies.

CHAPTER 27
TRADITION AND CHANGE IN EAST ASIA

INTRODUCTION

In the early modern age, powerful dynasties emerged in both China and Japan, featuring centralized, autocratic governments and efficient bureaucracies. In China, the Ming dynasty drove out the Mongols in 1368 and rebuilt the infrastructure of the empire, including the Great Wall, the Grand Canal, and irrigation systems. Ming Emperor Hongwu built a large navy and sponsored expeditions to southeast Asia and the Indian Ocean (see Chapter 23). However, later Ming rulers reversed this policy, destroyed the fleet, and restricted foreign contact.

In the mid-seventeenth century, Manchurian tribesmen invaded China, overthrew a corrupt Ming state, and established the Qing dynasty with a Manchu ruling class. Also in the seventeenth century, the Tokugawa shoguns of Japan broke the power of the provincial lords (the *daimyo*) and created a centralized military government. Although Chinese and Japanese traditions are very different, there are some common elements in this period, including

- A centralized bureaucracy. A hierarchy of Confucian-trained administrators ran the Qing Empire from the new capital at Nanjing. The Tokugawa shogunate required regular attendance by the *daimyo* at the capital city, Edo.

- Neo-Confucian values. Confucian teachings were appropriated by the state, stressing duty, order, and submission to authority. The patriarchal family was the basic social unit. Patriarchal values were grotesquely expressed in China in the practice of binding girls' feet.

- Agricultural economies with limited trade. Peasant farming fed the state, and crafts and luxury goods provided additional wealth. Both states severely restricted foreign trade to a few, carefully controlled port cities.

- Cultural insularity. For nearly two hundred years, Chinese and Japanese citizens did not travel abroad and had little knowledge of the outside world. By the eighteenth century, both dynasties had fallen behind the West in science and technology.

OUTLINE

I. The quest for political stability

    A. The Ming dynasty

        1. Ming government (1368–1644) drove the Mongols out of China

            a) Centralized government control; faced new invasions from the Mongols

            b) Rebuilt and repaired the Great Wall to prevent northern invasions

            c) Restored Chinese cultural traditions and civil service examinations

        2. Ming decline

            a) Coastal cities and trade disrupted by pirates, 1520s–1560s

    b)   Government corruption and inefficiency caused by powerful eunuchs

    c)   Famines and peasant rebellions during the 1630s and 1640s

    d)   Manchu invaders with peasant support led to final Ming collapse, 1644

B.   The Qing dynasty

    1.   The Manchus (1644–1911), invaders from Manchuria to the northeast

        a)   Overwhelmed the Chinese forces; proclaimed the Qing dynasty, 1644

        b)   Originally pastoral nomads, organized powerful military force

        c)   Captured Korea and Mongolia first, then China

        d)   Remained an ethnic elite; forbade intermarriage with Chinese

    2.   Kangxi (1661–1722) and his reign

        a)   Confucian scholar; effective, enlightened ruler

        b)   Conquered Taiwan; extended to Mongolia, central Asia, and Tibet

    3.   Qianlong (1736–1795) and his reign

        a)   A sophisticated and learned ruler, poet, and artist

        b)   Vietnam, Burma, and Nepal were made vassal states of China

        c)   Under his rule, China was peaceful, prosperous, and powerful

C.   The son of heaven and the scholar-bureaucrats

    1.   Emperor considered "the son of heaven"

        a)   Heavenly powers and an obligation to maintain order on the earth

        b)   Privileged life, awesome authority, and paramount power

    2.   Governance of the empire fell to civil servants, called scholar-bureaucrats

        a)   Schooled in Confucian texts, calligraphy

        b)   Had to pass rigorous examinations with strict quotas

    3.   The examination system and Chinese society

        a)   Civil service exam intensely competitive; few chosen for government positions

        b)   Others could become local teachers or tutors

        c)   System created a meritocracy with best students running the country

        d)   Wealthy families had some advantages over poor families

        e)   Confucian curriculum fostered common values

II. Economic and social changes

A.   The patriarchal family

    1.   The basic unit of Chinese society was the family; the highest value, filial piety

        a)   Included duties of children to fathers, loyalty of subjects to the emperor

        b)   Important functions of clan

2. Gender relations: strict patriarchal control over all females

    a) Parents preferred boys over girls; marriage was to continue male line

    b) Female infanticide; widows encouraged to commit suicide

    c) Footbinding of young girls increased

    d) Lowest status person in family was a young bride

B. Population growth and economic development

    1. Intense garden-style agriculture fed a large population

        a) American food crops in seventeenth century: maize, sweet potatoes, and peanuts

        b) Available land reached maximum productivity by mid-seventeenth century

    2. Population growth: 100 million in 1500, 225 million in 1750

    3. Manufacturing and trade benefited from abundant, cheap labor

        a) Exported large quantities of silk, porcelain, lacquerware, and tea

        b) Compensation for exports came in the form of silver bullion

    4. Foreign trade brought wealth to the dynasty, but threatened scholar-bureaucrats

        a) Kangxi began policy of strict control on foreign contact

        b) Western merchants restricted to Macao and Quangzhou

    5. Government and technology

        a) Ming and Qing dynasties considered technological change disruptive

        b) With abundant skilled labor, labor-saving technologies unnecessary

C. Gentry, commoners, soldiers, and mean people

    1. Privileged classes

        a) Scholar-bureaucrats and gentry occupied the most exalted positions

        b) Directed local government and society

    2. Peasants, the largest class, esteemed by Confucius for their honest labor

    3. Artisans and other skilled workers, some economic status

    4. Merchants often powerful and wealthy

    5. Lower classes or "mean people": slaves, servants, entertainers, prostitutes

III. The Confucian tradition and new cultural influences

A. Neo-Confucianism and pulp fiction

    1. Confucian education supported by Ming and Qing emperors

        a) Hanlin Academy in Beijing and provincial schools prepared students for civil service exams

        b) Imperial cultural projects: encyclopedias and libraries

    2. Popular culture expanded to include novels, romances, travel adventures

B. The return of Christianity to China

    1. Matteo Ricci (1552–1610), an Italian Jesuit in the Ming court

        a) A learned man who mastered written and oral Chinese

        b) Impressed Chinese with European science and mathematics

        c) Popular mechanical devices: glass prisms, harpsichords, clocks

    2. Confucianism and Christianity

        a) Jesuits respectful of Chinese tradition, but won few converts

        b) Chinese had problems with exclusivity of Christianity

    3. End of the Jesuit mission

        a) Rival Franciscan and Dominican missionaries criticized Jesuits' tolerance

        b) When the pope upheld critics, Emperor Kangxi denounced Christianity

        c) Jesuits had been an important bridge between Chinese and western cultures, introducing each to the achievements of the other

IV. The unification of Japan

A. The Tokugawa shogunate

    1. Tokugawa Ieyasu brought stability to Japan after 1600

        a) Japan divided into warring feudal estates

        b) As shogun, Ieyasu established a military government known as *bakufu*

    2. First need to control the daimyo, powerful local lords

        a) Each daimyo absolute lord within his domain

        b) Tokugawa shoguns required daimyo to live alternative years at Edo

        c) *Bakufu* controlled daimyo marriages, travel, expenditures

    3. Control of foreign relations

        a) The shoguns adopted policy of isolation from outside world, 1630s

        b) Foreign trade was under tight restriction at the port of Nagasaki

        c) Despite the policy, Japan was never completely isolated

B. Economic and social change

    1. Population growth

        a) Agricultural production doubled between 1600 and 1700

        b) Population rose by one-third from 1600 to 1700

        c) Then slow growth due to infanticide, contraception, late marriage, abortion

    2. Social change

        a) Peace undermined the social and economic role of warrior elites

        b) Merchants became prominent, and often wealthier than the ruling elites

C. Neo-Confucianism and floating worlds

   1. Neo-Confucianism (loyalty, submission) became the official ideology of the Tokugawa

   2. Scholars of "native learning" tried to establish distinctive Japanese identity

   3. "Floating worlds"—centers of urban culture

     a) Included teahouses, theaters, brothels, public baths

     b) Ihara Saikaku, poet and novelist

     c) *Kabuki* theater and *bunraku* (the puppet theater) popular

D. Christianity and Dutch learning

   1. Christian missions, under Jesuits, had significant success in sixteenth century

   2. Anti-Christian campaign launched by Tokugawa shoguns

     a) Feared any movement that might help daimyo

     b) Buddhists and Confucians resented Christian exclusivity

     c) After 1612, Christians banned from islands, thousands killed

   3. Dutch learning was one limited connection to the outside world

     a) Dutch merchants permitted to trade at Nagasaki

     b) Japanese scholars were permitted to learn Dutch and, after 1720, to read Dutch books

     c) Shoguns became enthusiastic proponents of Dutch learning by mid-eighteenth century

     d) European art, medicine, and science began to influence Japanese scholars

IDENTIFICATION: PEOPLE

What is the contribution of each of the following individuals to world history? Identification should include answers to the questions *who, what, where, when, how,* and *why is this person important?*

Yongle

Kangxi

Qianlong

Zheng He

Matteo Ricci

Ieyasu

IDENTIFICATION: TERMS/CONCEPTS

State in your own words what each of the following terms means and why it is significant to a study of world history. (Terms with an asterisk are defined in the glossary.)

Ming dynasty*

Great Wall

Forbidden City

Qing dynasty*

Scholar-bureaucrats

Footbinding

Neo-Confucianism*

Tokugawa shogunate*

Daimyo*

Floating worlds

STUDY QUESTIONS:

1. What steps did the Ming dynasty take to restore traditional Chinese culture and remove all foreign influences associated with Mongol rule?

2. What factors led to the collapse of the Ming dynasty? How did Manchurian invaders gain control of China?

3. Describe the structure of the typical Chinese family. What was the status of women within Ming and Qing societies?

4. What factors led to rapid population growth in China?

5. Why did the Qing dynasty discourage Chinese travel abroad and try to control contacts with foreigners? What was the impact of this policy?

6. How was Chinese society structured? Which classes enjoyed the greatest status? Which had the least?

7. What are some of the principles of Confucianism that influenced Chinese notions of government and society at this time?

8. How did the Tokugawa shogunate come to power in the sixteenth century in Japan? What steps did the shoguns take to control the daimyo?

9. What factors led to the economic and population growth of Japan under the Tokugawa shoguns?

10. To what extent was the culture of Japan influenced by China?

11. Why did the shoguns decide to cut off relations with the outside world? How was this isolation accomplished? What did this decision mean for the future of Japan?

INQUIRY QUESTIONS

1. Consider the process of becoming a scholar-bureaucrat. What might be the impact of this civil service system on the administration and culture of China? What were the future prospects for most of the students pictured on page 730 in the textbook?

2. What tone does Emperor Qianlong take in his letter to King George III of England (page 736)? How do you think King George and the English public reacted to this letter? Try to imagine an appropriate response.

3. Discuss the successes and failures of the Jesuit mission to China in the seventeenth and eighteenth centuries. Why was it so difficult for Christian missions to attract converts in China?

STUDENT QUIZ

1. Although the Ming emperor Yongle encouraged maritime exploration, later emperors discontinued that practice because
   a. Portuguese adventurers defeated the Chinese navy.
   b. new Mongol invasions turned China's attention to the north.
   c. the navy was considered too great a drain on the imperial resources.
   d. Qing emperors feared that new ideas would lead to political instability.
   e. all of the above.

2. Which of the following is *not* true of the Manchus?
   a. They were nomadic warriors from Manchuria.
   b. They spoke a different language from their ethnic Chinese subjects.
   c. They rejected Confucian principles in favor of a Mongol-style tribal council.
   d. They established the Qing dynasty.
   e. They ruled China from the Forbidden City in Beijing.

3. Which of the following is *not* true of the scholar-bureaucrats of China?
   a. They came almost entirely from aristocratic families.
   b. They were independent warlords, far from court and above the law.
   c. They were responsible for the security and stability of the country.
   d. Their appointment was based on their performance in the civil service exams.
   e. They enjoyed positions of power and prestige.

4. Which of the following is *not* true of China's civil service system?
   a. It was open to all men regardless of social standing.
   b. It provided the poor with an avenue for upward social mobility.
   c. It ensured that the most progressive men available governed China.
   d. It guaranteed the central place of Confucianism in Chinese education.
   e. It was very competitive with only a fraction of those applying gaining a government post.

5. The person with the *lowest* status in the Chinese household was
   a. an unmarried son.
   b. the mother of grown sons.
   c. a young husband.
   d. dead ancestors.
   e. a daughter-in-law.

6. All of the following are indicative of the low status of Chinese women in the Ming and Qing dynasties *except*
   a. the practice of footbinding.
   b. female infanticide.
   c. the forced burning of widows.
   d. a wife's obligations to her in-laws.
   e. arranged marriages.

7. Foreign traders sought all of the following Chinese products *except*
   a. silk.
   b. silver.
   c. porcelain.
   d. lacquerware.
   e. tea.

8. In the view of Emperor Qianlong, the trade between China and England was
   a. unnecessary to China but a favor to England.
   b. mutually beneficial to both countries.
   c. dangerous to both countries.
   d. dangerous to England but beneficial to China.
   e. none of the above.

9. By far the biggest social class in early modern China was the
   a. peasants.
   b. gentry class.
   c. workers and artisans.
   d. merchant class.
   e. "mean people."

10. According to traditional Confucian values, merchants were
    a. honored for their contributions to society.
    b. considered social parasites.
    c. considered "mean people."
    d. ineligible for civil service positions.
    e. all of the above.

11. Confucian education tended to support
    a. widespread literacy and popular fiction.
    b. an open mind to different religious traditions.
    c. conservative values such as filial piety and submission to authority.
    d. independent thinking and resistance to authority.
    e. none of the above.

12. Which of the following statements is *not* true of the Jesuit mission in China?
    a. Jesuits attracted many converts, and Christianity became a popular religion.
    b. Jesuits made an effort to learn Chinese and to understand Chinese culture.
    c. Jesuits captured Chinese interests with European science and technology.
    d. Other Catholic missionaries criticized the Jesuits' tolerance of Chinese traditions.
    c. Most Chinese were put off by Christian claims to be the only true religion.

13. Tokugawa Ieyasu ruled Japan as
    a. hereditary emperor.
    b. a temporary military ruler in support of the emperor.
    c. the elected lord of the daimyo.
    d. a powerful regional warlord.
    e. none of the above.

14. In order to control daimyo and maintain political stability, the Tokugawa *bakufu*
    a. obliged the daimyo to live in the capital on alternative years.
    b. limited contacts between individual daimyo.
    c. had final approval over all marriage alliances among the daimyo.
    d. limited contacts between daimyo and the outside world.
    e. all of the above.

15. The isolationism of the Tokugawa government included
    a. forbidding Japanese from going abroad.
    b. forbidding Chinese and Dutch merchants from trading at Nagasaki.
    c. forbidding scholars of neo-Confucianism from teaching in Japan.
    d. banning all foreign religions such as Confucianism and Buddhism.
    e. all of the above.

16. The population growth in Japan slowed after 1700 because of the practice of
    a. abortion.
    b. contraception.
    c. infanticide.
    d. late marriage.
    e. all of the above.

17. In the floating worlds in the major Japanese cities, one could find
    a. centers of neo-Confucian learning.
    b. important Shinto shrines and Buddhist temples.
    c. *kabuki* theaters, brothels, public baths, and teahouses.
    d. decorated luxury boats floating over the river water.
    e. all of the above.

18. What became of the Christian community in Japan under the Tokugawa shogunate?
    a. Christians were restricted to a few carefully controlled missions.
    b. Christians were brutally persecuted and driven into secrecy.
    c. Christianity merged with Buddhism and Shintoism into a new syncretic religion.
    d. Japanese Christians continued to worship but lost support after European trade was restricted.
    e. None of the above.

19. "Dutch learning" in Tokugawa Japan referred to all of the following areas *except*
    a. weapons and armaments.
    b. representational drawing and linear perspective.
    c. astronomy and calendars.
    d. anatomy and medicine.
    e. Dutch language.

20. In his treatise "Deus Destroyed," Fabian Fucan expressed his concerns that
    a. Japanese Christians were being persecuted by the shogunate.
    b. Japanese converts had too easily abandoned Christianity.
    c. Christian missionaries were misguided as to the true faith.
    d. Christian missionaries planned to subvert Buddhism and destroy traditional Japanese culture.
    e. without the Christian mission in Japan, the country would lose all contact with the outside world

MATCHING

Match these figures with the statements that follow.

A.	Yongle	F.	Qianlong
B.	Manchurians	G.	Matteo Ricci
C.	Ming dynasty	H.	Tokugawa Ieyasu
D.	Qing dynasty	I.	Tokugawa shogunate
E.	Kangxi	J.	Zheng He

1. ___ Shogun and effective ruler of Japan who established the *bakufu* government.

2. ___ Qing ruler who embodied the Confucian ideal: a scholar, an effective administrator, and a conqueror who expanded Chinese influence into Tibet and Taiwan.

3. ___ Ming emperor who sponsored the consolidation of Confucian learning into massive encyclopedias.

4. ___ Dynasty that defeated the Mongols and restored traditional Chinese values.

5. ___ Nomadic people who took advantage of the chaotic conditions in China in the seventeenth century and conquered the empire.

6. ___ Dynasty that began with sweeping economic reforms but grew increasingly isolated and conservative.

7. ___ Dynasty that effectively ruled Japan under the fiction that the military government was simply a temporary replacement for the emperor.

8. ___ Jesuit missionary who succeeded in introducing Western science and technology to China but was less successful in attracting converts to Christianity.

9. ___ Qing emperor who added Vietnam, Burma, and Nepal as vassal states to the empire.

10. ___ Ming-era admiral who led massive expeditions to southeast Asia and the Indian Ocean.

SEQUENCING

Place the following clusters of events in chronological order. Consider carefully how one event leads to another, and try to determine the internal logic of each sequence.

A.

_____ The fleet is mothballed and navigational charts are destroyed.

_____ Eunuch admiral Zheng He leads seven massive expeditions to southeast Asia and the Indian Ocean.

_____ The Ming dynasty begins by reasserting Chinese naval power in defense of coastal cities.

_____ Scholar-bureaucrats determine that the navy is too expensive and foreign influences too dangerous.

B.

_____ Several powerful daimyo and many commoners are converted.

_____ Tokugawa Ieyasu establishes the *bakufu* government and begins to rein in the daimyo.

_____ Francis Xavier establishes a Jesuit mission in Japan.

_____ Christian missionaries are banned and thousands of Japanese converts are persecuted.

_____ The shogunate closes off Japan to outside trade and influence.

C.

_____ Ming dynasty

_____ Qing dynasty

_____ Yuan (Mongol) dynasty

_____ Song dynasty

<u>QUOTATIONS</u>

For each of the following quotes, identify the speaker, if known, or the point of view. What is the significance of each passage?

1. "Japanese ships are strictly forbidden to leave for foreign countries. No Japanese is permitted to go abroad. If there is anyone who attempts to do so secretly, he must be executed. The ship so involved must be impounded and its owner arrested. . . . If any Japanese returns from overseas after residing there, he must be put to death."

2. "Our Celestial Empire possesses all things in prolific abundance and lacks no product within its own borders. There [is] therefore no need to import the manufactures of outside barbarians in exchange for our own produce. But, as the tea, silk, and porcelain which the Celestial Empire produces are absolute necessities to the European nations, we have permitted as a signal mark of favor, that trading agents should be established at Guangzhou."

3. "The study of mathematics and that of medicine are held in low esteem, because they are not fostered by honors as is the study of philosophy, to which students are attracted by the hope of the glory and the rewards attached to it. . . . The nine volumes of Confucius . . . present a collection of moral precepts for the future good and development of the kingdom."

4. "And therefore the adherent of Deus have no recourse but to subvert the Royal Sway, overthrow the Buddhas and the gods, eliminate the customs of Japan, and then to import the customs of their own countries; thus only will advance the plot they have concocted to usurp the country themselves."

MAP EXERCISE

Study Map 27.2 on page 727 in the textbook. On the outline map of east Asia below, locate and label the following:

- Boundaries of the Qing dynasty in 1644 and at its height in 1750
- Peripheral territories: Korea, Manchuria, Mongolia, Taiwan, Tibet, Vietnam
- Cities: Beijing, Nanjing, Macao, Guangzhou
- Features: Gobi Desert, Himalayas
- Bodies of water: Huang He River, Yangzi River, Yellow Sea, South China Sea

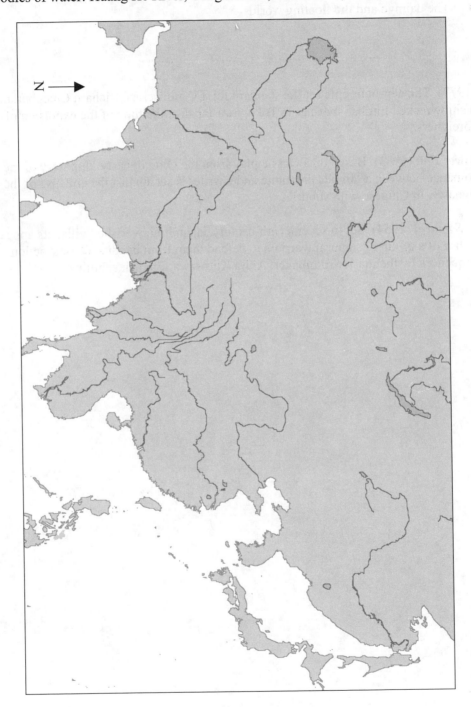

<u>CONNECTIONS</u>

In fifty words or less, explain the relationship between each of the following pairs. How does one lead to or foster the other? Be specific in your response.

- The Forbidden City and scholar-bureaucrats
- Confucianism and footbinding
- The Great Wall and Chinese technology
- Neo-Confucianism and Dutch learning
- The daimyo and the floating worlds

<u>FILMS</u>

Shogun (1977). This ten-hour epic set the standard for TV miniseries. Richard Chamberlain plays a shipwrecked English mariner in Tokugawa Japan at the time of the expulsion of foreigners.

Peach Flower Fan (1963). Based on a classic play from the Qing dynasty, this story of the romance between a famous prostitute and a writer is set against the collapse of the Ming dynasty. In Chinese with subtitles.

The Seven Samurai (1954). Set in seventeenth-century Japan, impoverished villagers appeal to the honor of a group of samurai warriors to defend them from bandits. Classic action sequences by the master filmmaker, Akira Kurosawa. English subtitles.

CHAPTER 28
THE ISLAMIC EMPIRES

<u>INTRODUCTION</u>

Three powerful Islamic empires emerged in India and southwest Asia after the fifteenth century. Beginning with the fall of Constantinople to the Ottoman Turks in 1453, Turkish warriors and charismatic leaders established first the Ottoman empire, then the Safavid dynasty in Persia (1502), and finally the Mughal dynasty in India (1526). Three distinct empires emerged with different cultures and traditions. Yet there are some striking similarities, including

- Autocratic rule. All three empires began as military states in which all power and prestige centered on the person of the ruler. All three were plagued by problems of succession from one ruler to the next.

- Islamic faith. All three empires embraced Islam. Sizable Christian minorities in the Ottoman Empire and a large Hindu majority in India forced those rulers to craft policies of religious toleration. The Safavid dynasty followed the Shia sect of Islam, which brought them into conflict with their Sunni Ottoman neighbors.

- Inward-looking policies. Although all three Islamic states maintained power through the military, neither the Safavid nor the Mughal dynasties developed a navy or a merchant fleet. Military resources were concentrated on defending inland borders. The Ottoman did have a powerful navy at one time, but by the eighteenth century, Ottoman armaments were outmoded and usually of European manufacture.

- Agricultural economies. Agriculture was the basis of the Islamic empires, and the majority of the population was engaged in raising and processing food. In the seventeenth and eighteenth centuries, the Ottoman and Safavid populations grew slowly; the population in India grew more dramatically.

- Ambivalence toward foreign trade. All three empires existed along important historic trade routes and derived benefit from their locations. The Safavids actively encouraged foreign trade. However, none of the three states sent merchants abroad or encouraged new industries.

- Cultural conservatism. The Islamic empires did not seek out new ideas or technologies and proved hostile to innovation by the eighteenth century. Like leaders in the Qing and Tokugawa dynasties (Chapter 27), Islamic conservatives feared that new ideas would lead to political instability.

<u>OUTLINE</u>

I. Formation of the Islamic empires

    A. The Ottoman empire (1289–1923)

        1. Founded by Osman Bey in 1289, who led Muslim religious warriors (*ghazi*)

        2. Ottoman expansion into Byzantine empire

a) Seized city of Bursa, then into the Balkans

   b) Organized *ghazi* into formidable military machine

   c) Central role of the Janissaries (slave troops)

   d) Effective use of gunpowder in battles and sieges

3. Mehmed the Conqueror (reigned 1451–1481)

   a) Captured Constantinople in 1453; it became Istanbul, the Ottoman capital

   b) Absolute monarchy; centralized state

   c) Expanded to Serbia, Greece, Albania; attacked Italy

4. Suleyman the Magnificent (reigned 1520–1566)

   a) Sultan Selim the Grim (reigned 1512–1520) occupied Syria and Egypt

   b) Suleyman the Magnificent expanded into southwest Asia and central Europe

   c) Suleyman also built a navy powerful enough to challenge European fleets

B. The Safavid empire

1. The Safavids, Turkish conquerors of Persia and Mesopotamia

   a) Founder Shah Ismail (reigned 1501–1524) claimed ancient Persian title of shah

   b) Proclaimed Twelver Shiism the official religion; imposed it on Sunni population

   c) Followers known as *qizilbash* (or "Red Hats")

2. Twelver Shiism

   a) Traced origins to twelve ancient Shiite imams

   b) Ismail believed to be the twelfth, or "hidden," imam, or even an incarnation of Allah

3. Battle of Chaldiran (1514)

   a) Sunni Ottomans persecuted Shiites within Ottoman empire

   b) *Qizilbash* considered firearms unmanly; were crushed by Ottomans at Chadiran

4. Shah Abbas the Great (1588–1629) revitalized the Safavid empire

   a) Modernized military; sought European alliances against Ottomans

   b) New capital at Isfahan; centralized administration

C. The Mughal empire

1. Babur (1523–1530), founder of Mughal ("Mongol") dynasty in India

   a) Central Asian Turkish adventurer invaded India in 1523, seized Delhi in 1526

   b) By his death in 1530, Mughal empire embraced most of India

2. Akbar (reigned 1556–1605), a brilliant charismatic ruler

   a) Created a centralized, absolutist government

   b) Expanded to Gujarat, Bengal, and southern India

        c) Encouraged religious tolerance between Muslims and Hindus

        d) Developed a syncretic religion called "divine faith"

    3. Aurangzeb (1659–1707)

        a) Expanded the empire to almost the entire Indian subcontinent

        b) Revoked policies of toleration: Hindus taxed, temples destroyed

        c) His rule troubled by religious tensions and hostility

II. Imperial Islamic society

  A. The dynastic state

    1. The emperors and Islam

        a) All three Islamic empires were military creations

        b) Authority of dynasty derived from personal piety and military prowess of rulers

        c) Devotion to Islam encouraged rulers to extend their faith to new lands

    2. Steppe traditions

        a) Autocratic: emperors imposed their will on the state

        b) Ongoing problems with royal succession

        c) Ottoman rulers could legally kill their brothers after taking the throne

    3. Royal women often wielded great influence on politics

  B. Agriculture and trade

    1. Food crops the basis of all three empires

        a) Major crops: wheat and rice

        b) Little impacted by new American crops

        c) Imports of coffee and tobacco very popular

    2. Population growth in the three empires less dramatic than in China or Europe

        a) Significant population growth in India from more intense agriculture

        b) Less dramatic growth in Safavid and Ottoman realms

    3. Long-distance trade important to all three empires

        a) Ottoman and Safavid empires shared segments of the east-west trade routes

        b) Safavids offered silk, carpets, and ceramics to European trading companies

        c) The Mughal empire less attentive to foreign or maritime trading

        d) Mughals permitted stations for English, French, and Dutch trading companies

  C. Religious affairs in the Islamic empires

    1. Religious diversity created challenges to the rule of the empires

    2. Religious diversity in India under the rule of Akbar

        a) Portuguese Goa was the center of Christian missions

b) Jesuits welcomed at court of Akbar, but he was not interested in an exclusive faith

c) Akbar tolerated Sikhism, a new faith combining elements of Hinduism and Islam

d) Advocated syncretic "divine faith," emphasizing loyalty to emperor

3. Religious minorities generally tolerated in Islamic states

a) In Ottoman empire, conquered peoples protected, granted religious and civil autonomy in their own communities

b) In India, the Muslim rulers closely cooperated with Hindu majority

c) Under Aurangzeb: Islam proclaimed official state religion, nonbelievers taxed

D. Cultural patronage of the Islamic emperors

1. All three sponsored arts and public works: mosques, palaces, schools, hospitals, etc.

2. Istanbul, the Ottoman capital, a bustling city of a million people

a) Topkapi palace housed government offices and sultan's residence

b) The Suleymaniye blended Islamic and Byzantine architectural elements

3. Isfahan, Safavid capital, the "queen of Persian cities"

4. Fatehpur Sikri, Mughal capital, created by Akbar

a) Combined Islamic style with Indian elements

b) Site abandoned because of bad water supply

c) The Taj Mahal, exquisite example of Mughal architecture

III. The empires in transition

A. The deterioration of imperial leadership, from the sixteenth to eighteenth centuries

1. Dynastic decline caused by negligent rulers, factions, and government corruption

2. Tensions increased when religious conservatives abandoned policies of tolerance

a) Ottoman conservatives resisted innovations like the telescope and printing press

b) In Safavid empire: Shiite leaders urged the shahs to persecute Sunnis, non-Muslims, and even the Sufis

c) In Mughal India, Aurangzeb's policies provoked deep animosity of Hindus

B. Economic and military decline

1. Strong economies in sixteenth century; stagnated by eighteenth century

a) End of territorial expansion; difficult to support armies and bureaucrats

b) Series of long and costly wars

c) Officials resorted to raising taxes or corruption to deal with financial problems

d) Failure to develop trade and industry; lost initiative to European merchants

2. Military decline

a) Importing European weapons only promoted European weapon industries

b) Imported arsenals outdated

c) Ottomans even purchased military vessels from abroad

C. Cultural conservatism

1. Neglect of cultural developments in the larger world

a) Ottoman cartographer, Piri Reis, gathered together European maps

b) Muslims seldom traveled to the West, confident of their superiority

c) Ignorant of European technological developments—hostile to telescope, 1703

2. Resistance to printing press

a) Introduced by Jewish refugees to Anatolia, late fifteenth century

b) At first, Ottoman authorities banned printing in Turkish and Arabic

c) Ban lifted in 1729, but conservatives forced closure of a Turkish press in 1742

d) In India, Mughal rulers showed little interest in printing technology

e) Aesthetic considerations: elegant, handwritten books favored over cheaply produced printed ones

f) Printed matter could introduce and spread subversive ideas

3. Foreign cultural innovations seen as a threat to political stability

IDENTIFICATION: PEOPLE

What is the contribution of each of the following individuals to world history? Identification should include answers to the questions *who, what, where, when, how,* and *why is this person important?*

Osman

Mehmed the Conqueror

Suleyman the Magnificent

Shah Ismail

Shah Abbas

Babur

Akbar

Aurangzeb

IDENTIFICATION: TERMS/CONCEPTS

State in your own words what each of the following terms means and why it is significant to a study of world history. (Terms with an asterisk are defined in the glossary.)

Ottoman empire*

Safavids*

Mughals*

*Ghazi**

Janissaries

Twelver Shiism*

*Qizilbash**

Sikhs*

Taj Mahal

STUDY QUESTIONS

1. How did the Ottoman Turks defeat the Byzantine empire? What was the basis of their military strength?

2. Discuss the religious and political issues that separated the Ottoman Turks and the Safavid Turks, two neighboring Islamic states, in the sixteenth century.

3. By what steps did Shah Abbas achieve a strong and unified Safavid state?

4. What was Babur's assessment of India? Why did he decide to remain?

5. Compare Akbar's policies with those of Aurangzeb.

6. What aspects of these Islamic empires made political succession so uncertain? What often happened when the ruler died?

7. What were some of the principal commodities traded in and out of the Islamic states? Which state had the most to offer Western merchants?

8. Identify and compare the status of religious minorities within the three Islamic empires. Which empire faced the greatest challenges in this regard?

9. What factors led to the economic and military decline of the Islamic empires?

INQUIRY QUESTIONS

1. How were Turkish and Mongol steppe traditions translated into political structures and ideologies? Which of these practices were most effective, and which seem to have been least effective?

2. What factors contributed to the increasing cultural conservatism in the Islamic states during the seventeenth century? What were the future implications of such resistance to science and technological change?

STUDENT QUIZ

1. In their rise of power the Ottomans were aided by the *ghazi,* who were
    a. Mongol mercenaries.
    b. Christian captives raised to fight for them.
    c. Muslim religious warriors.
    d. Anatolian peasants, eager to escape heavy taxes of the Byzantine empire.
    e. all of the above.

2. The Ottoman military made use of
    a. gunpowder weapons.
    b. siege warfare.
    c. specially trained Janissary forces.
    d. armored cavalry.
    e. all of the above.

3. Which of the following places did *not* come under the control of the Muslim Ottomans?
    a. Albania
    b. Anatolia
    c. Egypt
    d. the Iranian plateau
    e. Tunisia

4. The Janissaries were
    a. slave women who lived in the sultan's harem.
    b. Christian boys taken from conquered territories and raised as special forces.
    c. regional administrators, who were granted autonomy in exchange for loyalty and support.
    d. armored, light cavalry.
    e. eunuchs in service to the sultan.

5. Suleyman the Magnificent
    a. captured Belgrade and laid siege to the city of Vienna.
    b. conquered Russia.
    c. brought the entire Arabian peninsula under Ottoman rule.
    d. invaded the island of Sicily.
    e. all of the above.

6. In his "Turkish Letters," the Hungarian diplomat Ghislain de Busbecq expresses concerns that
    a. the Ottoman Turks are technologically superior to Europeans.
    b. Ottoman troops are numerically superior to European forces.
    c. Ottoman forces are hardier and more disciplined than European forces.
    d. Ottoman forces are better fed than European forces.
    e. all of the above.

7. The Safavid empire began with the reign of Shah Ismail, who claimed legitimacy to the throne by
    a. killing off competitors from the Mughal royal families.
    b. seizing the Peacock Throne.
    c. tracing his ancestry back to a Sufi religious leader.
    d. marrying the daughter of Suleyman the Magnificent.
    e. tracing his ancestry back to Tamerlane.

8. Twelver Shiism was a Muslim sect that claimed that
    a. Ismail was the "hidden" imam or even a reincarnation of Allah.
    b. Shah Ismail was a direct descendant of the Prophet Muhammad.
    c. all *ghazi* are true spokesmen of Allah.
    d. the Safavid were the lost tribe of Israel.
    e. the *qizilbash,* or "red heads," should be purged from the country.

9. At the Battle of Chaldiran in 1514,
    a. the Safavid *qizilbash* defeated the Ottoman Janissary forces.
    b. the Sunni Ottomans defeated the Shiite Safavids.
    c. an alliance of Safavids and Ottomans defeated European crusaders.
    d. European forces turned back the Ottoman advance into central Europe.
    e. none of the above.

10. Shah Abbas revitalized the Safavid regime by all of the following means *except*
    a. increasing the use of gunpowder weapons.
    b. making land grants to *qizilbash* officers.
    c. expelling the Portuguese from Hormuz.
    d. forging alliances with the Ottomans against Europeans.
    e. promoting trade with other lands.

11. The Mughal leader Babur originally invaded northern India in order to
    a. create a Shiite Muslim state.
    b. finance his military campaigns in central Asia.
    c. control the trade routes into southeast Asia.
    d. defeat his long-standing enemy, the sultan of Delhi.
    e. all of the above.

12. The reforms of Akbar included all the following *except*
    a. religious toleration for Hindus and Sikhs.
    b. a syncretic religion, called "divine faith," which stressed loyalty to the emperor.
    c. a centralized administrative structure with ministers appointed to regional provinces.
    d. education and basic rights for Indian women.
    e. conquest of Gujarat and Bengal.

13. The Mughal emperor Aurangzeb
    a. replaced many Hindu temples with mosques.
    b. required all nonbelievers to pay a special tax.
    c. extended Mughal authority into southern India.
    d. faced many rebellions and religious conflicts.
    e. all of the above.

14. Politically, all three of the Islamic states began as
    a. oligarchies, dominated by the merchant class.
    b. constitutional monarchies.
    c. military states.
    d. feudal aristocracies.
    e. tribal councils.

15. Foreign trade took hold primarily in
    a. the Ottoman and the Mughal empires.
    b. the Mughal and the Safavid empires.
    c. the Safavid and the Ottoman empires.
    d. all three empires.
    e. none of the empires.

16. One persistent problem within all three empires was
    a. maintaining the loyalty of the military.
    b. maintaining control over a vast slave population.
    c. communication between the central and provincial administrations.
    d. achieving a peaceful succession after the death of the emperor.
    e. all of the above.

17. Major trade commodities sought by European merchants from the Islamic empires included
    a. coffee and tobacco.
    b. sugar and rum.
    c. silks, carpets, and other crafts.
    d. wheat, rice, and other food staples.
    e. slaves.

18. Which of the following would *not* be an example of religious toleration under Muslim rule?
    a. the *millet* communities in the Ottoman empire.
    b. the *jizya* tax imposed by Aurangzeb
    c. the Jesuit mission at the court of Goa
    d. the syncretic "divine faith" of Akbar
    e. Christian monasteries permitted at Isfahan

19. A major reason for the decline in the Islamic empires was
    a. the refusal to accept new ideas and technologies from the West.
    b. an abandonment of religious toleration as a state policy.
    c. the decline in military leadership.
    d. the rigidity of the religious leaders.
    e. all of the above.

20. The Muslim resistance to new ideas and technologies by the eighteenth century is illustrated by
    a. the Ottoman ban on the printing press.
    b. the purchase of outmoded weapons from Europe.
    c. the banning of "impious" telescopes.
    d. reluctance of Muslims to travel abroad.
    e. all of the above.

MATCHING

Match these figures with the statements that follow.

A. Shah Abbas
B. *Ghazs*
C. Janissaries
D. *Qizilbash*
E. Shah Ismael
F. Mehmed the Conqueror

G. Osman
H. Babur
I. Akbar
J. Suleyman the Magnificent
K. Aurangzeb
L. Shah Jahan

1. ___ Thirteenth-century founder of the Ottoman dynasty.

2. ___ Sixteenth-century founder of the Safavid dynasty.

3. ___ Sixteenth-century founder of the Mughal dynasty.

4. ___ Religious warriors in service of the Ottoman empire.

5. ___ Followers of Twelver Shiism.

6. ___ Ottoman sultan who conquered Constantinople and created a unified Ottoman empire.

7. ___ Ottoman troops comprised of captive Christian boys, raised in Islam and devoted to the sultan.

8. ___ Seventeenth-century ruler who sponsored the creation of the Peacock Throne and the construction of the Taj Mahal, two symbols of the wealth of the Mughal empire.

9. ___ Ottoman sultan, known to his subjects as "the Lawgiver," who expanded his empire into central Europe.

10. ___ Ruler who extended Mughal rule into southern India but faced many challenges from his Hindu subjects.

11. ___ Effective Safavid ruler who modernized the army and retook Hormuz from the Portuguese.

12. ___ Mughal ruler who created a centralized administrative structure that included both Hindus and Muslims in positions of power.

SEQUENCING

Place the following clusters of events in chronological order. Consider carefully how one event leads to another, and try to determine the internal logic of each sequence.

A.

_____ With powerful forces and gunpowder weapons, Mehmed the Conqueror encircles and finally captures Constantinople.

_____ Moving into the Balkans, the Ottomans create a special military force comprised of captive Christian slaves.

_____ Osman Bey founds the Turkish dynasty in northwest Anatolia.

_____ Renamed Istanbul, the city is the capital of a vast and wealthy empire.

_____ Turkish *ghazi* seize territory in Anatolia from the Byzantine empire.

B.

_____ Safavid empire

_____ Abbasid empire

_____ Iran

_____ the Ilkhanate of Persia

QUOTATIONS

For each of the following quotes, identify the speaker, if known, or the point of view. What is the significance of each passage?

1. "The *Ghazi* is the instrument of the religion of Allah, a servant of God who purifies the earth from the filth of polytheism; the *Ghazi* is the sword of God, he is the protector and the refuge of the believers."

2. "I am the Sovereign of two lands and two seas."

3. "I tremble when I think of what the future must bring when I compare the Turkish system with our own; one army must prevail and the other be destroyed. . . . On their side are the resources of a mighty empire, strength unimpaired, experience in fighting, a veteran soldiery. . . . On our side is public poverty, private luxury, impaired strength, lack of endurance and training."

4. "For all these reasons, most of the best warriors were unwilling to stay in India; in fact, they determined to leave. . . . I summoned all the leaders and took counsel. I said, 'Without means and resources there is no empire and conquest, and without land and followers there is no sovereignty and rule. . . . Should we abandon a country taken at such risk of life?' "

5. "I perceive that there are varying customs and beliefs of varying religious paths. . . . But the followers of each religion regard the institution of their own religion as better than those of any other. . . . Wherefore I desire that on appointed days the books of all the religious laws be brought forward, and the doctors meet and hold discussion, so that I may hear them, and that each one may determine which is the truest and mightiest religion."

MAP EXERCISES

1. On a map of India and southwest Asia, draw the boundaries of the Ottoman, Safavid, and Mughal empires at their height (see Map 28.1, page 755 in the textbook). Add the following features:
    - Bodies of water: Arabian Sea, Black Sea, Caspian Sea, Mediterranean Sea, Persian Gulf, Red Sea, Euphrates River, Indus River, Ganges River, Nile River, Tigris River
    - Regions: Albania, Anatolia, Arabia, Armenia, Egypt, Greece, Gujarat, Iran, Lebanon, Punjab, Serbia
    - Cities: Alexandria, Cairo, Delhi, Goa, Hormuz, Isfahan, Istanbul, Kabul, Mecca

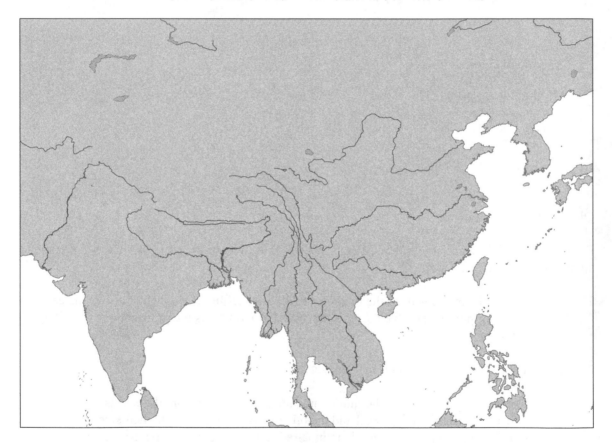

2. Graph the population growth of India, Persia, and Ottoman Anatolia between 1500 and 1800. Compare to China (Chapter 27) and Europe (Chapter 24). In what country and in what century was growth most dramatic? Where and when was there the least population growth? Explain the differences.

CONNECTIONS

In fifty words or less, explain the relationship between each of the following pairs. How does one lead to or foster the other? Be specific in your response.

- Janissaries and Topkapi palace
- Trading concessions and European weapons
- Muslim clerics and English muskets
- Treaty of Tordesillas and Mehmed the Conqueror

FILMS

Gabbeh (1997). A romantic fable set among a nomadic tribe in Iran. Gabbeh is both the name of a traditional handwoven carpet and the name of the heroine, who is forbidden by her father to marry the man she loves. In Farsi with subtitles.

Prince Ehtejab (1974). Dying of tuberculosis, the Safavid Prince Ehtejab shuts himself up in his palace, where he is assailed by the memories and guilt of his family's cruel deeds. Based on the classic Iranian novel about the Quajar dynasty, which ruled Persia from 1795 to 1925. In Farsi with subtitles.

Mughal-e-Azam, or *The Great Mughal* (1960). The conflict between love and duty is presented in this largely fictional tale of the doomed romance between the son of the Emperor Akbar and a common dancer. An uncritical view of Akbar as empire builder. In Hindi/Urdu with subtitles.

CHAPTER 29
REVOLUTIONS AND NATIONAL STATES
IN THE ATLANTIC WORLD

INTRODUCTION

The years 1776 and 1789 are pivotal dates in world history. The impact of the American revolution and the French revolution extended far beyond the borders of those two countries. Other revolts followed, and in spite of a conservative reaction in Europe, the world was not the same afterward. Some common elements of the revolutionary era:

- New ideals. The ideals of freedom, equality, and popular sovereignty first expressed by the philosophes of the Enlightenment (see Chapter 24) were now enacted. John Locke's theory of government as a contract between rulers and subjects inspired the leaders of the American revolution. Likewise, Jean-Jacques Rousseau's concept of a "social contract" based on the "general will" found expression in the National Assembly of France.

- New governments. Vastly different governments emerged in the United States, France, and Latin America. However, most revolutionary governments began with written constitutions, statements of individual rights, and elected assemblies. Political power was generally the privilege of men of property. Only Haiti empowered all men regardless of race.

- New ideologies. Political theories emerged to address the dramatic changes of the age. Conservatism, liberalism, and later, socialism (see Chapter 30) differed in the understanding of change and authority and came to express the social and economic currents of the nineteenth century.

- Uneven social progress. Some changes, such as the abolition of feudal rights and obligations in France, were profound and permanent. Other changes, like the abolition of slavery in the Americas, came more slowly and piecemeal. Equal rights for women did not gain momentum until late in the nineteenth century.

- Nationalism. Popular sovereignty gave voice to a new form of identity. Based on notions of a common cultural and historic experience, nationalism was a powerful force in the nineteenth century. Ethnic minorities like the Greeks within the Ottoman empire demanded national independence, and scattered cultural groups like the Italians and the Germans created new states to house their national identities.

OUTLINE

I. Popular sovereignty and political upheaval

    A. Enlightened and revolutionary ideas

        1. Popular sovereignty: relocating sovereignty in the people

            a) Traditionally monarchs claimed a "divine right" to rule

b) The Enlightenment challenged this right, made the monarch responsible to the people

c) John Locke's theory of contractual government: authority comes from the consent of the governed

2. Freedom and equality: important values of the Enlightenment

a) Demands for freedom of worship and freedom of expression

b) Demands for political and legal equality

(1) Condemned legal and social privileges of aristocrats

(2) Jean-Jacques Rousseau, *The Social Contract*

c) Equality not extended to women, peasants, laborers, slaves, or people of color

3. Ideals of Enlightenment were significant global influence

B. The American revolution

1. Tension between Britain and the North American colonies

a) Legacy of Seven Years' War: British debt, North American tax burden

b) Mounting colonial protest over taxes, trade policies, parliamentary rule

(1) Colonial boycott of British goods

(2) Attacks on British officials; Boston Tea Party, 1773

c) Political protest over representation in Parliament: Continental Congress, 1774

d) British troops and colonial militia skirmished at the village of Lexington, 1775

2. The Declaration of Independence, 4 July 1776

a) Thirteen United States of America severed ties with Britain

b) Declaration inspired by Enlightenment and Locke's theory of government

3. The American revolution, 1775–1781

a) British advantages: strong government, navy, army, plus loyalists in colonies

b) American advantages: European allies, George Washington's leadership

c) Weary of a costly conflict, British forces surrendered in 1781

4. Building an independent state: Constitutional Convention, 1787

a) Constitution guaranteed freedom of press, of speech, and of religion

b) American republic based on principles of freedom, equality, popular sovereignty

c) Full legal and political rights granted only to men of property

C. The French revolution

1. Summoning the Estates General

a) Financial crisis: half of government revenue went to national debt

b) King Louis XVI forced to summon Estates General to raise new taxes

    c) Many representatives wanted sweeping political and social reform

    d) First and Second Estates (nobles, clergy) tried to limit Third Estate (commoners)

2. The National Assembly formed by representatives of Third Estate, 17 June 1789

    a) Demanded a written constitution and popular sovereignty

    b) Angry mob seized the Bastille on 14 July, sparked insurrections in many cities

    c) National Assembly wrote the "Declaration of the Rights of Man and the Citizen"

3. "Liberty, equality, and fraternity" was the slogan and values of the National Assembly

    a) The National Assembly abolished the feudal system, altered the role of church

    b) France became a constitutional monarchy, 1791

4. The Convention replaced National Assembly under new constitution, 1791

    a) Austrian and Prussian armies invaded France to restore *ancien régime*

    b) France declared war on Spain, Britain, and the Netherlands

    c) Convention abolished the monarchy and proclaimed France a republic

    d) King Louis XVI and Queen Marie Antoinette executed, 1793

    e) Radical Jacobins dominated the Convention in 1793–94 in a "reign of terror"

    f) Revolutionary changes: in religion, dress, calendar, women's rights

5. The Directory, 1795–1799

    a) A conservative reaction against the excesses of the Convention

    b) Executed the Jacobin leader Robespierre, July 1794

    c) New constitution

D. The reign of Napoleon, 1799–1815

1. Napoleon Bonaparte (1769–1821)

    a) Brilliant military leader; became a general in the royal army at age twenty-four

    b) Supported the revolution; defended the Directory

    c) His invasion of Egypt was defeated by British army

    d) Overthrew the Directory and named himself consul for life

2. Napoleonic France brought stability after years of chaos

    a) Made peace with the Roman Catholic church and pope

    b) Extended freedom of religion to Protestants and Jews

    c) Civil Code of 1804: political and legal equality for all adult men

    d) French civil law a model for law codes elsewhere in Europe and North America

    e) Restricted individual freedom, especially speech and press

3. Napoleon's empire: 1804, proclaimed himself emperor

a) Dominated the European continent: Iberia, Italy, Netherlands

b) Defeated Austria and Prussia; fought British on high seas

c) Disastrous invasion of Russia in 1812 destroyed Grand Army

4. The fall of Napoleon

a) Forced by coalition of enemies to abdicate in 1814, exiled on Elba

b) Escaped, returned to France, raised army, but was defeated by British in 1815

II. The influence of revolution

A. The Haitian revolution: the only successful slave revolt in history

1. Saint-Domingue, rich French colony on western Hispaniola

a) Society dominated by small white planter class

b) 90 percent of population were slaves working under brutal conditions

c) Large communities of escaped slaves, or maroons

d) Free blacks fought in American war, brought back revolutionary ideas

e) Widespread discontent: white settlers sought self-governance, *gens de couleur* sought political rights, slaves wanted freedom

2. Slave revolt began in 1791

a) Factions of white settlers, *gens de couleur,* and slaves battled each other

b) French troops arrived in 1792; British and Spanish forces intervened in 1793

3. Toussaint Louverture (1744–1803)

a) Son of slaves, literate, skilled organizer, built a strong and disciplined army

b) Controlled most of Saint-Domingue by 1797, created a constitution in 1801

c) Arrested by French troops; died in jail, 1803

4. The Republic of Haiti

a) Yellow fever ravaged French troops; defeated and driven out by slave armies

b) Declared independence in 1803; established the Republic of Haiti in 1804

B. Wars of independence in Latin America

1. Latin American society rigidly hierarchical

a) Social classes: *peninsulares,* creoles, slaves, and indigenous peoples

b) Creoles sought to displace the *peninsulares* but retain their privileged position

2. Mexican independence

a) Napoleon's invasion of Spain in 1807 weakened royal control of colonies

b) 1810: peasant revolt in Mexico led by Hidalgo, defeated by conservative creoles

c) 1821: Mexico briefly a military dictatorship, then in 1822 a republic

d) South part of Mexico was split into several independent states in 1830s

3. Simón Bolívar (1783–1830) led independence movement in South America

    a) Inspired by George Washington, took arms against Spanish rule in 1811

    b) Creole forces overcame Spanish armies throughout South America, 1824

    c) Bolívar's effort of creating Gran Colombia failed in 1830s

4. Brazilian independence

    a) Portuguese royal court fled to Rio de Janeiro, 1807

    b) The king's son, Pedro, agreed to Brazilian independence, 1821

    c) Became Emperor Pedro I in the independent Brazil (reigned 1822–1834)

5. Creole dominance in Latin America

    a) Independence brought little social change in Latin America

    b) Principal beneficiaries were creole elites

C. The emergence of ideologies: conservatism and liberalism

1. Conservatism: resistance to change

    a) Importance of continuity, tradition

    b) Edmund Burke viewed society as an organism that changed slowly over time

        (1) American Revolution: a natural and logical outcome of history

        (2) French Revolution: violent and irresponsible

2. Liberalism: welcomed change as an agent of progress

    a) Championed freedom, equality, democracy, written constitutions

    b) Many liberals consider democracy dangerous because it promoted mass participation in politics

    c) John Stuart Mill championed individual freedom and minority rights

D. Testing the limits of revolutionary ideals: slavery

1. Movements to end slave trade: began in 1700s, gained momentum during revolutions

    a) In 1807 British Parliament outlawed slave trade

    b) Other states followed suit, though illegal slave trade continued from some time

2. Movements to abolish slavery: more difficult because of property rights

    a) In Haiti and much of South America, end of slavery came with independence

    b) In Europe and North America, campaign against slave trade became campaign to abolish slavery

    c) Abolition in Britain in 1833, France in 1848, the United States in 1865, Brazil in 1888

3. Abolition brought legal freedom for slaves but not political equality

E. Testing the limits of revolutionary ideals: women's rights

1. Enlightenment ideals and women

    a) Enlightenment call for equality not generally extended to women

    b) Women used logic of Locke to argue for women's rights

        (1) Mary Astell attacked male dominance in the family

        (2) Mary Wollstonecraft: women possessed same natural rights as men

2. Women crucial to revolutionary activities

    a) French revolution granted women rights of education and property, not the vote

    b) Olympe de Gouges's declaration of full citizenship for women too radical

    c) Women made no significant gains in other revolutions

3. Women's rights movements gained ground in the nineteenth century in United States and Europe

III. The consolidation of national states in Europe

A. Nations and nationalism

    1. Cultural nationalism: an expression of national identity

        a) Emphasized common historical experience

        b) Used folk culture and literature to illustrate national spirit (*Volkgiest*)

    2. Political nationalism more intense in the nineteenth century

        a) Demanded loyalty and solidarity from members of the national group

        b) Minorities sought independence as a national community

        c) Young Italy formed by Giuseppe Mazzini

    3. Zionism: Jewish nationalism as a response to widespread European anti-Semitism

        a) Movement founded by Theodor Herzl to create a Jewish state in Palestine

        b) Anti-Semitism practiced openly in many countries of Europe

        c) Jewish state of Israel finally created in 1948

B. The emergence of national communities

    1. Congress of Vienna, 1814–15

        a) Conservative leaders determined to restore old order after defeat of Napoleon

        b) Succeeded in maintaining balance of power in Europe for a century

        c) Failed in repressing nationalist and revolutionary ideas

    2. Nationalist rebellions against old order throughout nineteenth century

        a) Greek rebels overcame Ottoman rule in 1827

        b) 1830 and 1848, rebellions in France, Spain, Portugal, German states, Belgium, Italy, and Poland

        c) Conservative government usually restored afterward but ideals persisted

C. The unification of Italy and Germany

    1. Cavour and Garibaldi united Italy by 1870

        a) Mazzini's Young Italy inspired uprisings against foreign rule in Italy

        b) Cavour led nationalists and expelled Austrian authorities in northern Italy, 1859

        c) Garibaldi controlled southern Italy, delivered it over to King Vittore Emmanuele, 1860

    2. Prussian prime minister Otto von Bismarck (1815–1898) created a united Germany

        a) In Germany, nationalist rebellion was repressed in 1848

        b) Bismarck provoked three wars that swelled German pride

        c) 1871, Prussian king proclaimed emperor of the Second Reich

IDENTIFICATION: PEOPLE

What is the contribution of each of the following individuals to world history? Identification should include answers to the questions *who, what, where, when, how,* and *why is this person important?*

Olympe de Gouges

John Locke

George Washington

Louis XVI

Marie Antoinette

Maximilien Robespierre

Napoleon Bonaparte

Toussaint Louverture

Simón Bolívar

Edmund Burke

John Stuart Mill

Klemens von Metternich

Otto von Bismarck

IDENTIFICATION: TERMS/CONCEPTS

State in your own words what each of the following terms means and why it is significant to a study of world history. (Terms with an asterisk are defined in the glossary.)

Declaration of Independence*

Ancien régime

National Assembly

Jacobins

Directory

Civil Code

*Peninsulares**

Conservatism

Liberalism

Zionism

Congress of Vienna*

STUDY QUESTIONS

1. In what specific ways did the ideals of the Enlightenment challenge long-held assumptions about government and social order?

2. What specific issues and concerns led the British colonies of North America to revolt against their sovereign? What was the outcome of that rebellion?

3. What were the principal causes of the French revolution of 1789? Were these concerns addressed by the revolution?

4. How was French society restructured during the most radical phase of the revolution (1793–94)? Were these permanent changes or short-lived ones?

5. Conventional wisdom holds that Napoleon ended the revolution when he proclaimed himself emperor in 1804. In what ways did he continue the ideals of the revolution? In what ways did he reverse the revolution?

6. What events led to the slave revolt of Saint-Domingue (Haiti)? Why was this rebellion successful when so many other slave revolts failed?

7. Describe the basic social structure of Latin American society in 1800. What factors led to the revolutions that followed?

8. What kind of states emerged in Mexico, Gran Colombia, and Brazil after the revolutions?

9. What factors led the Western powers to abolish the slave trade and then slavery in the nineteenth century?

10. What was the impact of the ideals of the Enlightenment and the events of the revolutionary era on the status of women? Give some specific examples.

11. Compare the unification of Italy with the unification of Germany.

INQUIRY QUESTIONS

1. Compare the declarations on pages 789 and 804 in the textbook. Did Olympe de Gouges simply add the word *women* to the original declaration, or did she substantially change the meaning of the concept of citizenship in her declaration? Did she speak from the traditions of the Enlightenment, or did she challenge those traditions?

2. Under the ancien régime, the state was generally defined as the domain of the sovereign. How was this definition changed by the American and French revolutions? What are the elements of a national identity in the modern world? (And what is the place of minorities such as the Jews within this new concept of nationality?)

3. Compare the positions of a conservative and a liberal in the nineteenth century on the nature of political authority and political change. What would each ideology say about abolition of slavery? About women's rights?

STUDENT QUIZ

1. The ideas of the Enlightenment challenged the long-term assumptions about sovereignty and instead proposed that
    a. true government stems from religious authority.
    b. the best form of government is a democracy.
    c. governments are bound to the will of the people.
    d. all government is inherently unjust. Humans are better off living in a state of nature.
    e. church and state should be entirely separate.

2. Which of the following could be considered an expression of enlightened ideas about government?
    a. the Stamp Act of 1708
    b. the Quartering Act
    c. the Declaration of Independence
    d. the Committee of Public Safety
    e. the Congress of Vienna

3. The American colonists won their bid for independence primarily because
   a. they had superior generals.
   b. they were united in the cause of freedom.
   c. colonial militias were more disciplined and better marksmen than British troops.
   d. the French and the Dutch decided to support them against the British.
   e. all of the above.

4. Embedded in the American Constitution is the principle of
   a. universal male suffrage.
   b. the abolition of slavery.
   c. free enterprise.
   d. westward expansion.
   e. popular sovereignty.

5. Which of the following was *not* one of the causes of the French revolution of 1789?
   a. a staggering national debt
   b. accusation of treason against Louis XVI
   c. resentment at the privileges of the aristocracy
   d. the extravagance of Marie Antoinette and the court at Versailles
   e. the opportunity presented by the summoning of the Estates General

6. Which of the following was *not* one of the provisions of the new French constitution of 1791?
   a. France became a constitutional monarchy.
   b. Church property was confiscated and clergy lost their privileged status.
   c. Peasants were freed from the dues and services owed to their landlords.
   d. All adult males were given the right to vote in national elections.
   e. An elective, legislative body, the Convention, was established.

7. Under the rule of the Convention, French women
   a. gained important property rights and the right to a divorce.
   b. were proclaimed full citizens of the Republic.
   c. lost economic power to their husbands.
   d. were legally defined in terms of either their fathers or their husbands.
   e. were granted the right to vote in national elections.

8. Napoleon Bonaparte rose to power as
   a. a liberal noble who supported the Third Estate.
   b. a military hero.
   c. an opponent of Robespierre.
   d. a supporter of Marie Antoinette.
   e. none of the above.

9. In general, Napoleon championed
   a. political freedom but not social equality.
   b. equality under the law but not political freedom.
   c. freedom of expression but only for the aristocracy.
   d. all the rights of citizenship proclaimed by the National Assembly.
   e. the restoration of the *ancien régime*.

10. Which of the following is *not* a correct explanation of why the Haitian revolution succeeded?
    a. Five hundred *gens de couleur* were veterans of the American revolution.
    b. The large maroon population supported the revolution.
    c. Toussaint Louverture was an effective strategist.
    d. The revolutionaries had the support of British and Spanish forces.
    e. The French army was struck down with yellow fever.

11. In leading the revolutions of South America, Simón Bolívar advocated
    a. that Spanish colonial rule be replaced with an indigenous monarchy.
    b. that ethnic nationalism be the basis of the new states.
    c. popular sovereignty.
    d. the abolition of slavery and full male suffrage.
    e. all of the above.

12. Revolutions in Latin America were frequently a power struggle between what two groups?
    a. masters and slaves
    b. *peninsulares* and *crioles*
    c. European and indigenous peoples
    d. Europeans and mestizos
    e. colonial militias and European mercenaries

13. Which Latin American state gained independence as a monarchy?
    a. Brazil
    b. Haiti
    c. Mexico
    d. Peru
    e. Venezuela

14. A political conservative in the nineteenth century would be likely to advocate
    a. the restoration of the French monarchy after the defeat of Napoleon.
    b. limiting suffrage to men of property.
    c. censorship as a reasonable means of preventing social unrest.
    d. government support of the established church.
    e. all of the above.

15. A political liberal in the nineteenth century would be likely to advocate
    a. returning freed slaves to Africa.
    b. the confiscation of church property by the state.
    c. universal suffrage for all men and women, regardless of race.
    d. written constitutions and representative government.
    e. all of the above.

16. The first European power to abolish the slave trade was
    a. Britain.
    b. France.
    c. Portugal.
    d. Spain.
    e. the United States.

17. The last country to abolish slavery was
    a. Brazil.
    b. Britain.
    c. France.
    d. Haiti.
    e. the United States.

18. The American women's rights movement began
    a. at the Constitutional Convention.
    b. concurrent with the antislavery movement.
    c. after the Civil War, when women saw how freed slaves benefited from the vote.
    d. not until the twentieth century.
    e. none of the above.

19. Which of the following would *not* be an example of cultural nationalism?
    a. the study of language
    b. the study of history
    c. collecting folk songs and fairy tales
    d. anti-Semitism
    e. All are examples of cultural nationalism.

20. Theodor Herzl's Zionism was the direct result of
    a. his shock at a government order revoking the citizenship of all French Jews.
    b. his shock at the army's persecution of Alfred Dreyfus.
    c. his frustrated desire to emigrate to America.
    d. a religious revelation that European Jews should return to the Holy Land.
    e. a wave of persecution against Jews living in the Ottoman empire.

21. The German people united behind King Wilhelm because
    a. he promised them a constitutional monarchy.
    b. he was the rightful heir to the Holy Roman Empire.
    c. the wars engineered by Bismarck generated strong nationalist sentiment.
    d. the Prussian army defeated all other claimants to the throne.
    e. all of the above.

MATCHING

Match these figures with the statements that follow.

A. Simón Bolívar
B. Mary Wollstonecraft
C. John Locke
D. John Stuart Mill
E. Toussaint Louverture
F. Edmund Burke

G. Louis XVI
H. Maximilien Robespierre
I. Olympe de Gouges
J. Napoleon Bonaparte
K. Otto von Bismarck
L. Klemens von Metternich

1. ____ Conservative Austrian diplomat who sought a balance of power between the nations of Europe.

2. ____ Radical Jacobin leader associated with the worst excesses of the French revolution.

3. ____ Political theorist of the seventeenth century who inspired the revolutions of the eighteenth century.

4. ____ Leader who, when he plotted with Austria to invade France, destroyed the possibility of a constitutional monarchy and invited his own execution.

5. ____ English feminist who argued that the ideals of the Enlightenment—natural rights, consent of the governed—should also be applied to women.

6. ____ Revolutionary who, armed with an education, organizational skills, and a determined army, liberated his island colony from French rule.

7. ____ Considered the "George Washington" of Latin America.

8. ____ Leader who, although regarded as one of the greatest military leaders of any age, committed the fatal mistake of overconfidence.

9. ____ French feminist who insisted that women should become full citizens of revolutionary France, an idea for which she was eventually executed.

10. ____ Prime minister of Prussia and architect of German unification.

11. ____ Spokesman for British conservatism who accepted change that was gradual and consistent with tradition.

12. ____ Spokesman for British liberalism who argued for complete freedom of speech and freedom of religion.

SEQUENCING

Place the following clusters of events in chronological order. Consider carefully how one event leads to another, and try to determine the internal logic of each sequence.

A.   Napoleon:

_____   Taking advantage of a chaotic politic scene, he is appointed to the Directory, then disbands the Directory and proclaims himself consul for life.

_____   An alliance of his enemies defeats him, twice—and exiles him from France.

_____   After successfully defeating the enemies of France, he crowns himself emperor.

_____   He establishes his reputation as a general in defense of the revolution.

_____   An impoverished noble from Corsica, he secures a military appointment at a young age.

_____   In his worst military decision, he invades Russia in the winter and loses most of his army.

B.

_____   The Stamp Act and Tea Act

_____   The Declaration of Independence

_____   The Boston Tea Party

_____   The Peace of Paris

_____   End of the Seven Years' War

C.

_____   Radical Jacobins seize control of the Convention.

_____   Napoleon seizes power and proclaims himself emperor.

_____   A hereditary monarchy rules France.

_____   The Directory executes Robespierre and ends the "reign of terror."

_____   A hereditary monarchy again rules France.

_____   The Third Estate forms a National Assembly.

For each of the following quotes, identify the speaker, if known, or the point of view. What is the significance of each passage?

1. "The great questions of the day will not be settled by speeches or majority votes—that was the great mistake of 1848 and 1849—but by *blood and iron*."

2. "Liberty and justice consist of restoring all that belongs to others; thus, the only limits on the exercise of the natural rights of women are perpetual male tyranny; these limits are to be reformed by the laws of nature and reason."

3. "Those who have served the revolution have plowed the sea."

4. "Liberty, fraternity, equality!"

5. "We hold these truths to be self-evident: that all men are created equal; that they are endowed by their Creator with certain unalienable rights; that among these are life, liberty, and the pursuit of happiness."

6. "No taxation without representation!"

1. On an outline map of Europe, indicate all the states that were directly controlled by Napoleon and those states that were at one time allied with Napoleon. Assume that the states not included in this system were enemies of Napoleon. From this map alone, can you predict some of the reasons for Napoleon's downfall? (See Map 29.2, page 794 in the textbook.)

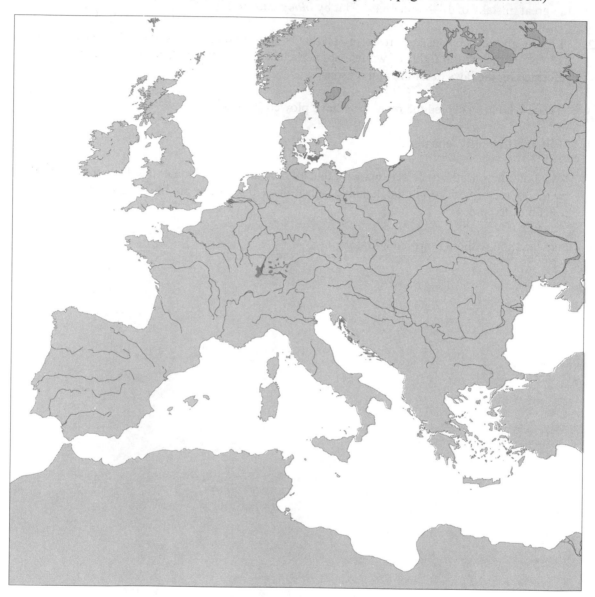

2. On an outline map of Latin America, locate and label all the following countries. Indicate as well the date of independence for each one. (See Map 29.3, page 800.)

- Argentina, Bolivia, Brazil, Central America, Chile, Gran Columbia, Haiti, Mexico, Paraguay, Peru, United States of America, Uruguay

- Simón Bolívar dreamed of a United States of South America. What were some of the barriers to this vision?

<u>CONNECTIONS</u>

In fifty words or less, explain the relationship between each of the following pairs. How does one lead to or foster the other? Be specific in your response.

- John Locke and the Declaration of Independence
- Olympe de Gouges and Toussaint Louverture
- *The Social Contract* (Rousseau) and the Committee of Public Safety
- The Congress of Vienna and Bismarck

<u>FILMS</u>

The Crossing (2000). By December of 1776, the revolution was unraveling. Washington badly needed a victory to regain the confidence of his men and the Continental Congress. On Christmas Eve, he led his troops across the Delaware River and surprised the British celebrating the holiday in their barracks. With Jeff Daniels.

The Patriot (1999). Although British forces were notoriously brutal in the South, this film grossly overstates British atrocities toward civilians. That the hero owns a plantation but no slaves is also not credible. Watch this one for the battle scenes. With Mel Gibson.

Jefferson in Paris (1995). Nick Nolte plays Thomas Jefferson as the United States ambassador to Paris just before the French Revolution. Interesting character study: Jefferson enjoys high-minded discussions about rights and freedom, while still dominating his family and his slaves. With Thandie Newton as the slave girl Sally Hemmings and Gwyneth Paltrow as Jefferson's daughter.

Revolution (1985). Al Pacino is an unwilling foot soldier in the Continental Army; Donald Sutherland is a sadistic British general. Historically accurate, particularly the battle sequences.

A Tale of Two Cities. Charles Dickens's classic tale about the French Revolution has been filmed many times. The 1935 black-and-white version is a classic. The more recent Masterpiece Theatre production is longer, but faithful to the book—avoid the 1980 film. Whichever you see, count on an epic tale of love, heroism, and sacrifice.

The Scarlet Pimpernel (1982). Anthony Andrews plays a British agent who acts the part of a simpering dandy while smuggling French aristocrats out of Paris to safety during the Revolution. Jane Seymour plays his French wife. There is also a splendid 1934, black-and-white version starring Leslie Howard.

War and Peace (1956). Tolstoy's sweeping romance set in Russia at the time of Napoleon's invasion. Starring Audrey Hepburn, Mel Torme, and Henry Fonda. (Or watch the 1967 Russian version with subtitles.)

CHAPTER 30
THE MAKING OF INDUSTRIAL SOCIETY

<u>INTRODUCTION</u>

The previous chapter describes the dramatic political changes that followed the American and French revolutions. Equally profound were the social and economic changes that accompanied what has sometimes been called the Industrial Revolution. Beginning in Great Britain about 1750, the processes of manufacturing were transformed. Britain held the lead in industrialization, but eventually the following changes reached western Europe, the United States, Russia, and Japan.

- New sources of energy. The coal-fired steam engine replaced traditional sources of power such as wood, wind, and water. Nations with abundant coal—Britain, Germany, the United States—could benefit from the new technology. Railroads and steamships, fired by the steam engine, created important links between raw materials, industry, and market.

- New labor-saving technologies. Phases in textile production once done by hand, such as spinning and weaving, were mechanized. Factories replaced cottage industry and became more efficient through the use of interchangeable parts and the assembly line.

- Increased standard of living. The factory system was tremendously productive. Efficiencies of scale and improved transportation links meant cheaper consumer goods for everyone. The accumulation of great wealth provided the capital for further industrialization.

- New patterns of work. The factory system transformed rural laborers into industrial workers with rigid timetables and strict discipline. Workers faced long hours of tedious and often dangerous work.

- New social patterns. Industrialization separated work from home life and created separate spheres for men and women. Women, especially middle-class women, were expected to take care of home and children. Men were expected to work and provide for the family.

- Urbanization. Industrial centers grew rapidly through the nineteenth century. Large cities struggled to provide such services as water delivery, sewage disposal, police and fire protection, public education.

<u>OUTLINE</u>

I. Patterns of industrialization

    A. Foundations of industrialization

        1. Coal critical to the early industrialization of Britain

            a) Shift from wood to coal in eighteenth century; deforestation caused wood shortages

            b) Abundant, accessible coal reserves in Britain

2. Overseas colonies provided raw materials

    a) Plantations in the Americas provided sugar and cotton

    b) Colonies also became markets for British manufactured goods

    c) Grain, timber, and beef shipped from United States to Britain after 1830

3. Demand for cheap cotton spurred mechanization of cotton industry

    a) John Kay invented the flying shuttle, 1733

    b) Samuel Crompton invented the spinning "mule," 1779

    c) Edmund Cartwright invented a water-driven power loom, 1785

4. James Watt's steam engine, 1765

    a) Burned coal, which drove a piston, which turned a wheel

    b) Widespread use by 1800 meant increased productivity, cheaper prices

5. Iron and steel also important industries, with continual refinement

    a) Coke (purified coal) replaced charcoal as principal fuel

    b) Bessemer converter (1856) made cheaper, stronger steel

6. Transportation improved with steam engines and improved steel

    a) George Stephenson invented the first steam-powered locomotive, 1815

    b) Steamships began to replace sailing ships in the mid-nineteenth century

    c) Railroads and steamships lowered transportation costs and created dense transportation networks

B. The factory system

1. The factory gradually replaced the putting-out system

    a) Most industrial workers from rural areas, where economic opportunities were declining

    b) Factory system required division of labor; each worker performed a single task

    c) Required a high degree of coordination, work discipline, and close supervision

2. Working conditions often harsh

    a) Workers lost status; not skilled, just wage earners

    b) Harsh work discipline, fast pace of work, frequent accidents

3. Industrial protest

    a) Luddites struck against mills and destroyed machines, 1811 and 1816

    b) Fourteen Luddites hung in 1813, and the movement died

C. The early spread of industrialization

1. Industrialization in western Europe

        a) British industrial monopoly, 1750 to 1800, forbade immigration of skilled workers

        b) Napoleon abolished internal trade barriers in western Europe, dismantled guilds

        c) Belgium and France moved toward industrialization by mid-nineteenth century

        d) After German unification, Bismarck sponsored heavy industry, arms, shipping

    2. Industrialization in North America slow to start, few laborers, little capital

        a) British craftsmen started cotton textile industry in New England in 1820s

        b) Heavy iron and steel industries in 1870s

        c) Rail networks developed in 1860s; integrated various regions of United States

D. Industrial capitalism

    1. Mass production provided cheaper goods

        a) Eli Whitney promoted mass production of interchangeable parts for firearms

        b) Later (1913), Henry Ford introduced assembly line to automobile production

    2. Industrialization expensive; required large capital investment

        a) Encouraged organization of large-scale corporations with hundreds of investors

        b) New laws protected investors from liability

    3. Monopolies, trusts, and cartels: competitive associations

        a) Trusts and cartels formed to control supply of a product (and therefore its price)

        b) Vertical organization: Rockefeller's Standard Oil Co.

        c) Horizontal organization (or cartel): IG Farben, world's largest chemical company

II. Industrial society

A. The fruits of industry

    1. Population growth

        a) Industrialization raised material standards of living

        b) Populations of Europe and America rose sharply from 1700 to 1900

        c) Better diets and improved sanitation reduced death rate of adults and children

    2. Demographic transition: population change typical of industrialized countries

        a) Pattern of declining birthrate in response to declining mortality

        b) Voluntary birth control through contraception

B. Urbanization and migration

    1. Industrialization drew migrants from countryside to urban centers

        a) By 1900, 50 percent of population of industrialized countries lived in towns

        b) By 1900, more than 150 cities with over one hundred thousand people in Europe and North America

    c) Urban problems: shoddy houses, fouled air, inadequate water supply

    d) By the late nineteenth century, governments passed building codes, built sewer systems

  2. Transcontinental migration: some workers sought opportunities abroad

    a) 1800–1920, 50 million Europeans migrated to North and South America

    b) Fled: famine in Ireland, anti-Semitism in Russia, problems elsewhere

C. Industry and society

  1. New social classes created by industrialization

    a) Captains of industry: a new aristocracy of wealth

    b) Middle class: managers, accountants, other professionals

    c) Working class: unskilled, poorly paid, vulnerable

  2. Dramatic changes to the industrial family

    a) Sharp distinction between work and family life, worked long hours outside home

    b) Family members led increasingly separate lives

  3. Men gained increased stature and responsibility in industrial age

    a) Middle- and upper-class men were sole providers

    b) Valued self-improvement, discipline, and work ethic

    c) Imposed these values on working-class men

      (1) Workers often resisted work discipline

      (2) Working-class culture: bars, sports, gambling, outlets away from work

  4. Opportunities for women narrowed by industrialization

    a) Working women could not bring children to work in mines or factories

    b) Middle-class women were expected to care for home and children

    c) Increased opportunities for women to work in domestic service

  5. Many children forced to work in industry to contribute to family support

    a) 1840s, Parliament began to regulate child labor

    b) 1881, primary education became mandatory in England

D. The socialist challenge

  1. Utopian socialists: Charles Fourier, Robert Owen, and their followers

    a) Established model communities based on principle of equality

    b) Stressed cooperative control of industry, education for all children

  2. Marx (1818–1883) and Engels (1820–1895), leading nineteenth-century socialists

    a) Scorned the utopian socialists as unrealistic, unproductive

    b) Critique of industrial capitalism

          (1) Unrestrained competition led to ruthless exploitation of working class

          (2) State, courts, police: all tools of the capitalist ruling class

      3. *The Communist Manifesto,* 1848

         a) Claimed excesses of capitalism would lead communist revolution

         b) "Dictatorship of the proletariat" would destroy capitalist order

         c) Socialism would follow—a fair, just, and egalitarian society

         d) Ideas dominated European and international socialism throughout nineteenth century

      4. Social reform came gradually, through legislative measures

         a) Regulated hours and restricted work for women and children

         b) Under Bismarck, Germany provided medical insurance and social security

      5. Trade unions formed to represent interests of industrial workers

         a) Faced stiff opposition from employers and governments

         b) Forced employers to be more responsive to workers' needs; averted violence

III. Global effects of industrialization

    A. The continuing spread of industrialization beyond Europe and North America

      1. Industrialization in Russia promoted by tsarist government

         a) Between 1860 and 1900, built thirty-five thousand miles of railroads

         b) Finance minister, Sergei Witte, promoted industry

           (1) Oversaw the construction of the trans-Siberian railroad

           (2) Reformed commercial law to protect industries and steamship companies

           (3) Promoted nautical and engineering schools

           (4) Encouraged foreign investors

         c) By 1900 Russia produced half the world's oil, also significant portion of its iron and armaments

      2. Industrialization in Japan also promoted by government

         a) Hired thousands of foreign experts to establish modern industries

         b) Created new industries; opened technical institutes and universities

         c) Government-owned businesses then sold to private entrepreneurs (*zaibatsu*)

         d) Japan was the most industrialized land in Asia by 1900

    B. The international division of labor

      1. Industrialization increased demand for raw materials

         a) Nonindustrialized societies became suppliers of raw materials

         b) Cotton from India, Egypt; rubber from Brazil, Malaya, and Congo River basin

2. Economic development stronger in lands colonized by Europe
   a) High wages encouraged labor-saving technologies
   b) Canada, Argentina, South Africa, Australia, New Zealand: later industrialized
3. Economic dependency more common in other countries
   a) Latin America, sub-Saharan Africa, south Asia, and southeast Asia
   b) Foreign investors owned and controlled plantations and production
   c) Free-trade policy favored foreign products over domestic
   d) World divided into producers and consumers

IDENTIFICATION: PEOPLE

What is the contribution of each of the following individuals to world history? Identification should include answers to the questions *who, what, where, when, how,* and *why is this person important?*

James Watt

Eli Whitney

Henry Ford

J. D. Rockefeller

Thomas Malthus

Robert Owen

Karl Marx

Sergei Witte

IDENTIFICATION: TERMS/CONCEPTS

State in your own words what each of the following terms means and why it is significant to a study of world history. (Terms with an asterisk are defined in the glossary.)

Bessemer converter

Luddites*

Crystal Palace

Demographic transition

Socialism*

Communism*

Proletariat*

Trade unions

*Zaibatsu**

Economic dependency

STUDY QUESTIONS

1. What inventions led to the mechanization of the cotton industry after 1750? Why was the textile industry so prominent at this time?

2. Explain how Great Britain took such a commanding lead in the Industrial Revolution.

3. Summarize the changes in iron and steel production and in transportation in the nineteenth century.

4. When and how did industrialization spread to the European continent and to the United States? What factors in those countries tended to support industry?

5. What are some of the characteristics of "industrial capitalism"? How did industrial giants like J. D. Rockefeller achieve such dominance over the marketplace?

6. What was the impact of the Industrial Revolution on the material standard of living in Europe and America? Who benefited the most from this?

7. What are the significant demographic (population) trends of the nineteenth century in Europe and America? What factors account for these changes?

8. What was the impact of the industrial revolution on working-class families? Consider the changes for working-class men, women, and children.

9. In what ways did the major industrial nations of the west become more responsive to the needs and interests of working people?

10. Compare the process of industrialization in Russia and Japan in the late nineteenth century.

11. What was the impact of Western industrialism on the nonindustrial countries of Asia and South America?

INQUIRY QUESTIONS

1. Compare the conditions for workers under the putting-out system with the working conditions in the factory system. Which system would be preferable to most workers? Who benefits from the new system of labor?

2. What were living conditions like in the industrial cities of the late nineteenth century? What systems and agencies needed to be developed to address some of these problems?

3. What was Karl Marx's criticism of industrial capitalism? What solutions did he envision? How well did he foresee the evolution of industrial society? (Did his predictions come to pass?)

STUDENT QUIZ

1. Which of the following was *not* an economic advantage enjoyed by Britain in the eighteenth century?
   a. abundant and accessible coal deposits
   b. local sources of raw cotton
   c. abundant skilled and unskilled labor
   d. access to water transportation
   e. sources of capital for investment

2. Cotton cloth was valued by European consumers in the eighteenth century because
   a. it was rare and considered a luxury.
   b. it was comfortable and convenient.
   c. it was a British product and thus considered patriotic.
   d. it lasted longer than wool.
   e. all of the above.

3. Improvements in transportation, such as the railroads and steamships,
   a. lowered transportation costs.
   b. linked industrial centers with overseas resources.
   c. facilitated the movement of people as well as goods.
   d. facilitated delivery of manufactured products to consumers.
   e. all of the above.

4. Which of the following was *not* a significant labor-saving invention in the production of cotton cloth?
   a. the flying shuttle
   b. the steam-driven spinning "mule"
   c. chemical dyes
   d. the power loom
   e. the cotton gin

5. From the perspective of the worker, the factory system meant
    a. better working conditions than piecework done at home.
    b. better pay for skilled work.
    c. greater opportunities for advancement within a free market system.
    d. harsh discipline and close supervision.
    e. an opportunity to families to work together.

6. From the perspective of the consumer, the factory system meant
    a. cheaper manufactured goods.
    b. lower quality manufactured goods.
    c. fewer choices in manufactured goods.
    d. manufactured goods priced beyond the means of many consumers.
    e. acute shortages of many manufactured items.

7. Rural laborers new to the factory had difficulty adjusting to
    a. the relative freedom of the factory system.
    b. the segregation of men and women in the workplace.
    c. the absence of children in the workplace.
    d. the rigid timetables of industrial work.
    e. all of the above.

8. The Luddites were threatened by industrialization of what industry in particular?
    a. ironworks
    b. pottery
    c. railroads
    d. steelworks
    e. textiles

9. The British maintained their head start in industrialization by
    a. sabotaging the efforts of their competitors.
    b. forbidding the export of machinery and expertise.
    c. constant innovation and renovation.
    d. significant government support of industry.
    e. all of the above.

10. In what nation did the government give significant support to industry in the late nineteenth century?
    a. Britain
    b. Canada
    c. France
    d. Germany
    e. the United States

11. One advantage of the industrial corporation over the older joint-stock company was
    a. the limited liability for investors.
    b. the possibility for government-sponsored monopoly.
    c. the ability to remain flexible and small-scale.
    d. the opportunity to improve the standard of living of many more workers.
    e. all of the above.

12. All of the following are examples of vertical organization *except*
    a. Standard Oil's control of all phases of petroleum production and distribution.
    b. Krupp's integration of mines, steel mills, and munitions plants.
    c. British East India Company's monopoly on the tea trade.
    d. U.S. Steel's control of mines, steel mills, and railroad manufacture.
    e. All of the above are examples of vertical integration.

13. The population of the industrial world grew dramatically in the nineteenth century, in part because
    a. improved transportation networks resulted in cheaper food and therefore better diets.
    b. families did not yet know how to limit the number of births.
    c. new urban centers were healthier environments than rural villages were.
    d. aggressive public health programs eradicated childhood diseases.
    e. all of the above

14. By 1900, birthrates had sharply declined in most industrialized countries because
    a. raising children was more expensive in an industrial society than in an agricultural one.
    b. declining infant mortality meant that more of the children born were likely to survive.
    c. improved health and nutrition reduced overall death rates.
    d. married couples actively practiced birth control.
    e. all of the above.

15. Which of the following was *not* a typical inducement for Europeans to emigrate abroad in the nineteenth century?
    a. famine in Ireland
    b. difficult political, social, and economic circumstances in Europe generally
    c. unemployment in Britain
    d. anti-Semitism in Russia
    e. economic opportunities in the United States

16. Middle-class family life in the new industrial society was characterized by
    a. substantial social and political gains by women.
    b. equal participation of men and women in the industrial economy.
    c. gendered division of labor and space.
    d. children leaving school to work in the mills at an early age.
    e. all of the above.

17. In Britain, one outcome of the laws against child labor in the late nineteenth century was that
    a. all children were required to attend public school.
    b. poor children were forced to do piecework at home.
    c. children spent more time away from their parents than when they had been working.
    d. working-class parents were obliged to find child care.
    e. all of the above.

18. In their critique of industrial capitalism, Karl Marx and Friedrich Engels claimed that
    a. the trade union movement would force industry to accept social reforms.
    b. the most equitable and just society could be found in an industrial commune.
    c. the bourgeois class needed to exercise responsibility toward their workers.
    d. democracy had failed because most workers did not understand their true interests; a dictatorship would serve them better.
    e. only a communist revolution would change the abuses of capitalism and create a just and equal society.

19. In response to socialist demands for social and economic reform, most governments
    a. treated trade unions as illegal organizations.
    b. supported business and prosecuted strikers.
    c. passed laws restricting child labor.
    d. extended the vote to the working class.
    e. all of the above.

20. In Russia, the government sponsored industrialization by all of the following measures *except*
    a. constructing the Trans-Siberian Railroad.
    b. supporting steamship companies and establishing nautical schools.
    c. encouraging foreign investment.
    d. reforming commercial law and protecting infant industries
    e. setting minimum wages for Russian workers.

MATCHING

Match these figures, groups, or items with the statements that follow.

A. Proletariat	G. Eli Whitney
B. Bourgeoisie	H. Robert Owen
C. *Zaibatsu*	I. J. D. Rockefeller
D. Thomas Malthus	J. Karl Marx
E. Henry Ford	K. Luddites
F. James Watt	L. Sergei Witte

1. ___ A philanthropic industrialist who created utopian societies for his workers and their families.

2. ___ English handicraft workers who tried to halt the industrialization of the textile industry through sabotage.

3. ___ Inventor who, by manufacturing with interchangeable parts, streamlined industrial production.

4. ___ The industrial empires built by wealthy Japanese industrialists.

5. ___ Inventor of the steam engine, which provided the energy that ran the Industrial Revolution.

6. ___ Entrepreneur who advanced mass production with a mechanized assembly line that moved the product through the factory.

7. ___ Economist whose dire predictions about population growth suggested that nothing could be done to relieve poverty.

8. ___ The wealthy middle class, often the managers or industrialists.

9. ___ The urban working class, the wage earners in industry.

10. ___ Finance minister who aggressively promoted the industrial development of Russia.

11. ___ An aggressive and often ruthless industrialist who built a vertical empire around oil production.

12. ___ An outspoken critic of industrial capitalism who envisioned a classless society where all would share equally in the benefits of industry.

SEQUENCING

Place the following clusters of events in chronological order. Consider carefully how one event leads to another, and try to determine the internal logic of each sequence.

A.

____ Putting-out system

____ Interchangeable parts

____ Assembly line

____ Factory system

B.

____ Wind and water power

____ Manpower

____ Coal-fired steam engines

____ Oil and electricity

QUOTATIONS

For each of the following quotes, identify the speaker, if known, or the point of view. What is the significance of each passage?

1. "I have a belt round my waist, and a chain passing between my legs, and I go on my hands and feet. The road is very steep, and we have to hold by a rope; and when there is no rope, by anything we can catch hold of. . . . I am very tired when I get home at night; I fall asleep sometimes before I get washed. I am not so strong as I was, and cannot stand my work so well as I used to. I have drawn till I have had the skin off me; the belt and chain is worse when we are in the family way."

2. "Population, when unchecked, goes on doubling itself every twenty-five years, or increases in a geometrical ratio . . . [while] the means of subsistence . . . could not possibly be made to increase faster than in an arithmetic ratio. The ultimate check to population appears then to be want of food, arising necessarily from the different ratios according to which population and food increase."

3. "Domestic life is the chief source of her influence. . . . There is something unfeminine in independence."

4. "The history of all hitherto exiting society is the history of class struggles. . . . Our epoch, the epoch of the bourgeoisie, possesses, however, this distinctive feature: it has simplified the class antagonism. Society as a whole is more and more splitting up into two great hostile camps, into two great classes facing each other: Bourgeoisie and Proletariat."

MAP EXERCISES

1. Consider the network of railroads in Europe in 1850 (Map 30.1, page 823 in the textbook). What factors seem to dictate the placement of railroads? In Britain, which regions are well connected and which are more isolated? How would you characterize the nature of railroads on the continent?

2. Consider the population distribution in Europe by 1850 (also Map 30.1). Does population density correspond to the other indications of industrialization, such as railroads, coal deposits, and industrial centers? How do you explain the discrepancies?

3. Graph the population growth between 1700 and 1900 for Britain, Europe, Japan, and the United States. What factors account for this dramatic growth? What factors might account for the differences within the industrialized nations?

CONNECTIONS

In fifty words or less, explain the relationship between each of the following pairs. How does one lead to or foster the other? Be specific in your response.

- Steam engine and urbanization
- Luddites and trade unions
- Mass production and the demographic transition
- Thomas Malthus and *The Communist Manifesto*

FILMS

Germinal (1994). A grim portrait of life in the mines of rural France, based on the novel by the French realist Émile Zola. Workers struggle against brutal conditions to maintain some semblance of normal life and eventually are persuaded to go on strike. Stars Gerard Depardieu. In French with subtitles.

Matewan (1987). Gritty story about the labor struggles of West Virginia coal miners in the 1920s. A cut in pay prompts a call for a strike by the union with tragic results. Directed by John Sayles.

Molly Maguires (1970). In the coal mines of Pennsylvania in the 1870s, Irish miners were resented by "native-born" Americans and brutally treated by their employers. They fought back with secret labor unions, such as the Molly Maguires. With Sean Connery and Richard Harris.

CHAPTER 31
THE AMERICAS
IN THE AGE OF INDEPENDENCE

<u>INTRODUCTION</u>

In 1800, the United States was a shaky new republic, and the rest of the Americas were controlled by European states. By 1900, the United States and Canada had claimed the entire North American continent, and most of Latin America had broken free from colonial rule. The states that emerged were vastly different from one another. Some of those differences had been apparent since the colonial era (see Chapter 25). Events of the nineteenth century further defined the societies that emerged in the Americas:

- Territorial expansion. A booming population and continual immigration impelled American and Canadian settlers to press onto the western lands. Railroad construction in the late nineteenth century facilitated that expansion.

- Conflicts with indigenous peoples. Across the Americas, expansion brought settlers into lands claimed by indigenous peoples. Conflicts between Native Americans and military forces in the United States, Canada, Argentina, and Chile invariably ended badly for the natives. Survivors were usually forced onto marginal lands.

- Constitutional issues in North America. After 1800, the United States became increasingly divided, north and south, over slavery and related issues. The Civil War determined that the American "house" would no longer be "divided" and that the federal government would be more powerful than the state governments. Canada achieved independence within the framework of the British empire, but faced challenges in creating a government that respected both British and French citizens.

- Constitutional issues in Latin America. Independence left many unresolved questions. What system would best address the inequities between creole elites and the vast majority of landless peasants? How would order be maintained? How best to advance reforms? Often, the solution seemed to be a military dictator.

- Economic development in North America. Foreign capital, a stable government, free enterprise, and abundant cheap labor: all contributed to the dramatic economic expansion of the United States in the nineteenth century. Canadian economic expansion was less spectacular but steady, especially after completion of the Canadian Pacific Railroad in 1885.

- Economic colonialism in Latin America. With a few exceptions, the economies of Latin America did not develop or diversify. Instead, Latin America continued the colonial pattern of exporting raw materials to industrial powers. While wealthy elites profited, the peasants saw their standard of living decline.

OUTLINE

I. **The building of American states**

A. The United States: westward expansion and civil war

1. By 1820s all adult white men could vote and hold office

2. Rapid westward expansion after the revolution

a) Britain ceded all lands east of the Mississippi River to the United States after the revolution

b) 1803, the United States purchased France's Louisiana Territory, west to the Rocky Mountains

c) By 1840s, coast-to-coast expansion was claimed as the manifest destiny of the United States

3. Conflict with indigenous peoples followed westward expansion

a) 1830, Indian Removal Act forced eastern natives to move west of the Mississippi

b) Thousands died on the "Trail of Tears" to Oklahoma

c) Stiff resistance to expansion: Battle of Little Big Horn, 1876, Sioux victory

d) U.S. massacre at Wounded Knee, 1890, ended Indian Wars

4. The Mexican-American War, 1845–1848

a) Texas declared independence from Mexico in 1836, was annexed by the United States in 1845

b) U.S.-Mexican conflict over the border ended with resounding U.S. victory

c) By Treaty of Guadalupe Hidalgo, the United States purchased Texas, California, New Mexico

5. Sectional conflict: north versus south over slavery

a) Nineteenth-century cotton cultivation in the south was dependent on slave labor

b) Northern states did not want slavery expanded into new territories

c) Abraham Lincoln elected president, 1860; publicly opposed to slavery

6. The U.S. Civil War, 1861–1865

a) With Lincoln's election, eleven southern states seceded from the Union

b) Southerners believed their economy of cotton and slaves was self-sufficient

c) Northerners fought to preserve the Union as much as in opposition to slavery

d) In 1863, Lincoln's Emancipation Proclamation made abolition a goal of the war

e) By 1865, the industrial north defeated the agricultural south

f) The war ended slavery, enhanced authority of the federal government

B. The Canadian Dominion: independence without war

1. Autonomy and division characterized Canadian history
    a) French Quebec taken by Britain after the Seven Years' War
    b) British authorities made large concessions to French Canadians
    c) After 1781, many British loyalists fled the United States to seek refuge in Canada
2. The War of 1812 unified Canada against U.S. invaders
    a) Anti-U.S. sentiments created sense of unity among French and British Canadians
    b) 1830s, tensions between French citizens and growing English population
    c) 1840–1867, British authorities granted home rule to Canadians
3. Dominion of Canada created in 1867
    a) A federal government with a governor-general acting as the British representative
    b) Britain retained jurisdiction over foreign affairs until 1931
4. Prime Minister John Macdonald strengthened Canadian independence and unity
    a) Persuaded western and maritime provinces to join the Dominion, 1860s
    b) Transcontinental railroad completed, 1885

C. Latin America: fragmentation and political experimentation
    1. Creole elites faced political instability after independence
        a) Creole leaders had little experience with self-government
        b) White minority dominated politics; peasant majority was without power
        c) Political instability aggravated by division among elites
    2. Conflicts between farmers and ranchers and indigenous peoples common
        a) Intense fighting in Argentina and Chile; modern weapons against native peoples
        b) Colonists had pacified most productive land by 1870s
    3. *Caudillos:* military leaders who held power after revolutionary era
        a) Juan Manuel de Rosas dominated Argentina from 1835 to 1852
        b) Took advantage of chaotic times; brought order to Argentina
        c) Used personal army to crush opposition; opposed liberal reforms
    4. Mexico: war and reform from 1821 to 1911
        a) Shifted from monarchy to republic to *caudillo* rule
        b) *La Reforma:* liberal movement in 1850s led by President Benito Juarez as an effort to create a rural middle class
        c) Granted universal male suffrage; limited power of priests and military
        d) Land reforms converted corporate lands to private property, which ended up in hands of large landowners
        e) Bitter division between liberals and conservatives ensued

        f) Juarez suspended loan payments to foreign countries, provoking intervention by France, Britain, and Spain

        g) Napoleon III attempted to end chaos in Mexico by creating monarchy

        h) French forces defeated at Puebla in May 1862

        i) Napoleon III proclaimed empire; forced to withdraw troops in 1867 and Maximilian, his appointee, was executed

        j) Juarez restores order but great political division continues

   5. Mexico: revolution (1911–1920)

        a) Fundamentally a class conflict: 95 percent of people were landless and impoverished

        b) Middle class joined with peasants and workers to overthrow the dictator Diaz

        c) Emiliano Zapata and Pancho Villa led popular uprisings in countryside

        d) With U.S. support, Mexican government regained control

        e) New constitution of 1917 brought sweeping reform

II. American economic development

  A. Migration to the Americas

    1. Industrial migrants to United States and Canada

        a) In 1850s, 2.3 million Europeans migrated to the United States, and the number increased after that

        b) The low cost of immigrant labor contributed to U.S. industrial expansion

        c) 1852–1875, two hundred thousand Chinese migrated to California to work in mines and railroads

    2. Latin American migrants mostly worked on agricultural plantations

        a) Italians migrated to Brazil and Argentina

        b) Asians migrated to Cuba and the Caribbean sugar fields

  B. Economic expansion in the United States

    1. British capital crucial for early development of U.S. industries

        a) Foreign capital supported textile, iron and steel, railroads

        b) Helped create an industrial rival that soon surpassed Britain

    2. Railroads integrated national economy by late nineteenth century

        a) Two hundred thousand miles of railroad in the United States by 1900, coast to coast

        b) Economic stimulus: 75 percent of steel went to railroads, supported other industries

    3. Railroads changed American landscape and timetables; set time zones by 1880s

4. Dramatic economic growth between 1870 and 1900

    a) New inventions and technologies: electric lights, telephones, and so on

    b) Labor conflicts over wages and working conditions: big business usually won

C. Canadian prosperity

  1. The National Policy: plan to develop national economy

    a) Wanted to attract migrants and British capital but to protect Canadian industries

    b) Construction of Canadian Pacific Railroad opened the west to settlement

    c) Boom in agricultural and industrial production in late nineteenth and early twentieth centuries

  2. Heavy U.S. investment in Canada; owned 30 percent of Canadian industry by 1918

D. Latin American dependence

  1. Colonial legacy prevented industrialization of Latin American states

    a) Spain and Portugal never encouraged industries

    b) Creole elites continued land-based economies after independence

  2. British didn't invest in industry in Latin America; no market for manufactured goods

    a) Instead invested in cattle and sheep ranching in Argentina

    b) Supplied British wool and beef; most of profits returned to Britain

  3. Some attempts at industrialization with limited success

    a) Diaz encouraged foreign investors to build rails, telegraphs, and mines

    b) Profits went to Mexican oligarchy and foreign investors, not used for further development

    c) While Mexican industry boomed, average Mexican standard of living declined

  4. Economic growth in Latin America driven by exports such as silver, copper, beef, wheat, bananas, rubber, coffee, sugar, and tobacco

  5. Other regions of world increased export of these products, resulting in lower prices

III. American culture and social diversity

A. Multicultural society in the United States

  1. By late nineteenth century, the United States was a multicultural society but was dominated by white elites

  2. Native peoples had been pushed onto reservations

    a) Dawes Act, 1887: encouraged natives to take up farming, often on marginal land

    b) Slaughter of buffalo threatened Indians' survival

    c) Children sent to boarding schools, lost native language and traditions

  3. Freed slaves often were denied civil rights

a) Northern armies forced the south to undergo Reconstruction (1867–68)

b) After Reconstruction, a violent backlash overturned reforms

c) South was rigidly segregated; blacks were denied opportunities, political rights

4. American women's movement had limited success in nineteenth century

a) "Declaration of Sentiments" issued by American feminists in 1848

b) Sought education, employment, and political rights

5. Migrants: 25 million Europeans to America from 1840–1914

a) Hostile reaction to foreigners from "native-born" Americans

b) Newcomers concentrated in districts like Little Italy and Chinatown

c) Antagonism to Asians led to legal exclusion of Chinese and Japanese migrants

B. Canadian cultural contrasts

1. Ethnic diversity beyond dominant British and French populations

a) Significant minority of indigenous people displaced by whites

b) Blacks free after 1833 but not equal; former slaves, some escaped from United States

c) Chinese migrants came to goldfields of British Columbia, worked on railroad

d) Late nineteenth and early twentieth century, waves of European migrants

e) Expansion into Northwest Territories increased British and French conflicts

2. Northwest Rebellion by the métis, descendants of French traders and native women

a) Conflict between natives, métis, and white settlers in west, 1870s and 1880s

b) Louis Riel, leader of western métis and indigenous peoples

c) Riel organized a government and army to protect land and trading rights

d) Canadian authorities outlawed his government and exiled him, 1870s

e) In 1885 Riel again led métis resistance against railroads and British settlements

f) Rebels were subdued, and Riel was executed for treason

3. French Canadians suspicious of British elites after Northwest Rebellion

C. Ethnicity, identity, and gender in Latin America

1. Latin American societies organized by ethnicity and color, legacy of colonialism

2. Large-scale migration in nineteenth century brought cultural diversity

a) Small number of Chinese in Cuba assimilated through intermarriage

b) Larger group of East Indians in Trinidad and Tobago preserved cultural traditions

c) European migrants made Buenos Aires "the Paris of the Americas"

3. Gauchos: Argentine cowboys on the pampas

a) Gaucho society: ethnic egalitarianism, mostly *mestizos* or *castizos* (mixed race)

b) Distinctive gaucho dress, independent, celebrated in legend and song

c) Caudillo rule disrupted gaucho life: impressed into armies, lands enclosed

4. Male domination central feature of Latin American society in nineteenth century

a) Machismo: culture of male strength, aggression

b) No significant women's movement; some efforts to improve education for girls

IDENTIFICATION: PEOPLE

What is the contribution of each of the following individuals to world history? Identification should include answers to the questions *who, what, where, when, how,* and *why is this person important?*

Andrew Jackson

Abraham Lincoln

John Macdonald

Benito Juarez

Juan Manuel de Rosas

Porfirio Diaz

Emiliano Zapata

Louis Riel

IDENTIFICATION: TERMS/CONCEPTS

State in your own words what each of the following terms means and why it is significant to a study of world history. (Terms with an asterisk are defined in the glossary).

Louisiana Purchase

Manifest destiny

The Trail of Tears*

Mexican-American War

Emancipation Proclamation

Dawes Act

Caudillos*

La Reforma*

Northwest Rebellion

Gauchos*

Golindrinas

STUDY QUESTIONS

1. How did the United States gain control over the territory from the east to the west coast in the nineteenth century?

2. What specific issues and events led to the American Civil War? What was the outcome of that conflict, and what did it mean for the nation as a whole?

3. Summarize the steps by which Canada became politically united and independent of Britain. How was the government of the Dominion of Canada like and unlike that of the United States?

4. What kinds of constitutions emerged in the independent republics of Latin America? Which groups held political power?

5. How did the *caudillos* rise to power in Latin America? Who benefited most from their rule?

6. What factors led to *La Reforma,* the reform movement in Mexico? What was the ultimate outcome of this conflict?

7. Compare nineteenth-century migration patterns to North America and Latin America. Where did migrants come from in each case? What opportunities did they find in each region?

8. What factors contributed to the tremendous economic growth of the United States in the late nineteenth century? What were some of the problems generated by that economic growth?

9. Compare the economic development of Canada with that of Latin America. Neither became an economic powerhouse like the United States. What are the similarities and differences?

10. Note the political and economic status of each of the following groups in the United States in the late nineteenth century: native Americans, African Americans, women, and foreign-born immigrants.

11. What have been the central ethnic conflicts in Canadian history?

12. Summarize the political and cultural conflict between city and pampas in Argentina.

INQUIRY QUESTIONS

1. Compare the treatment of indigenous peoples in the United States and Canada. Why was there not a significant *métis* population in the United States? What does this difference mean?

2. Migration to the United States soared in the late nineteenth century. Why did these people come to America? What were their experiences? How would the experience of an Italian coming to New York City in 1890 compare with that of another Italian migrating to Argentina at the same time?

3. What have been the obstacles to the industrial development of Latin America? Consider the export products named on page 866 in the textbook. Who profits from this trade? How is it that "even as agriculture, railroad construction and mining were booming, the standard of living for average Mexicans was declining in the late nineteenth century" (page 866)?

STUDENT QUIZ

1. The United States gained western territory by all of the following means *except*
   a. treaty with Britain.
   b. purchase from France.
   c. treaty with Spain.
   d. war and purchase from Mexico.
   e. purchase from indigenous people.

2. The term *manifest destiny* was used to describe
   a. the inevitability of American independence from Britain.
   b. the superiority of the U.S. Constitution.
   c. the inevitability of American dominion over all of North America.
   d. the superiority of the North to the South during the Civil War.
   e. all of the above.

3. At Wounded Knee in 1890,
   a. Colonel George Armstrong Custer was defeated by an army of Lakota Sioux.
   b. thousands of eastern Cherokee were crowded onto a desolate reservation in Oklahoma.
   c. Sioux warriors, emboldened by the Ghost Dance movement, attacked and massacred a community of white settlers.
   d. U.S. cavalry massacred a settlement of 200 Sioux men, women, and children.
   e. Blackfeet warriors tried unsuccessfully to escape across the border into Canada.

4. Which of the following is *not* a territory acquired as a result of the Mexican-American War?
   a. Arizona
   b. California
   c. Nevada
   d. Oregon
   e. Utah

5. The constitutional issue at the center of the American Civil War was
   a. the balance of power between the president and the Congress.
   b. the balance of power between the state governments and the federal government.
   c. conflicting claims between the individual and society.
   d. the rights of immigrant labor versus the rights of slave labor.
   e. how to fulfill ideals of the Enlightenment.

6. The Emancipation Proclamation
    a. freed all slaves in the western hemisphere.
    b. freed all slaves who took up arms against the South.
    c. had little immediate effect on the status of slaves.
    d. freed all slaves in the western territories.
    e. promised to free all slaves at the end of the Civil War.

7. British Canada gained a large French population as a result of
    a. France's loss of its Canadian colonies in the Seven Years' War.
    b. the flight to Canada of French Protestants in the eighteenth century.
    c. French citizens fleeing the Napoleonic wars.
    d. French fur traders being driven out of the United States.
    e. all of the above.

8. Which of the following provinces was *not* part of the Dominion of Canada by 1900?
    a. Alberta
    b. British Columbia
    c. Nova Scotia
    d. Ontario
    e. Quebec

9. In Latin America, the road to a stable state was hindered by
    a. an elite conspiracy against lower classes.
    b. the ignorance and apathy of the lower classes.
    c. sharp divisions among the creole classes.
    d. the *caudillos'* reign of terror.
    e. all of the above.

10. The Mexican Revolution was fundamentally a conflict between
    a. supporters of the Catholic church and anti-cleric revolutionaries.
    b. liberal and socialist programs for social reform.
    c. supporters of Emiliano Zapata and supporters of Pancho Villa.
    d. Mexican business interests and foreign investors.
    e. conservative landowners and landless peasants.

11. All of the following contributed to American economic development in the nineteenth century *except*
    a. foreign investment.
    b. cheap labor provided by immigration.
    c. the transcontinental railroad.
    d. lack of competition from Europe.
    e. abundant natural resources, including coal and iron.

12. New inventions toward the turn of the century included all of the following *except*
    a. electric lights.
    b. electric motor.
    c. radio.
    d. phonograph.
    e. telephone.

13. The National Policy for economic development of Canada included
    a. tariffs to protect Canadian industry.
    b. recruitment of immigrants.
    c. construction of the Canadian Pacific Railroad.
    d. attracting foreign investment without losing control of the national economy.
    e. all of the above.

14. Economic development in Latin America was limited because
    a. the market for manufactured goods was too small.
    b. most goods were manufactured on self-sufficient haciendas.
    c. state control discouraged foreign investment.
    d. there were insufficient natural resources in Latin America.
    e. there wasn't enough cheap labor in Latin America.

15. During the dictatorship of Porfirio Diaz, Mexico achieved all of the following *except*
    a. construction of rail and telegraph lines.
    b. industrial expansion.
    c. paved streets and electric lights in Mexico City.
    d. improved public health and education.
    e. significant foreign investment in the Mexican economy.

16. The purpose of the Dawes Severalty Act of 1887 was to
    a. provide useful industrial skills to Native Americans.
    b. break tribal reservations into small family farms.
    c. undermine Native religions and inculcate Christian values.
    d. regulate relations between Indians and settlers on the plains.
    e. allow for autonomous self-government on the reservations.

17. After Reconstruction, former slaves in the American south
    a. elected biracial governments for the first time in U.S. history.
    b. remained free, but lost many of their civil rights.
    c. became independent farmers and landowners.
    d. gained control of their own schools and local institutions.
    e. all of the above.

18. The Northwest Rebellion in Canada in 1885 was sparked by
    a. the loss of land and trading rights by *métis* and natives because of western expansion.
    b. tensions between British and French settlers on the frontier.
    c. conflicts between settlers and the railroad over land rights.
    d. tensions between British and French residents and newcomers from Eastern Europe.
    e. a border dispute between Canadian and American settlers on the western plains.

19. The *gaucho* in Argentina is similar to what widely romanticized figure in American history?
    a. the fur trader
    b. the solitary prospector
    c. the homesteader
    d. the cattle rustler
    e. the western cowboy

20. By 1900 Latin American women had achieved
    a. expanded educational opportunities.
    b. the right to vote in national elections.
    c. the right to divorce.
    d. property rights within marriage.
    e. nothing at all.

MATCHING

Match these figures with the statements that follow.

A. *Gauchos*	G. Andrew Jackson
B. *Caudillos*	H. Juan Manuel de Rosas
C. Benito Juarez	I. Abraham Lincoln
D. John Macdonald	J. Porfirio Diaz
E. Louis Riel	K. Emiliano Zapata
F. *Métis*	L. *Mestizos*

1. ___ In Canada, people of mixed French and Native American ancestry.

2. ___ In Latin America, people of mixed European and Native American ancestry.

3. ___ Powerful Mexican dictator who represented the interests of wealthy merchants, landowners, and foreign investors at the expense of the Mexican people.

4. ___ Dictator, known as the "Argentine Nero," whose dictatorship was notorious for brutally crushing all opposition to his rule.

5. ___ Highly romanticized Argentine cowboys, the embodiment of machismo.

6. ___ A *mestizo* revolutionary leader who enjoyed great support in the countryside but not in the cities of Mexico.

7. ___ Liberal Mexican president who attempted to curtail the power of the church and redistribute land to the poor.

8. ___ Leader of a rebellion of *métis* and indigenous peoples against the steady encroachment of white settlers of western lands in Canada.

9. ___ President who expressed his concern for the welfare of eastern Indians and authorized their forced removal to Oklahoma territory.

10. ___ Military dictators who brought order to Latin America in the chaotic years following independence; posing as supporters of the people, they limited freedom and reform.

11. ___ Signer of the Emancipation Proclamation who ensured that the American Civil War would end slavery.

12. ___ Visionary Canadian president who forged the union of provinces from British Columbia to Newfoundland.

SEQUENCING

Place the following clusters of events in chronological order. Consider carefully how one event leads to another, and try to determine the internal logic of each sequence.

A.

_____ Indian removal

_____ Completion of transcontinental railroad line

_____ Louisiana Purchase

_____ Mexican War

_____ Annexation of Texas

B.

_____ *Caudillos* take over with popular support and restore order.

_____ Creole elites seize power but fail to unite the country.

_____ Military oppression and lack of freedom invite further rebellion.

_____ Colonial rule excludes wealthy local creoles.

C.

_____ Louis Riel is executed for treason.

_____ British settlers move west, seeking farmland.

_____ French *courier de bois* (fur traders) reach the Northwest Territories. Many stay and marry native women.

_____ An army of *métis* and indigenous peoples tries to shut down construction of the Canadian Pacific Railroad.

_____ The National Economic Policy seeks to unite British North America by rail.

QUOTATIONS

For each of the following quotes, identify the speaker, if known, or the point of view. What is the significance of each passage?

1. "A house divided against itself cannot stand. I believe this government cannot endure permanently half slave and half free. . . . It will become all one thing, or all the other."

2. "We hold these truths to be self-evident: that all men and women are created equal."

3. "That on the first day of January, in the year of our Lord one thousand eight hundred and sixty-three, all persons held as slaves within any State or designated part of a State, the people whereof shall then be in rebellion against the United States, shall be then, thenceforward, and forever free."

4. "While a few individuals possess immense areas of uncultivated land that could support millions of people, the great majority of Mexicans languish in a terrible poverty and are denied property, homes, and work. Such a people cannot be free, democratic, much less happy, no matter how many constitutions and laws proclaim abstract rights and beautiful but impracticable theories."

5. "There is urgent necessity for prompt legislation on the subject of Chinese immigration. . . . The popular demand for legislation excluding the Chinese from this country is urgent and imperative and almost universal. Their presence here is inimical to our institutions and is deemed injurious and a source of danger. . . . They have no attachment to our country, its laws or its institutions, nor are they interested in its prosperity. They never assimilate with our people, our manners, tastes, religion, or ideas. With us they have nothing in common."

MAP EXERCISES

1. Without looking, how many of the twelve provinces and territories of Canada can you name? Make a list, then look at Map 31.2 on page 855 in the textbook.

2. Before 1840, territorial acquisitions by the U.S. government tended to follow geographic boundaries, such as rivers and mountain ranges. After 1840, new territories tended to follow geometric survey lines. Explain this, using Map 31.1 on page 850.

3. Aside from the cultural and political challenges, what were the *geographic* barriers to the unification of Canada? Use Map 31.2 on page 855 to explain your answer. What was the significance of the transcontinental railroad to the unification of Canada? Why do you think British Columbia joined the Dominion so long before Alberta and Saskatchewan?

CONNECTIONS

In fifty words or less, explain the relationship between each of the following pairs. How does one lead to or foster the other? Be specific in your response.

- Manifest destiny and the Trail of Tears
- British North America Act and the Northwest Rebellion
- *La Reforma* and Portiforio Diaz
- The Mexican War and the Civil War
- Creole elites and Emiliano Zapata

FILMS

A Thousand Pieces of Gold (1991). A Chinese girl, sold into slavery by her father, is delivered to a mining town on the Oregon frontier. In spite of her ignorance of American culture and the prejudice toward Chinese in the mining camps, she endures and eventually prospers. Based on the life story of a pioneer woman.

Dances with Wolves (1990). Kevin Costner plays a Civil War veteran who is sent to a remote frontier post where he learns to respect the neighboring Lakota Sioux. As he becomes more sympathetic to their struggles, the army questions his loyalty. Beautifully photographed.

Hester Street (1975). A tale of assimilation and identity among Eastern European Jews on New York's Lower East Side at the turn of the last century. A Russian Jew, Jake, has been living in the United States for five years and is joined by his wife and son from the old country. He is thoroughly Americanized, but she honors the old traditions.

Reed, Insurgent Mexico (1971). American journalist John Reed is a sympathetic witness to the Mexican Revolution of 1911. Director Paul Leduc received an award in 1972 for the best film by a new director. In Spanish with subtitles.

Viva Zapata! (1952). Acclaimed film about the struggle and disappointments of the Mexican Revolution. Marlon Brando is the empassioned, illiterate Zapata; Anthony Quinn won an Oscar as his older brother, Eufemio. John Steinbeck wrote the screenplay.

CHAPTER 32
SOCIETIES AT CROSSROADS

INTRODUCTION

The dramatic economic expansion of western Europe and the United States in the nineteenth century was not matched by the older empires of Asia. The Ottoman empire, the Qing dynasty, the Russian empire, and Tokugawa shogunate had all been vibrant and dynamic cultures at one time, but by 1800 had become isolated and backward. By 1900, all four had been challenged and changed profoundly. Some common dimensions of those changes are:

- Conservative autocratic regimes. None of the regimes discussed here shared in the liberal ideals of the Enlightenment or the revolutionary era. Rulers were absolute; individuals had few rights; and dissent was viewed as dangerous.

- Military unpreparedness. Since these regimes failed to modernize, they found themselves outgunned by the western powers. Often this realization followed a humiliating defeat—the loss of Egypt for the Ottomans, the Opium War for China, the Crimean War for Russia, and the unequal treaty forced on Japan by the United States. For most regimes, this realization led to a radical restructuring of the military.

- Weak economies. All four regimes lacked the basic elements for industrialization: capital, free workers, and infrastructure. China and Japan had been closed economies and had little contact with the outside world. The Ottoman and Russian empires had been agricultural societies with large unskilled peasant populations.

- Imperial pressures. All four had to fight off the imperialistic encroachments of the industrializing powers. The Qing dynasty was the least successful and, by the end of the century, had lost control of its economy and much of its territorial sovereignty. Japan was most successful in competing economically and militarily with the west.

- Reform from the top down. Change, when it came, was entirely at the discretion of the rulers. Japanese reformers, for example, perceived that a written constitution would give credibility to their new state, so that the emperor "gave" a constitution to the people that retained all power to the emperor. The Russian tsar granted, then rescinded, an elected legislature after the revolution of 1905.

OUTLINE

I. **Introduction: Ottoman empire, Russia, China, and Japan**

   A. Common problems

      1. Military weakness, vulnerability to foreign threats

      2. Internal weakness due to economic problems, financial difficulties, and corruption

   B. Reform efforts

      1. Attempts at political and educational reform and at industrialization

2. Turned to Western models

C. Different results of reforms

 1. Ottoman empire, Russia, and China unsuccessful; societies on the verge of collapse

 2. Reform in Japan was more thorough; Japan emerged as an industrial power

II. The Ottoman empire in decline

A. The nature of decline

 1. Military decline since the late seventeenth century

 a) Ottoman forces behind European armies in strategy, tactics, weaponry, training

 b) Janissary corps politically corrupt, undisciplined

 c) Provincial governors gained power, private armies

 2. Extensive territorial losses in nineteenth century

 a) Lost Caucasus and central Asia to Russia; western frontiers to Austria; Balkan provinces to Greece and Serbia

 b) Egypt gained autonomy after Napoleon's failed campaign in 1798

 (1) Egyptian general Muhammad Ali built a powerful, modern army

 (2) Ali's army threatened Ottomans, made Egypt an autonomous province

 3. Economic difficulties began in seventeenth century

 a) Less trade through empire as Europeans shifted to the Atlantic Ocean basin

 b) Exported raw materials, imported European manufactured goods

 c) Heavily depended on foreign loans, half of the revenues paid to loan interest

 d) Foreigners began to administer the debts of the Ottoman state by 1882

 4. The "capitulations": European domination of Ottoman economy

 a) Extraterritoriality: Europeans exempt from Ottoman law within the empire

 b) Could operate tax-free, levy their own duties in Ottoman ports

 c) Deprived empire of desperately needed income

B. Reform and reorganization

 1. Attempt to reform military led to violent Janissary revolt (1807–1808)

 2. Reformer Mahmud II (1808 1839) became sultan after revolt

 a) When Janissaries resisted, Mahmud had them killed; cleared the way for reforms

 b) He built a European-style army, academies, schools, roads, and telegraph

 3. Legal and educational reforms of the Tanzimat ("reorganization") era (1839–1876)

 a) Ruling class sought sweeping restructuring to strengthen state

 b) Broad legal reforms, modeled after Napoleon's Civil Code

 c) State reform of education (1846), free and compulsory primary education (1869)

d) Undermined authority of the *ulama,* enhanced the state authority

4. Opposition to Tanzimat reforms

a) Religious conservatives critical of attack on Islamic law and tradition

b) Legal equality for minorities resented by some, even a few minority leaders

c) Young Ottomans wanted more reform: freedom, autonomy, decentralization

d) High-level bureaucrats wanted more power, checks on the sultan's power

C. The Young Turk era

1. Cycles of reform and repression

a) 1876, coup staged by bureaucrats who demanded a constitutional government

b) New sultan Abdül Hamid II (1876–1909) proved an autocrat: suspended constitution, dissolved parliament, and punished liberals

c) Reformed army and administration: became source of the new opposition

2. The Young Turks, after 1889, an active body of opposition

a) Called for universal suffrage, equality, freedom, secularization, women's rights

b) Forced Abdül Hamid to restore constitution, dethroned him (1909)

c) Nationalist: favored Turkish dominance within empire, led to Arab resistance

d) The empire survived only because of distrust among European powers

III. The Russian empire under pressure

A. Military defeat and social reform

1. The Crimean War (1853–1856)

a) Nineteenth-century Russia expanded from Manchuria, across Asia to Baltic Sea

b) Sought access to Mediterranean Sea, moved on Balkans controlled by Ottomans

c) European coalition supported Ottomans against Russia in Crimea

d) Crushing defeat forced tsars to take radical steps to modernize army, industry

2. Emancipation of serfs in 1861 by Alexander II

a) Serfdom supported landed nobility, an obstacle to economic development

b) Serfs gained right to land, but no political rights; had to pay a redemption tax

c) Emancipation did not increase agricultural production

3. Political and legal reforms followed

a) 1864, creation of *zemstvos,* local assemblies with representatives from all classes

b) A weak system: nobles dominated, tsar held veto power

c) Legal reform more successful: juries, independent judges, professional attorneys

B. Industrialization

1. The Witte system: developed by Sergei Witte, minister of finance, 1892–1903

a) Railway construction stimulated other industries; trans-Siberian railway

b) Remodeled the state bank, protected infant industries, secured foreign loans

c) Top-down industrialization effective; steel, coal, and oil industries grew

2. Industrial discontent intensified

a) Rapid industrialization fell hardest on working classes

b) Government outlawed unions, strikes; workers increasingly radical

c) Business class supported autocracy, not reform

C. Repression and revolution

1. Cycles of protest and repression

a) Peasants landless, no political power, frustrated by lack of meaningful reform

b) Antigovernment protest and revolutionary activity increased in 1870s

c) Intelligentsia advocated socialism and anarchism, recruited in countryside

d) Repression by tsarist authorities: secret police, censorship

e) Russification: sparked ethnic nationalism, attacks on Jews tolerated

2. Terrorism emerges as a tool of opposition

a) Alexander II, the reforming tsar, assassinated by a bomb in 1881

b) Nicholas II (1894–1917), more oppressive, conservative ruler

3. Russo-Japanese War, 1904–05: Russian expansion to east leads to conflict with Japan

4. Revolution of 1905: triggered by costly Russian defeat by Japan

a) Bloody Sunday massacre: unarmed workers shot down by government troops

b) Peasants seized landlords' property; workers formed soviets

c) Tsar forced to accept elected legislature, the Duma; did not end conflict

IV. The Chinese empire under siege

A. The Opium War and the unequal treaties

1. Opium trade a serious threat to Qing dynasty by nineteenth century

a) Chinese *cohong* system restricted foreign merchants to one port city

b) China had much to offer, but little demand for European products

c) East India Company cultivated opium to exchange for Chinese goods

d) About forty thousand chests of opium shipped to China yearly by 1838

2. The Opium War (1839–1842)

a) Commissioner Lin Zexu was directed to stop opium trade

b) British refused; Lin confiscated and destroyed twenty thousand chests of opium

c) British retaliated, easily crushed Chinese forces, destroyed Grand Canal

3. Unequal treaties forced trade concessions from Qing dynasty

a) Treaty of Nanjing, 1842: Britain gained right to opium trade, most-favored-nation status, Hong Kong, open trade ports, exemptions from Chinese laws

b) Similar unequal treaties made to other Western countries and Japan

c) By 1900, China lost control of economy, ninety ports to foreign powers

B. The Taiping rebellion

1. Internal turmoil in China in the later nineteenth century

a) Population grew by 50 percent; amount of land and food increased more slowly; poverty strained resources

b) Other problems: official corruption, drug addiction

c) Four major rebellions in 1850s and 1860s; the most dangerous was the Taiping

2. The Taiping ("Great Peace") program proposed by Hong Xiuquan

a) Called for end of Qing dynasty; resented Manchu rule

b) Radical social change: no private property, footbinding, concubinage

c) Popular in southeast China; seized Nanjing (1853), moved on Beijing

3. Taiping defeat by combined Qing and foreign troops

a) Gentry sided with government; regional armies had European weapons

b) Taipings defeated in 1864; the war claimed twenty to thirty million lives

C. Reform frustrated

1. The Self-Strengthening Movement (1860–1895)

a) Sought to blend Chinese cultural traditions with European industrial technology

b) Built shipyards, railroads, weapon industries, steel foundries, academies

c) Not enough industry to make a significant change

d) Powerful empress dowager Cixi opposed changes

2. Spheres of influence eroded Chinese power

a) Foreign powers seized Chinese tribute states of Vietnam, Burma, Korea, Taiwan

b) 1898, they carved China into spheres of economic influence, each a different province

3. The Hundred-Days reforms (1898)

a) Two Confucian scholars advised radical changes in imperial system

b) Young Emperor Guangxu inspired to launch wide-range reforms

c) Movement crushed by Cixi and supporters; emperor imprisoned; reformers killed

4. The Boxer rebellion (the Society of Righteous and Harmonious Fists), 1899–1900

a) Local militia attacked foreigners, Chinese Christians

b) Crushed by European and Japanese troops

c) Collapse of Qing dynasty in 1912

V. The transformation of Ja

VI. pan

A. From Tokugawa to Meiji

1. Crisis and reform in early nineteenth century

    a) Crisis: crop failure, high taxes, rising rice prices all led to protests and rebellions

    b) Tokugawa *bakufu* tried conservative reforms, met with resistance

2. Foreign pressure for Japan to reverse long-standing closed door policy

    a) 1844 requests by British, French, and United States for the right of entry rebuffed

    b) 1853, U.S. Commodore Perry sailed U.S. fleet to Tokyo Bay, demanded entry

    c) Japan forced to accept unequal treaties with United States and other Western countries

3. The end of Tokugawa rule followed these humiliations

    a) Widespread opposition to shogun rule, especially in provinces

    b) Dissidents rallied around emperor in Kyoto

4. The Meiji restoration, 1868

    a) After brief civil war, Tokugawa armies defeated by dissident militia

    b) The boy emperor Mutsuhito, or Meiji, regained authority

    c) End of almost seven centuries of military rule in Japan

B. Meiji reforms

1. Meiji government welcomed foreign expertise

    a) Fukuzawa Yukichi studied Western constitutions and education

    b) Ito Hirobumi helped build Japanese constitutional government

2. Abolition of the feudal order essential to new government

    a) Daimyo and samurai lost status and privileges

    b) Districts reorganized to break up old feudal domains

    c) New conscript army ended power of samurai; rebelled in 1877 but lost

3. Revamping the tax system

    a) Converted grain taxes to a fixed money tax: more reliable income for state

    b) Assessed taxes on potential productivity of arable land

4. Constitutional government, the emperor's "gift" to the people in 1889

    a) Emperor remained supreme, limited the rights of the people

    b) Less than 5 percent of adult males could vote

    c) Legislature, the Diet, was an opportunity for debate and dissent

5. Remodeling the economy and infrastructure

   a) Transportation: railroads, telegraph, steamships

   b) Education: universal primary and secondary; competitive universities

   c) Industry: privately owned, government controlled arms industry

   d) *Zaibatsu:* powerful financial cliques, similar to trusts but filial

6. Costs of economic development borne by Japanese people

   a) Land tax cost peasants 40 percent to 50 percent of crop yield, provided 90 percent of state revenue

   b) Peasant uprisings crushed; little done to alleviate suffering

   c) Labor movement also crushed; Meiji law treated unions and strikes as criminal

7. Japan became an industrial power in a single generation

   a) Ended unequal treaties in 1899

   b) Defeated China in 1895 and Russia in 1904

IDENTIFICATION: PEOPLE

What is the contribution of each of the following individuals to world history? Identification should include answers to the questions *who, what, where, when, how,* and *why is this person important?*

Muhammad Ali

Mahmud II

Abdül Hamid II

Alexander II

Sergei Witte

Lin Zexu

Hong Xiuquan

Empress Dowager Cixi

Commodore Matthew Perry

Emperor Mutsuhito (Meiji)

Ito Hirobumi

IDENTIFICATION: TERMS/CONCEPTS

State in your own words what each of the following terms means and why it is significant to a study of world history. (Terms with an asterisk are defined in the glossary.)

Janissaries

The "capitulations"*

Tanzimat*

Young Turks*

Crimean War

*Zemstvos**

Soviets*

Duma*

Cohong system*

Opium War

Unequal treaties

Taiping rebellion*

Self-Strengthening Movement*

Spheres of influence

Boxer rebellion

Tokugawa shogunate*

Meiji restoration*

Daimyo*

Bakufu

Neo-Confucianism*

1. What factors led to the territorial decline of the Ottoman empire over the course of the nineteenth century? What territories were lost?

2. Compare the reforms of the Tanzimat era with the program of the Young Turks.

3. What significant political and legal reforms did the Russian government implement in the late nineteenth century?

4. What was Count Witte's program for the industrialization of Russia? What were the results?

5. What were the sources of social discontent and agitation in Russia in the late nineteenth century? How did the government respond?

6. What events led to the Russian revolution of 1905? What was the outcome of this revolution?

7. Why was the opium trade so important to the British? What factors led to the Opium War and how was this war resolved?

8. What was the impact of the Treaty of Nanjing on the Chinese empire? What nations benefited from this treaty?

9. What were the causes of the Taiping revolution? What was the outcome?

10. Overall, what weaknesses led to the collapse of the Qing dynasty?

11. What factors led to the collapse of the Tokugawa government and the restoration of the emperor Meiji in 1868?

12. How did Japanese reformers achieve rapid industrialization of Japan? What were the results of this effort? What were the costs?

INQUIRY QUESTIONS

1. Before 1800, both China and Japan had limited contact with the outside world. The leaders of both nations considered theirs to be a superior culture and did not seek or welcome change. Discuss changes in the Chinese and Japanese attitudes toward Western ideas and Western technology over the course of the nineteenth century.

2. Both Russia and Japan undertook ambitious programs of modernization and industrialization in the late nineteenth century. Compare the results and account for the differences.

3. Why were the states considered in this chapter so reluctant to grant political freedoms? Is it possible to reform a society without granting basic freedoms such as free speech, free press, freedom of religion, and the right to vote? Before answering "no," consider the experience of Japan.

1. At the end of the nineteenth century, the Ottoman empire, Russian empire, Qing dynasty, and Tokugawa Japan were "societies at crossroads" because
    a. they were all dealing with the challenges of rapid industrialization.
    b. they discovered through wars and confrontations that they were militarily much weaker than the Western powers.
    c. they were all forced to grant equal rights and political freedom to their people.
    d. they were all competing for the same colonies and resources.
    e. all of the above.

2. The Ottoman military had declined by the nineteenth century because
    a. the Janissary Corps was more interested in palace intrigues than in military training.
    b. the Janissaries resisted all efforts to modernize the army.
    c. many provincial rulers had private mercenary armies.
    d. Ottoman forces carried outmoded equipment.
    e. all of the above.

3. By 1913, all of the following provinces had gained either independence or autonomy from Ottoman control *except*
    a. Anatolia.
    b. Egypt.
    c. Greece.
    d. Serbia.
    e. All of the above had gained independence.

4. The "capitulations" were humiliating concessions to the West that
    a. allowed Western powers to establish spheres of influence within Ottoman territory.
    b. forbade the manufacture of cotton cloth and obliged Ottomans to buy textiles from Britain.
    c. held European citizens exempt from Ottoman laws and taxes.
    d. restricted the exchange of technology and prevented the emergence of domestic industry in the Ottoman Empire.
    e. permitted unrestricted traffic in and out of the Black Sea.

5. The most significant achievement of the sultan Mahmud II was the
    a. creation of a system of primary education.
    b. legal emancipation of women.
    c. creation of a modern army.
    d. creation of a legislative assembly.
    e. reconquest of Egypt.

6. Tanzimat legal reforms included all of the following rights *except*
    a. equality before the law for all subjects.
    b. public trials in civil courts.
    c. right to privacy.
    d. women's right to sue for divorce.
    e. All of the above *were* Tanzimat legal reforms.

7. Which of the Young Turk proposals caused the most dissension in the Ottoman empire?
    a. Turkish as the official language of the empire
    b. equality before the law
    c. free public education
    d. freedom of religion
    e. universal suffrage

8. The Russian empire was defeated in the Crimean War because
    a. the Ottoman army was superior in arms and training.
    b. Britain and France joined forces to prevent Russian expansion into the Ottoman empire.
    c. Russian troops mutinied and demanded a new constitution.
    d. the people of the Balkan Peninsula resisted Russian advances.
    e. the Russian troops were inadequately trained.

9. The emancipation of Russian serfs in 1861
    a. was achieved at the tsar's insistence.
    b. was intended to avert a revolution.
    c. brought freedom but few political rights for the peasants.
    d. did not significantly increase agricultural production.
    e. all of the above.

10. Which of the following was *not* part of Count Witte's policy of industrialization?
    a. construction of the trans-Siberian railroad
    b. banking reform to encourage domestic savings and investment
    c. protective tariffs to support emerging Russian industries
    d. nationalization of key industries such as coal and steel
    e. promotion of foreign investment in Russian industry

11. The Russian intelligentsia promoted terrorism as a strategy for political reform because
    a. their attempts at peaceful reform were crushed by the tsarist authorities.
    b. Tsar Alexander II refused to consider any reform measures.
    c. socialists elsewhere in Europe had found assassination to be an effective way to make their case to the public.
    d. they were affiliated with Zionists, who advocated the use of terrorism when necessary.
    e. all of the above.

12. Which of the following could *not* be considered a contributing cause of the Russian revolution of 1905?
    a. the lack of a representative legislative body
    b. the defeat of Russia in the Russo-Japanese war
    c. the Bloody Sunday massacre
    d. the government's failure to address the inequities of land ownership
    e. All of the above *were* factors in the revolution of 1905.

13. The British insisted on their right to trade opium with China because
    a. they were unaware of the social and health risks of opium addiction.
    b. it was the only trade good that they could sell in China at a profit.
    c. they planned to weaken the Chinese people with opium and then take over the Chinese economy.
    d. they argued that opium was only a fraction of the volume of trade delivered to China.
    e. the Chinese government had welcomed the opium trade in earlier times.

14. Which of the following was *not* a provision of the Treaty of Nanjing in 1842?
    a. Britain gained control of Hong Kong Island.
    b. British merchants gained the right to conduct the opium trade unimpeded.
    c. Chinese ports were open to foreign trade and residence.
    d. Christian missionaries were permitted to come into China.
    e. Japan gained control of the island of Taiwan.

15. The Taiping rebellion was defeated when
    a. the dowager empress imprisoned the emperor and ended the hundred-days reforms.
    b. Nanjing was defeated by a combined force of imperial and European soldiers.
    c. the dowager empress died, leaving a two-year-old child as emperor.
    d. the British seized the Grand Canal and cut off north-south trade in the empire.
    e. all of the above.

16. In China, a "sphere of influence" was
    a. a city designated for trade between Chinese and European merchants.
    b. a Christian mission where Chinese converts could live free of state persecution.
    c. a district in which a foreign power had exclusive trade, transportation, and mineral rights.
    d. a tributary state beyond the borders of the empire that paid taxes to the Qing dynasty in exchange for protection.
    e. a state-sponsored academy based on European science.

17. The Tokugawa shogunate was overthrown because
    a. the Japanese were outraged by the unequal treaty forced on them by Commodore Perry.
    b. the samurai were in debt to the merchant class.
    c. the emperor had failed in his obligations to protect the Japanese people.
    d. the daimyo led a tax revolt.
    e. Japanese merchants wanted more access to Western goods and technology.

18. The success of the Meiji restoration depended on destroying the power of
    a. the daimyo and samurai classes.
    b. the emperor and his court.
    c. the Japanese military.
    d. the independent merchants.
    e. all of the above.

19. The capital for the early industrialization of Meiji Japan came primarily from
    a. the export of textile products.
    b. land taxes.
    c. commercial taxes.
    d. private investors.
    e. foreign investors.

20. Which of the following was *not* a provision of the Meiji constitution?
   a. Japan became a constitutional monarchy.
   b. The right to vote was based on property qualifications.
   c. The emperor could disregard the recommendations of the Diet.
   d. The lower classes were represented in the lower chamber of the Diet.
   e. Individual rights were affirmed but made secondary to the needs of the state.

MATCHING

Match these figures with the statements that follow.

A.	Young Turks	G.	Lin Zexu
B.	Muhammad Ali	H.	Sergei Witte
C.	Matthew Perry	I.	Abdül Hamid
D.	Hong Xiuquan	J.	Mahmud II
E.	Alexander II	K.	Cixi
F.	Janissaries	L.	Mutsuhito

1. ___ Leader who, although never officially the ruler, was effectively the last of the Qing dynasty.

2. ___ Village schoolmaster whose vision of a radically reformed Chinese society inspired the Taiping revolution.

3. ___ Moderate tsar who emancipated the serfs but denied them political rights.

4. ___ Egyptian general who successfully challenged the Ottoman empire.

5. ___ Leader who rose to power in a palace coup and promised to honor a new constitution, but soon revoked that promise and ruled as an autocrat.

6. ___ American who forced Japan at gunpoint to open its doors and who brought down the Tokugawa government.

7. ___ Sultan who built a modern army and destroyed the Janissaries.

8. ___ Chinese commissioner who tried unsuccessfully to stop the flood of opium into his country.

9. ___ Liberal reformers who forced the Ottoman sultan to accept a written constitution, with greater freedom and equality.

10. ___ Group that was once the military elite of the Ottoman empire; by the nineteenth century, they had become corrupt and reactionary.

11. ___ Boy emperor who reclaimed his power after the collapse of the Tokugawa shogunate.

12. ___ Russian finance minister who pursued a program of aggressive modernization and industrialization.

<u>SEQUENCING</u>

Place the following clusters of events in chronological order. Consider carefully how one event leads to another, and try to determine the internal logic of each sequence.

A.   In the Ottoman empire:

_____ An autocratic state becomes increasingly corrupt, economically backward, and militarily vulnerable.

_____ Within a year, the new sultan, Abdül Hamid, suspends the constitution and rules as an autocrat.

_____ Sultan Mahmud II restructures the military and reforms the imperial bureaucracy, all of which enhances the power of the sultan.

_____ The Young Turks stage a coup and restore the constitution and Parliament but also alienate ethnic minorities.

_____ Dissatisfied with the pace of reform, young dissidents stage a coup and demand a written constitution.

_____ Broad legal and educational reforms inspired by Western societies had the net effect of undermining the Muslim foundations of society and strengthening the state.

_____ By 1913, the Ottoman empire was brittle and vulnerable.

B.   In the Russian empire:

_____ An autocratic state becomes increasingly corrupt, economically backward, and militarily vulnerable.

_____ The tsar is forced to agree to a legislative assembly, the Duma.

_____ In order to avert civil unrest, Tsar Alexander II emancipates the serfs in 1861.

_____ Workers and peasants across the empire rise up in protest, governing themselves through local councils or soviets.

_____ Peasants serve in local assemblies but have little real power. Government censorship and repression prevent meaningful political participation.

_____ Government troops fire on a peaceful demonstration of workers, killing 130.

_____ By 1913, the Russian empire has made significant progress in industry but remains economically backward and politically unstable.

C.   In the Qing dynasty:

_____   An autocratic state becomes increasingly corrupt, economically backward, and militarily vulnerable.

_____   With European arms and assistance, Qing forces crush the Taiping rebellion; twenty to thirty million people are killed.

_____   The imperial family and powerful gentry crush the reform movement and imprison the emperor.

_____   The dowager empress decides that "foreign devils" are responsible for the civil unrest and promotes the disastrous Boxer rebellion against all foreigners in China.

_____   A young, idealistic emperor launches an ambitious reform program with a constitution, civil liberties, and public education.

_____   A desperate peasant army embraces the vision of Hong Xiuquan for an egalitarian society without class distinctions or private property.

_____   By 1911, the Qing dynasty has lost control of the Chinese economy and much of its territory; the last emperor is forced to abdicate.

D.   In Tokugawa Japan:

_____   An autocratic state, the shogunate, becomes increasingly corrupt, economically backward, and militarily vulnerable.

_____   Power is centralized, and the powerful daimyo and samurai lose their feudal privileges.

_____   Peasants cannot vote, cannot strike or organize protests, and yet they bear the primary expense for the modernization of Japan.

_____   In a "gift" to his people, the emperor presents a constitution that provides an elected legislative body but retains ultimate power for the emperor.

_____   Opposition to the shogunate coalesces around the boy emperor, Meiji, who is restored to his rightful authority in 1868.

_____   An American naval officer forces the Tokugawa government to receive U.S. merchant ships and to sign an unequal treaty, demonstrating the military superiority of the United States.

_____   By 1905, Japan has emerged as a new industrial power, largely through the discipline and dedication of its people.

<u>QUOTATIONS</u>

For each of the following quotes, identify the speaker, if known, or the point of view. What is the significance of each passage?

1. "Chinese learning at the base, Western learning for use."

2. "Every citizen will enjoy complete liberty and equality, regardless of nationality or religion, and be submitted to the same obligations. All Ottomans, being equal before the law as regards rights and duties relative to the State, are eligible for government posts, according to their individual capacity and their education. Non-Muslims will be equally liable to the military law."

3. "It is better to abolish serfdom from above than to wait until the serfs begin to liberate themselves from below."

4. "If the merchants of your honorable country wish to enjoy trade with us on a permanent basis, they must fearfully observe our law by cutting off, once and for all, the supply of opium."

5. "We know that the ancient laws of your Imperial Majesty's government do not allow of foreign trade except with the Dutch. But as the state of the world changes, and new governments are formed, it seems to be wise from time to time to make new laws. . . . If your Imperial Majesty were so far to change the ancient laws so as to allow a free trade between [our] two countries, it would be extremely beneficial to both."

<u>MAP EXERCISES</u>

1. Compare the map of the Ottoman empire (Map 32.1, page 882 in the textbook) with the modern map of the same region (Map 39.3, page 1110). How many modern nations did the Ottoman empire control in 1800? How many of these countries were still under Ottoman control in 1913, on the eve of World War I?

2. Locate and label the following on the map of the Russian empire (see Map 32.2, page 888).

- Cities: Archangel, Irtkutsk, Kiev, Moscow, Port Arthur, St. Petersburg, Vladivostok
- Bodies of water: Aral Sea, Baltic Sea, Barents Sea, Bering Sea, Black Sea, Caspian Sea, Lake Baikal, Sea of Okhotsk
- Features: Ural Mountains, Kamchatka, Trans-Siberian Railroad
- Surrounding states: Finland Japan, Manchuria, Mongolia, Ottoman empire, Persia, Poland

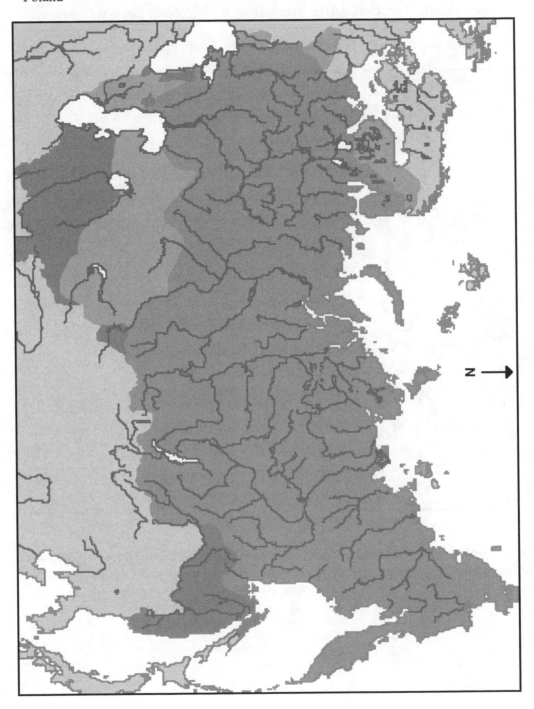

155

3. Explain how Russian territorial acquisitions in the nineteenth century enhanced trade and transportation for the empire.

4. Locate and label the following on the outline map of east Asia below (see Map 32.3, page 896).

   - States: Burma, China, India, Japan, Korea, Manchuria, Mongolia, Philippines, Russia, Siam, Taiwan, Tibet, Vietnam
   - Cities: Beijing, Edo, Guangzhou, Hanoi, Hong Kong, Macao, Nagasaki, Nanjing, Shanghai
   - Bodies of water: Huang He River, Yangzi River, South China Sea, East China Sea

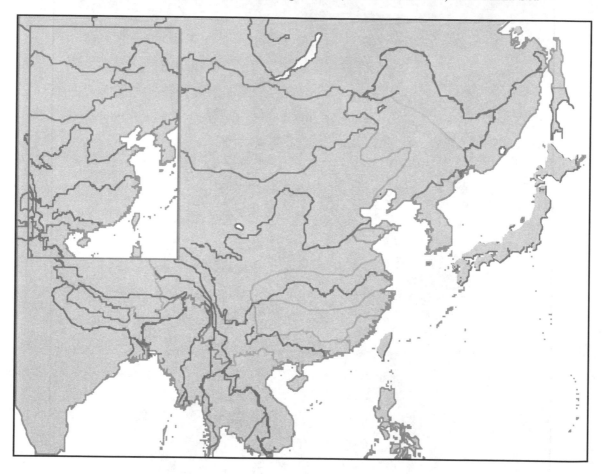

5. On the outline map of east Asia, indicate the spheres of influence in China held by each of the following imperial powers: Britain, France, Germany, Japan, Russia (see Map 32.3). What does this picture reveal about the economic viability of the late Qing dynasty?

CONNECTIONS

In fifty words or less, explain the relationship between each of the following pairs. How does one lead to or foster the other? Be specific in your response.

- The "capitulations" and the Young Turks
- The soviets and the Duma
- Emancipation of the serfs and the Revolution of 1905
- *Cohong* system and the Boxer Rebellion
- The Treaty of Nanjing and Commodore Perry
- Meiji restoration and the Russo-Japanese War

FILMS

Charge of the Light Brigade (1968). A sharp antiwar film, set during the Crimean War, that shows both the flag-waving patriotism and the cynical balance-of-power diplomacy of the age.

The Fixer (1968). Based on a novel by Bernard Malamud, this story of a Jew falsely accused of murder in tsarist Russia is based on an actual event that provided the pretext for official persecution of Jews. Starring Alan Bates. In English.

Samuari Assassin (1965). Considered by many to be one of the greatest samurai films, this one tells the story of a samurai whose family stands to lose everything if plans for the Meiji restoration proceed. In Japanese with subtitles.

55 Days at Peking (1963). Foreign troops and diplomats defend the besieged international compound in Peking (Beijing) during the 1900 Boxer Rebellion. An uncritical view of Western imperialism. Starring Charlton Heston, Ava Gardner, and David Niven.

Battleship Potemkin (1925). Depicts the real-life mutiny aboard the battleship *Potemkin* during the Russian Revolution of 1905 as celebrated by the Communist regime twenty years later. A silent film by the Russian master Sergei Eisenstein.

CHAPTER 33
THE BUILDING OF GLOBAL EMPIRES

<u>INTRODUCTION</u>

In the latter half of the nineteenth century, the industrial powers of western Europe swiftly extended their control over vast areas of Africa and Asia. This new imperialism was rationalized by theories of racial and cultural superiority; it was made possible by new technologies of warfare. The United States and Japan, and to a lesser extent Russia, were late arrivals on the imperial stage but soon established themselves as well. Modern imperialism is characterized by the following:

- Mixed motives. Imperial powers claimed economic necessity, strategic imperatives, and a high-minded "civilizing mission." Frequently motives were confused, so it became "the white man's burden" to convert Africans to Christianity while at the same time enslaving them.

- Competition between imperial powers. The scramble for Africa and later for the Pacific islands illustrates the intense competition among imperial nations. The United States took over the Philippines in order to be on an equal footing with other powers already in China. Japan seized Korea and Taiwan for the same reason.

- Different models of colonial rule. In practice, the new imperialism varied considerably; including settler colonies such as Australia, indirect rule as in British Africa, direct rule as in French Indochina, and even the private fiefdom of Leopold II in the Belgian Congo. In all cases, ultimate authority rested with the imperial state, and local rulers had little real power.

- Economic colonialism. The purpose of the colony was to supply cheap raw commodities to the imperialist state and to be a market for manufactured goods. All resources, natural and human, were directed to this effort. Forests were transformed into plantations, and workers impressed into service. There was no effort to develop a colonial industry that might compete with the imperial state.

- Contempt for local cultures. With few exceptions, the imperial powers regarded colonial people as their inferiors and treated them as such. The French made an effort to convert and educate colonial peoples. The British also employed colonials as soldiers and minor civil servants, but made little provision for education. This disrespect contributed to a growing nationalism in India.

<u>OUTLINE</u>

I. Foundations of empire

    A. Motives for imperialism

        1. Modern imperialism

            a) Refers to domination of industrialized countries over subject lands

b) Domination achieved through trade, investment, and business activities

2. Two types of modern colonialism

a) Colonies ruled and populated by migrants

b) Colonies controlled by imperial powers without significant settlement

3. Economic motives of imperialism

a) European merchants and entrepreneurs made personal fortunes

b) Overseas expansion for raw materials: rubber, tin, copper, petroleum

c) Colonies were potential markets for industrial products

4. Political motives

a) Strategic purpose: harbors and supply stations for industrial nations

b) Overseas expansion used to defuse internal tensions

5. Cultural justifications of imperialism

a) Christian missionaries sought converts in Africa and Asia

b) "Civilizing mission" or "white man's burden" was a justification for expansion

B. Tools of empire

1. Transportation technologies supported imperialism

a) Steam-powered gunboats reached inland waters of Africa and Asia

b) Railroads organized local economies to serve imperial power

2. Western military technologies increasingly powerful

a) Firearms: from muskets to rifles to machine guns

b) In Battle of Omdurman 1898, British troops killed eleven thousand Sudanese in five hours

3. Communication technologies linked imperial lands with colonies

a) Oceangoing steamships cut travel time from Britain to India from years to weeks

b) Telegraph invented in 1830s, global reach by 1900

II. European imperialism

A. The British empire in India

1. Company rule under the English East India Company

a) EIC took advantage of Mughal decline in India, began conquest of India in 1750s

b) Built trading cities and forts at Calcutta, Madras, Bombay

c) Ruled domains with small British force and Indian troops called *sepoys*

d) Sepoy Mutiny, 1857: attacks on British civilians led to swift British reprisals

2. British imperial rule replaced the EIC, 1858

a) British viceroy and high-level British civil service ruled India

       b) British officials appointed a viceroy and formulated all domestic and foreign policy

       c) Indians held low-level bureaucratic positions

   3. Economic restructuring of India and Ceylon (Sri Lanka)

       a) Introduction of commercial crops: tea in Ceylon, also coffee and opium

       b) Built railroads and telegraph lines, new canals, harbors, and irrigation methods

   4. British rule did not interfere with Indian culture or Hindu religion

       a) Established English-style schools for Indian elites

       b) Outlawed Indian customs considered offensive, such as the *sati*

B. Imperialism in central Asia and southeast Asia

   1. "The Great Game" refers to competition between Britain and Russia in central Asia

       a) By 1860s Russian expansion reached northern frontiers of British India

       b) Russian and British explorers mapped, scouted, but never colonized Afghanistan

       c) Russian dominance of central Asia lasted until 1991

   2. Dutch East India Company held tight control of Indonesia (Dutch East India)

   3. British colonies in southeast Asia

       a) Established colonial authority in Burma, 1880s

       b) Port of Singapore founded 1824; was base for conquest of Malaya, 1870s

   4. French Indochina created, 1859–1893

       a) Consisted of Vietnam, Cambodia, Laos—former tribute states of Qing dynasty

       b) French encouraged conversion to Christianity, established western-style schools

   5. Kingdom of Siam (Thailand) left in place as buffer between Burma and Indochina

C. The scramble for Africa

   1. Between 1875 and 1900, European powers seized almost the entire continent

       a) Early explorers charted the waters, gathered information on resources

       b) Missionaries like David Livingstone set up mission posts

       c) Henry Stanley sent by Leopold II of Belgium to create colony in Congo, 1870s

       d) To protect their investments and Suez Canal, Britain occupied Egypt, 1882

   2. South Africa settled first by Dutch farmers (Afrikaners) in seventeenth century

       a) By 1800, it was a European settler colony with enslaved black African population

       b) British seized Cape Colony in early nineteenth century, abolished slavery in 1833

       c) British-Dutch tensions led to Great Trek of Afrikaners inland to claim new lands

       d) They established Orange Free State in 1854, Transvaal in 1860

    e) Discovery of gold and diamonds in Afrikaner lands; influx of British settlers

    f) Boer War, 1899–1902: British defeated Afrikaners, Union of South Africa

3. The Berlin Conference, 1884–1885

    a) European powers set rules for carving Africa into colonies

    b) Occupation, supported by European armies, established colonial rule in Africa

    c) By 1900 all of Africa, except Ethiopia and Liberia, was controlled by European powers

4. Colonial rule challenging and expensive

    a) "Concessionary companies": granted considerable authority to private companies

        (1) empowered to build plantations, mines, railroads

        (2) made use of forced labor and taxation, as in Belgian Congo

        (3) unprofitable, often replaced by more direct rule

    b) Direct rule: local rulers replaced with Europeans—French model

        (1) justified by "civilizing mission"

        (2) hard to find enough European personnel

    c) Indirect rule: control over subjects through local institutions—British model

        (1) worked best in African societies that were highly organized

        (2) assumed firm tribal boundaries where often none existed

D. European imperialism in the Pacific

1. Settler colonies in the Pacific

    a) 1770, Captain James Cook reached Australia, reported it suitable for settlement

    b) 1788, one thousand settlers established colony of New South Wales

    c) 1851, gold discovered; surge of European migration to Australia

    d) Fertile soil and timber of New Zealand attracted European settlers

    e) European diseases dramatically reduced aboriginal populations

    f) Large settler societies forced indigenous peoples onto marginal lands

2. Imperialists in paradise: delayed colonization of Pacific islands until late nineteenth century

    a) Early visitors to the Pacific were mostly whalers, merchants, some missionaries

    b) Late nineteenth century, European states sought coaling stations and naval ports

    c) By 1900, all islands but Tonga claimed by France, Britain, Germany, and United States

    d) Island plantations produced sugarcane, copra, guano

III. The emergence of new imperial powers

A. U.S. imperialism in Latin America and the Pacific

1. The Monroe Doctrine, 1823: proclamation by U.S. president James Monroe

   a) Opposed European imperialism in the Americas; justified U.S. intervention

   b) United States purchased Alaska from Russia in 1867

   c) Hawai`i became a protectorate in 1875, formally annexed in 1898

2. The Spanish-American War (1898–99)

   a) United States defeated Spain and took over Cuba, Puerto Rico, Guam, and Philippines

   b) United States backed Filipino revolt against Spain, purchased and took over the colony

   c) 1902–1904, bitter civil war killed two hundred thousand Filipinos, ended in U.S. victory

3. The Panama Canal, 1903–1914

   a) Colombian government refused U.S. request to build canal at Panama isthmus

   b) United States helped rebels establish the state of Panama for the right to build a canal

   c) Completed in 1914; gave United States access to Atlantic and Pacific

4. Roosevelt Corollary to Monroe Doctrine: U.S. asserted right to intervene in affairs of nations of Central and South America to protect U.S. investments

B. Imperial Japan

1. Japanese resented unequal treaties of 1860s, resolved to become imperial power

2. Early Japanese expansion in nearby islands

   a) 1870s, to the north: Hokkaido, Kurile Islands

   b) By 1879, to the south: Okinawa and Ryukyu Islands

3. Meiji government bought British warships, built up navy, established military academies

   a) 1876, imposed unequal treaties on Korea at gunpoint

   b) Made plans to invade China

4. The Sino-Japanese War (1894–95)

   a) Rebellion in Korea: Chinese army sent to restore order, reassert authority

   b) Meiji leaders declared war against China, demolished Chinese fleet

   c) China forced to cede Korea, Taiwan, Pescadores Islands, Liaodong peninsula

5. The Russo-Japanese War (1904–05)

a) Russia also had territorial ambitions in Liaodong peninsula, Korea, Manchuria

b) Japanese navy destroyed local Russian forces; Baltic fleet sent as reinforcements

c) Japan now a major imperial power

IV. Legacies of imperialism

A. Empire and economy: two patterns of changes

1. Colonial rule transformed traditional production of crops and commodities

a) Indian cotton grown to serve British textile industry

b) Inexpensive imported textiles undermined Indian production

2. New crops transformed landscape and society

a) Rain forests of Ceylon converted to tea plantations

b) Ceylonese women recruited to harvest tea

c) Rubber plantations transformed Malaya and Sumatra

B. Labor migrations

1. European migration

a) Fifty million Europeans migrated 1800–1914, over half to the United States

b) Other settler colonies in Canada, Argentina, Australia, New Zealand, South Africa

c) Most European migrants became cultivators, herders, or skilled laborers

2. Indentured labor migration more typical from Asia, Africa, and Pacific islands

a) About 2.5 million indentured laborers globally during 1820–1914

b) Indentured migrants tended to work on tropical and subtropical plantations

c) Example: Indian laborers to Pacific island and Caribbean plantations

d) Japanese laborers to Hawaiian sugar plantations

3. Large-scale migrations reflected global influence of imperialism

C. Empire and society

1. Colonial conflict not uncommon in nineteenth century

a) In India, numerous insurrections, such as the Sepoy Mutiny of 1857

b) 1905, Maji Maji rebellion in east Africa thought traditional magic would defeat the Germans

c) Resistance included boycotts, political parties, anticolonial publications

d) Conflict among different groups united under colonial rule, for example, Hawai`i

2. "Scientific racism" popular in nineteenth century

a) Race became the measure of human potential; Europeans considered superior

b) Gobineau divided humanity into four main racial groups, each with peculiar traits

      c)   Social Darwinism: "survival of fittest" used to justify European domination

   3. Colonial experience only reinforced popular racism

      a)   Assumed moral superiority of Europeans

      b)   Racist views in U.S. treatment of Filipinos, Japanese treatment of Koreans

D. Nationalism and anticolonial movements

   1. Ram Mohan Roy (1772–1833), "father of modern India"

      a)   Sought an Indian society based on European science and traditional Hinduism

      b)   Used press to mobilize educated Hindus and advance reform

   2. The Indian National Congress, founded 1885

      a)   Educated Indians met, with British approval, to discuss public affairs

      b)   Congress aired grievances about colonial rule, sought Indian self-rule

      c)   1906, All-India Muslim League formed to advance interests of Indian Muslims

   3. Limited reform, 1909; wealthy Indians could elect representatives to local councils

      a)   Indian nationalism a powerful movement, achieved independence in 1947

      b)   India served as a model for anticolonial campaigns in other lands

IDENTIFICATION: PEOPLE

What is the contribution of each of the following individuals to world history? Identification should include answers to the questions *who, what, where, when, how,* and *why is this person important?*

Cecil Rhodes

Rudyard Kipling

Leopold II

Queen Victoria

Queen Lili`uokalani

Theodore Roosevelt

Charles Darwin

Ram Mohan Ray

IDENTIFICATION: TERMS/CONCEPTS

State in your own words what each of the following terms means and why it is significant to a study of world history. (Terms with an asterisk are defined in the glossary.)

Imperialism*

Battle of Omdurman

Suez Canal

Panama Canal

Sepoys

Great Game

Roosevelt Corollary

Sepoy Mutiny*

Boer

Great Trek

Berlin Conference*

Maori*

Maji Maji rebellion

Social Darwinism*

Indian National Congress

STUDY QUESTIONS

1. Summarize the economic, political, and cultural motives of nineteenth-century imperialists. To what extent did those motives overlap, and to what extent did they conflict with one another?

2. What were the principal "tools of empire"—the various technologies that gave the Europeans such an advantage?

3. How did the British establish control over India in the early nineteenth century? How did the Sepoy Mutiny contribute to this process?

4. Which Asian states managed to maintain their sovereignty in the nineteenth century? Why these states?

5. Who were the major players in the "scramble for Africa"? What was the principal objective of this landgrab?

6. Compare the British conquest of South Africa with that of Egypt and Sudan.

7. Why were the great powers less interested in the Pacific islands? What did they want from these islands?

8. What did the United States gain from the Spanish-American War? Note the political status of each of these acquisitions.

9. Where did the Japanese direct their ambitions as a new imperial power? How successful were they?

10. How did the imperial powers transform the economies of their colonies? Consider especially India and Ceylon.

11. Summarize some of the significant migrations of the late nineteenth century. What were the typical destinations?

12. How did subject peoples resist colonial rule? How did imperialism foster conflicts within colonial societies?

INQUIRY QUESTIONS

1. Nineteenth-century imperialists claimed that they were fulfilling a "civilizing mission" in their overseas conquests. To what extent was this claim true? Specifically, what significant reforms and changes did the British bring to India? What changes did the British *not* make?

2. The status of indigenous peoples was an important problem for the imperial powers of the nineteenth century. Compare the British treatment of Australian aborigines and New Zealand Maoris with the treatment of Native Americans by the U.S. government.

3. Compare the French model of direct rule with the British model of indirect rule. What are the relative advantages and disadvantages for both the rulers and their African subjects? Consider this: under which system would an African find the most opportunities for personal advancement?

STUDENT QUIZ

1. Cecil Rhodes was
   a. the British military leader who was responsible for a boom in naval expansion.
   b. the American politician who articulated the belief in manifest destiny.
   c. responsible for the philosophy known as social Darwinism.
   d. the first leader of an independent Canada.
   e. a leading British imperialist active in South Africa.

2. Which of the following was *not* an economic motivation for imperialism?
   a. Cheap raw materials from overseas colonies were needed to sustain industrialization.
   b. Overseas colonies offered markets for manufactured goods.
   c. Overseas colonies offered a haven for the settlement of surplus populations.
   d. European and American industry needed more sources of coal.
   e. All were economic motives for imperialism.

3. The "white man's burden" proposed by Rudyard Kipling refers to
   a. the cost of creating and supporting an empire.
   b. the moral duty of the West to work to "civilize" the rest of the world.
   c. the cost of abolishing slavery in Africa.
   d. the need for Christian missionaries to undermine Islam in Africa and Asia.
   e. all of the above.

4. All of the following improved communication between India and Britain *except*
   a. the completion of the Panama Canal.
   b. the use of steamships.
   c. the invention of the telegraph.
   d. the laying of submarine cables.
   e. All of the above improved communication between India and Britain.

5. The Battle of Omdurman clearly demonstrated that
   a. Europeans were morally superior to Africans.
   b. Japan had become a major world power.
   c. European troops with modern weapons could subdue a vast native army.
   d. Britain had fallen behind Germany by the end of the nineteenth century.
   e. none of the above.

6. The Mughal dynasty fell primarily because
   a. the state had been weakened by conflicts during the reign of Aurangzeb.
   b. the East India Company established powerful, coastal trading forts.
   c. British merchants gained access to interior territories.
   d. the Sepoy Mutiny failed to drive the British out of India.
   e. all of the above.

7. Under British imperial rule, India was governed
   a. as a private colony of Queen Victoria.
   b. as an independent sovereign state, but subject to British authority in foreign affairs.
   c. as the private domain of the East India Company.
   d. by a viceroy working in collaboration with Indian princes.
   e. with British bureaucrats and officers overseeing Indian civil servants.

8. One social goal of the British authorities in India was to
   a. abolish the caste system.
   b. establish a system of public education.
   c. convert the local population to Christianity.
   d. abolish the custom of burning widows with their husbands' bodies.
   e. none of the above.

9. Unlike the British in India, the French in Indochina
   a. encouraged conversion to Christianity.
   b. recruited local peoples into their colonial army.
   c. worked closely with local elites.
   d. promoted domestic industries.
   e. had no obvious racial bias.

10. The colonization of the Belgian Congo is noted for
    a. the spirited resistance of the Congolese people.
    b. the brutal treatment of the Congolese people by King Leopold II.
    c. a policy of free trade that encouraged merchants from all countries.
    d. the humane policies of the Belgian government toward the Congolese people.
    e. all of the above.

11. The term "Great Game" refers to the
    a. British and French rivalry for control of India.
    b. German conflict with the British and French for control of Africa.
    c. U.S. view of their easy victory in the Spanish-American War.
    d. Japanese and Chinese contest for domination of Manchuria.
    e. Russian contest with Britain for central Asia.

12. The Berlin Conference in 1884–1885 established
    a. the procedures for purchasing African lands from local rulers.
    b. the rules of military engagement for European forces overseas.
    c. that the Americas were off-limits for further European colonization.
    d. that Africa would be carved into spheres of influence similar to China.
    e. that, if a European power indicated its intention to colonize and then proceeded to occupy an African territory, it could claim that colony.

13. Why had most European governments abandoned concessionary companies in Africa by the early twentieth century?
    a. The companies provoked rebellion, and the governments had to come to their defense.
    b. The companies became so profitable that the governments decided to take over management of the colonies.
    c. The companies became so powerful that they threatened to break away from the mother country.
    d. The brutal use of forced African labor by companies provoked a public outcry in Europe.
    e. None of the above.

14. One striking difference between the British and the French imperial models in Africa is that
    a. the British preferred to use local institutions to control subject populations.
    b. the French preferred to employ local rulers to govern their colonies.
    c. the British established schools and academies to train African civil servants to run their colonies, while the French did not.
    d. many more British citizens relocated to Africa to administer their colonies than did French citizens.
    e. the British actively sought to convert Africans to Christianity, while the French did not.

15. Which of the following is *not* true about the settlement of Australia?
    a. The British defined the continent as land belonging to no one.
    b. The first settlers were mostly convicts, banished from Britain.
    c. Smallpox and measles reduced the aboriginal populations by 86 percent.
    d. Australia became a multicultural society, drawing settlers from all over the Pacific.
    e. Settlement increased significantly after the discovery of gold.

16. The scramble for Pacific island colonies in the late nineteenth century was motivated by
    a. the desire for the tropical produce.
    b. the need to defend the whaling industry.
    c. concerns about the Japanese expansion to nearby islands.
    d. the desire for strategic ports and refueling stations in the Pacific Ocean.
    e. items a and d above.

17. Panama was supported in its uprising against Colombia by U.S. president
    a. Grover Cleveland.
    b. William Howard Taft.
    c. Theodore Roosevelt.
    d. William McKinley.
    e. Woodrow Wilson.

18. The United States acquired Hawai`i by
    a. secretly sponsoring a rebellion against the Hawaiian monarchy.
    b. a purchase treaty with the Hawaiian people.
    c. seizing the islands by force in order to provide a naval base in the Pacific.
    d. purchasing the islands from Spain in the wake of the Spanish-American War.
    e. annexing the islands after American planters had overthrown the monarchy.

19. Japanese imperial expansion in the late nineteenth century was primarily motivated by
    a. the need for land for settlement by a growing population.
    b. the desire to spread Buddhism to other lands..
    c. resentment at the unequal treaties forced on them by the United States.
    d. a long-standing rivalry between China and Japan.
    e. all of the above.

20. Which of the following would *not* be typical of labor migration patterns in the age of empire?
    a. Chinese migrants to plantations in Cuba
    b. German migrants to plantations in the Congo
    c. Indian migrants to plantations in the Caribbean
    d. Irish migrants to factories and railroads in the United States
    e. Japanese migrants to plantations in Hawai`i

21. British rule undermined the Indian cotton industry by
    a. undercutting the cost of Indian cloth with cheap British textiles.
    b. forbidding the manufacture of cotton cloth in India.
    c. imposing tariffs on cotton cloth into India.
    d. imposing tariffs on cotton cloth shipped from India to Britain.
    e. monopolistic practices by the East India Company.

22. Colonial rule dramatically altered the environment in which of the following places?
    a. India, due to tea production
    b. Ceylon, due to tea production
    c. Malaya, due to rubber production
    d. Sumatra, due to rubber production
    e. all of the above

23. Proponents of "scientific racism" argued that
    a. race could be biologically defined and characterized.
    b. Western dominance was justified on the basis on racial superiority.
    c. the theories of Charles Darwin supported world dominance by the "fittest" races.
    d. people of European descent were morally superior to other races.
    e. all of the above.

24. Pressure for reform in British India came from
    a. educated Indians seeking self-rule.
    b. educated Indian women seeking greater independence.
    c. Indian Muslims seeking independence from the Hindu majority.
    d. Indian peasants and workers mobilized into unions.
    e. enlightened British rulers who felt that India was ready for self-government.

MATCHING

Match these figures and groups with the statements that follow.

A.	Charles Darwin	G.	Andrew Jackson
B.	Maori	H.	Ram Mohan Ray
C.	Leopold II	I.	Rudyard Kipling
D.	Afrikaners	J.	Theodore Roosevelt
E.	Sepoys	K.	Cecil Rhodes
F.	James Monroe	L.	Victoria I

1. ___ American president who informed the states of Europe that no further colonization of the New World would be tolerated by the U.S. government.

2. ___ Name taken by the descendants of Dutch settlers in South Africa.

3. ___ Scientist whose theory of evolution by natural selection was corrupted to justify Western imperialism over the so-called inferior races of the world.

4. ___ British poet, author, and apologist for imperialism, which he regarded as the "white man's burden."

5. ___ Name given to the aboriginal people of New Zealand.

6. ___ Indian soldiers in service of the East India Company and later of the British government.

7. ___ American president who oversaw the construction of the Panama Canal and secured U.S. rights to the Canal Zone.

8. ___ British adventurer who carved a personal empire out of South Africa.

9. ___ Educated Indian reformer whose ideas of Indian nationalism led to the creation of the Indian National Congress.

10. ___ Ruler of Britain for most of the nineteenth century and first empress of India.

11. ___ Belgian monarch who claimed the Congo as his personal domain and impressed the Congolese people to work on his plantations.

12. ___ American president who engineered the forcible removal of various tribes from the eastern woodlands to reservations on the western prairies.

SEQUENCING

Place the following clusters of events in chronological order. Consider carefully how one event leads to another, and try to determine the internal logic of each sequence.

A.

_____ After the British abolish slavery in Cape Colony, hundreds of Dutch families abandon the coast and reestablish themselves in the interior.

_____ The discovery of gold and diamonds lures thousands of British miners into the interior.

_____ During the Napoleonic Wars, the British seize Cape Town, which becomes an important station for trade to India.

_____ Tensions between Dutch and British settlers culminate in the Boer War, a nasty colonial conflict that pits whites against whites but kills thousands of blacks in the process.

_____ Dutch settlers establish farms near Cape Town and eventually displace the local Khoikhoi population.

_____ The Union of South Africa is created as a British colony.

B.

_____ Concessionary companies have full authority over the resources and labor of Africa.

_____ Systems of either direct or indirect rule prove to be costly colonial ventures.

_____ The brutality of forced labor on company plantations forces most imperial governments to intervene.

_____ European slave traders confine their contacts with Africans to coastal forts and trading posts.

C.

_____ Victory in the Sino-Japanese War gives Japan control of Korea, Taiwan, and the Liaodong peninsula.

_____ The Meiji restoration makes industrialization and militarization top national priorities.

_____ A resounding Japanese victory proves that Japan has become a major imperial power.

_____ The Tokugawa government is forced at gunpoint to accept an unequal treaty with the United States.

_____ Japan establishes control over the neighboring islands of Hokkaido and Okinawa and relocates settlers there to consolidate their claims.

_____ Japanese activity on the Asian mainland alarms the Russian empire and leads to the Russo-Japanese War.

QUOTATIONS

For each of the following quotes, identify the speaker, if known, or the point of view. What is the significance of each passage?

1. "[We assert] as a principle in which the rights and interests of the United States are involved, that the American continents, by the free and independent condition which they have assumed and maintain, are henceforth not to be considered as subjects for future colonization by any European powers."

2. "We are the finest race in the world, and the more of the world we inhabit, the better it is for the human race."

3. "If they are sufficiently complete to live, they do live, and it is well they should live. If they are not sufficiently complete to live, they die, and it is best they should die."

4. "Fill full the mouth of Famine/And bid the sickness cease;
And when your goal is nearest/the end for others sought,
Watch Sloth and heathen Folly/Bring all your hope to nought."

5. "There are some who say we have no *right* in Africa at all, that 'it belongs to the natives.' I hold that our right is the necessity that is upon us to provide for our ever-growing population. . . . Nor do we deprive the natives of their birthright of freedom, to place them under a foreign yoke. It has ever been the key-note of British colonial method to rule through and by the natives."

MAP EXERCISES

1. Use Map 33.1 on page 918 in the textbook to locate and label the following on the outline map of Asia.
    *   Countries and colonies: Burma, Ceylon, China, Dutch East Indies, Hokkaido, India, Indochina, Japan, Korea, Malay states, Philippines, Siam, Taiwan
    *   Cities: Bombay, Calcutta, Delhi, Goa, Guangzhou, Hong Kong, Macao, Manila, Saigon, Seoul, Shanghai, Singapore, Vladivostok
    *   Indicate which was controlled by Britain, France, Japan, the United States, the Netherlands, Russia, or Portugal.

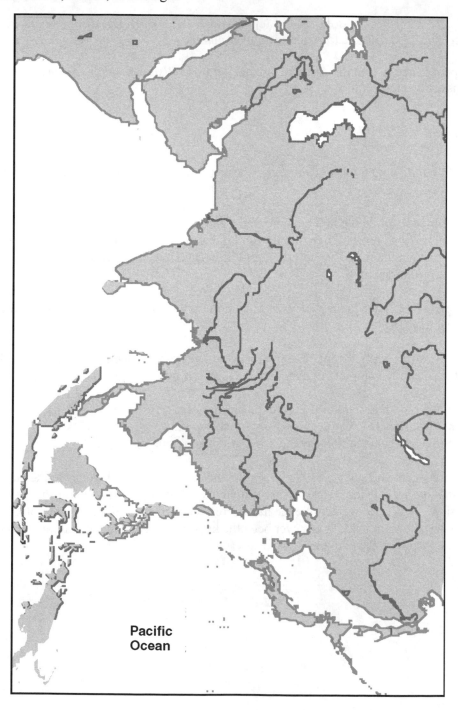

On the outline map of Africa (Map 33.2, page 923), label the colonies and color code by imperial state. Cecil Rhodes hoped to give the British control from "Cape to Cairo." How close did they come?

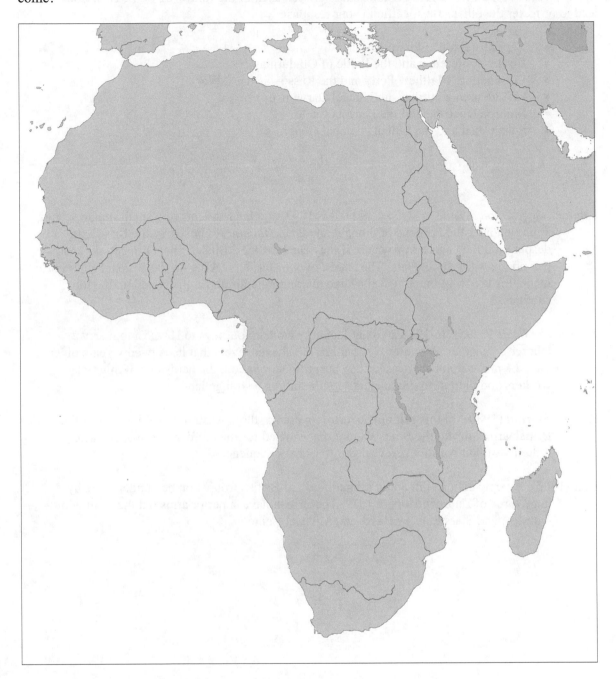

2. Assume that all the political boundaries of Africa were established at the convenience of the imperial powers. Note, for example the "hook" on the northeast corner of German Southwest Africa. This was intended to give the Germans access to the Zambezi River. What possible explanation could there be for such oddities as Cabinda, Gambia, or Rio Muni? What other anomalies do you see in the boundaries of Africa?

<u>CONNECTIONS</u>

In fifty words or less, explain the relationship between each of the following pairs. How does one lead to or foster the other? Be specific in your response.

- Capitalism and colonialism
- Berlin Conference and the Battle of Omdurman
- Commodore Matthew Perry and the Russo-Japanese War
- "White man's burden" and Social Darwinism
- Monroe Doctrine and the Panama Canal
- Suez Canal and the Indian National Congress

<u>FILMS</u>

Lagaan: Once Upon a Time in India (2001). It is 1893, and the residents of a small Indian village struggle under the burdens of drought and taxes (*lagaan*) imposed by the British. In desperation they agree to a wager: if they can beat the British team at cricket, they will pay no taxes for three years. The notion of poor farmers taking on the British Empire has made this lavish Indian musical a huge international hit. In English and Hindi with subtitles.

The Picture Bride (1995). In 1918 a young Japanese woman journeys to Hawai`i to marry a laborer on a sugar plantation. On her arrival, she discovers that he is twenty years older than the photograph she was sent. A beautiful story about the hardships of migrant workers and their struggle to create community in a strange land.

Breaker Morant (1980). In this gripping courtroom drama, three Australian soldiers serving in the British army during the Boer War are scapegoated for the murder of prisoners. The brutality of that conflict is revealed in flashback sequences.

Zulu (1965). An epic action film about a small force of British troops trapped under siege by a huge force of Zulu warriors in 1879. The British have superior arms but the Zulu win their respect. Stars Stanley Baker and Michael Caine.

CHAPTER 34
THE GREAT WAR:
THE WORLD IN UPHEAVAL

<u>INTRODUCTION</u>

The Great War of 1914–1919 was a nearly global conflagration that included all the major powers of Europe, their colonies, and overseas allies. The immediate provocation was a relatively minor incident—the assassination of the heir to the Austro-Hungarian empire—but the causes were long-standing and much more complex. Pressure to seek war and resist compromise had been mounting in the late nineteenth and early twentieth centuries, fed by aggressive nationalism, ambitious militarism, and complex national alliances. The war, when it came, was not what anyone expected.

- New kind of warfare. New technologies transformed the experience of war. Offensive battle plans stalled in the trenches, where soldiers were pounded by heavy artillery, trapped by machine-gun fire, and vulnerable to poisonous gas. Casualties were counted in the hundreds of thousands, and progress was measured in yards gained.

- Total war. World War I engaged civilian populations to an unprecedented degree. On the home front, women took up the work abandoned by recruits. Governments took control of wartime production, and propaganda campaigns demonized the enemy and glorified the war effort. Civilians were also targets of war through aerial bombing and naval blockades.

- The Russian revolution. The revolution was triggered by the war but sprang from the long-standing failure of the tsarist government to meet the needs of the Russian people. For a while it seemed that a liberal democracy might emerge, but within months the Bolshevik Party under the direction of Lenin overthrew the provisional government.

- Peace and unresolved questions. Armistice came in 1918, shortly after the United States entered the war. At the Paris Peace Conference, the victors, especially Britain and France, dictated harsh terms to the defeated Central Powers, dismantled their colonial empires, and imposed economic penalties. The bitterness engendered by the peace settlement virtually ensured that another conflict would follow.

<u>OUTLINE</u>

I. The drift toward war

    A. Nationalist aspirations

        1. Nationalism spread by the French revolution and Napoleonic Wars

            a) Self-determination suggested that each ethnic group had a right to a sovereign state

            b) Concept was ignored or opposed by dynastic powers

            c) Considerable nationalistic tensions in Ottoman, Hapsburg, and Russian empires

2. Slavic nationalism: stressed kinship of all Slavic peoples

    a) Ottoman empire shrank as first Greece, then others, gained independence

    b) Serbs of Austria-Hungary sought unification with independent Serbia

    c) Russians promoted Pan-Slavism in Austro-Hungarian empire

    d) Germany backed Austria-Hungary to fight ethnic nationalism

B. National rivalries

  1. The naval race between Germany and Britain increased tensions

    a) Germany's rapid industrialization threatened British economic predominance

    b) Both states built huge battleships, called dreadnoughts

  2. Colonial disputes of the late nineteenth century

    a) Germany unified in 1871; came late to the colonial race

    b) German resentment and antagonism toward both France and Britain

    c) France and Germany nearly fought over Morocco in 1905

    d) Balkan Wars (1912–13) further strained European diplomatic relations

  3. Public opinion supported national rivalries

    a) Attitudes of aggressive patriotism among European citizens

    b) Leaders under pressure to be aggressive, to take risks

C. Understandings and alliances

  1. Rival systems of alliance obligated allies to come to one another's defense

  2. The Central Powers

    a) Germany and Austria-Hungary formed a Dual Alliance in 1879

    b) In fear of France, Italy joined the Dual Alliance in 1882, thus, the Triple Alliance

    c) Ottoman empire loosely affiliated with Germany

  3. The Allies

    a) Britain, France, and Russia formed the Triple Entente, or the Allies

    b) Shifting series of treaties ended with a military pact, 1914

  4. War plans: each power poised and prepared for war

    a) Military leaders devised inflexible military plans and timetables

    b) France's Plan XVII focused on offensive maneuvers and attacks

    c) Germany's Schlieffen plan: swift attack on France, then defensive against Russia

II. Global war

A. The guns of August: triggered a chain reaction

  1. June 1914, Austrian Archduke assassinated by Serbian nationalist

  2. Austria-Hungary declared war on Serbia, July 28

3. Russia mobilized troops to defend its Serbian ally against the Central Powers

4. Germany: July 31, sent ultimatums to Russia and France, which were ignored

5. Germany declared war on Russia and France, invaded Belgium to reach France

6. August 4: to protect Belgium's neutrality, Britain declared war on Germany

B. Mutual butchery

1. War was greeted with enthusiasm on all sides; was expected to be brief

2. The western front

   a) German invasion of France halted along the River Marne for three years

   b) Trenches on the western front ran from the English Channel to Switzerland

   c) Italy entered war with Allies, maintained defensive line against Austria-Hungary

3. Stalemate and new weapons

   a) New technologies favored defensive tactics over offensive tactics

      (1) Poisonous gas: introduced by Germans, used by both sides

      (2) Eight hundred thousand casualties from mustard gas

   b) Armored tanks used to break down trenches toward end of the war

   c) Airplanes used mainly for reconnaissance

   d) Submarines used especially by Germans against Allied shipping

4. No-man's-land littered with dead, the grim reality of trench warfare

5. On the eastern front, battle lines more fluid

   a) Austrian-German forces overran Serbia, Albania, and Romania

   b) Russia invaded Prussia 1915, but was soon driven out

   c) Russians' counterattacks in 1916–1917 collapsed in a sea of casualties

6. Bloodletting: long, costly battles

   a) At Verdun: French "victory" with 315,000 dead, defeated Germans lost 280,000

   b) At the Somme, Britain and Germany saw losses of 420,000 each

7. New rules of engagement

   a) Civilians became targets of enemy military operations

   b) Air raids against civilians; naval blockades common

C. Total war: the home front

1. On the home front: the economy mobilized to support the war effort

   a) Governments militarized civilian war production

   b) Imposed wage and price controls

   c) Extended military draft in Germany from ages sixteen to sixty

2. Women served the war by entering the workforce

a) Took over jobs vacated by soldiers

b) Did hazardous work with explosives, shells, TNT

c) A liberating experience, especially for middle- and upper-class women

d) Women granted the vote in Western nations after the war

3. Propaganda campaigns to maintain national support for the war

a) Included censorship and restrictions on civil liberties

b) Criticism of the war regarded as treasonous

c) Propaganda designed to dehumanize the enemy

D. Conflict in east Asia and the Pacific

1. Expansion of the war beyond Europe

a) European animosities extended to the colonies

b) British and French forces recruited colonials into their armies

c) Eventually, Japan, United States, Ottoman empire entered the war

2. Japan entered war with the Allies, 1914

a) Seized German-leased territory in China

b) New Zealand and Australia likewise seized German-held lands in the Pacific

3. The Twenty-One Demands

a) Japan advanced its imperial interests in China

b) The Twenty-One Demands were designed to reduce China to Japanese protectorate

c) Britain intervened, prevented total capitulation of China to Japan

E. Battles in Africa and southwest Asia

1. The war in sub-Saharan Africa

a) Allies targeted the four German colonies in Africa

b) Togoland fell quickly, but not the others

c) Many Allied soldiers and workers died from tropical diseases

2. Battle of Gallipoli, 1915, in Ottoman Turkey

a) British decided to strike at the weakest Central Power, the Ottomans

b) Battle of Gallipoli a disaster, with 250,000 casualties on each side

c) Weakened ties of loyalty between Canada, Australia, New Zealand, and Britain

3. The Ottoman empire lost ground after Gallipoli

a) Lost Caucasus to Russians

b) Successful Arab revolt aided by British

III. The end of the war

A. Revolution in Russia

  1. February Revolution of 1917: uprising against shortages, mounting deaths in the war

    a) Facing mutinies, Nicholas II abdicated throne

    b) Provisional government established

  2. Struggle for power between provisional government and Petrograd soviet

    a) New government passed many liberal reforms

    b) Did not undertake land reform, did not withdraw from the war

  3. V. I. Lenin (1870–1924) stepped into unstable situation

    a) A revolutionary Marxist, exiled in Switzerland

    b) Saw importance of a well-organized, disciplined party for revolution

    c) German authorities delivered Lenin to Russia, 1917, to take Russia out of war

    d) Headed radical Bolshevik Party: demanded power to soviets, withdrawal from war

  4. The October Revolution

    a) Minority Bolsheviks gained control of Petrograd soviet

    b) Bolsheviks' slogan "Peace, Land, and Bread" appealed to workers and peasants

    c) Armed force seized power from provisional government in name of all soviets

  5. Russia withdrew from war, made a separate peace with Germany, lost one-third of Ukraine

B. U.S. intervention and collapse of the Central Powers

  1. 1914–1916, United States under President Woodrow Wilson officially neutral

    a) American public opposed participation in a European war

    b) U.S. companies sold supplies, gave loans to Allies

    c) By 1917, Allied ability to repay loans depended on Allied victory

  2. The submarine warfare helped sway American public opinion

    a) German blockade sank merchant ships, intended to strangle Britain

    b) 1915, Germans sank *Lusitania,* a British passenger liner, killing 1,198 passengers

  3. United States declared war on Germany, 6 April 1917

  4. Collapsing fronts after years of bloodletting

    a) April 1916, Irish nationalists attempted to overthrow British rule

    b) Central Powers: shortages, food riots, mutinies

    c) 1917, mutiny of fifty thousand French soldiers

    d) Spring 1918, massive Germany offensive on western front failed

    e) With fresh American troops, Allies broke the front and pushed the Germans back

      f)   Central Powers collapsed, one after another; accepted armistices November 1918

C. The Paris Peace Conference, 1919

    1. In the end, the Great War killed fifteen million people, wounded twenty million

    2. The Paris settlement was dominated by heads of Britain, France, and United States

        a)   Twenty-seven nations with conflicting aims participated

        b)   Leaders of Central Powers and Soviet Union not included

    3. Woodrow Wilson's Fourteen Points: proposal for a just and lasting peace

        a)   Included free trade, arms treaties, rights for colonials, an association of nations

        b)   Most of the program rejected by Allies; Central Powers felt betrayed

    4. The Peace Treaties, 1919

        a)   French insisted on destroying German military

        b)   Central Powers forced to accept war guilt and pay reparations for cost of war

        c)   Austria and Hungary were separated and reduced; the new states were added to eastern Europe

        d)   Overall, the peace settlement was a failure; left a bitter legacy

    5. Ataturk: Mustafa Kemal, father of modern Turkey

        a)   1923, drove out occupying Allied forces, proclaimed Republic of Turkey

        b)   Implemented reforms: emancipation of women, Western dress, European law

        c)   Secular rule replaced Muslim authorities

        d)   Constitutional democracy, although Ataturk ruled as virtual dictator until 1938

    6. The League of Nations created to maintain world peace

        a)   Forty-two members, twenty-six of them outside Europe

        b)   The league had no power to enforce its decisions

        c)   Collective security depended on all major powers, but United States never joined

    7. Self-determination for ethnic nationalities: urged by Wilson at Paris Conference

        a)   Basis for redrawing map of eastern Europe: Poland, Czechoslovakia, Yugoslavia

        b)   Difficult to draw lines: German minorities left in Poland and Czechoslovakia

        c)   Yugoslavia: land of southern Slavs, uneasy mix of Serbs, Croats, and Slovenes

    8. The mandate system

        a)   United States opposed direct colonization; Allies proposed system of trusteeships

        b)   Colonies of Central Powers divided into three classes of mandates

        c)   Allies divided up Germany's African colonies, Ottoman territories in southwest Asia

        d)   Arabs outraged at betrayal by their British allies

D. Challenges to European preeminence

    1. Great War weakened Europe, set the stage for decolonization after World War II

        a) Economic crises: inflation, debt, loss of overseas investments, foreign markets

        b) Economic relationship between Europe and United States reversed; United States now creditor

        c) Loss of prestige overseas weakened European grip on colonies

    2. Revolutionary ideas

        a) The war helped spread concept of self-determination

        b) Nationalist movements also sought inspiration from the Soviet Union

IDENTIFICATION: PEOPLE

What is the contribution of each of the following individuals to world history? Identification should include answers to the questions *who, what, where, when, how,* and *why is this person important?*

Archduke Franz Ferdinand

Kaiser Wilhelm

T. E. Lawrence

Mustapha Kemal (Ataturk)

V. I. Lenin

Woodrow Wilson

IDENTIFICATION: TERMS/CONCEPTS

State in your own words what each of the following terms means and why it is significant to a study of world history. (Terms with an asterisk are defined in the glossary.)

Dreadnought*

Balkan Wars 1912–1913

Allies

Central Powers*

Schlieffen Plan

Gallipoli

Bolsheviks*

Lusitania

Treaty of Versailles

League of Nations*

Mandate system*

STUDY QUESTIONS

1. What goals and values were expressed in the various nationalistic movements of the early twentieth century? Which ethnic groups in particular asserted the right of self-determination?

2. How did the imperialistic rivalries of the European powers contribute to international tensions before World War I? Be specific.

3. Summarize the forces set in motion by the assassination of the Archduke Ferdinand in 1914. When and why did the war begin?

4. What was the typical experience of the soldier in World War I? Explain how new technologies changed the experience of war.

5. What role did women play in the war effort? Were these changes long- or short-term?

6. How else did the war transform civilian life? Consider especially the enlarged role of the government.

7. Why did Japan enter WWI? What did it gain?

8. What factors caused the Russian revolutions in February and October of 1917? What changes emerged initially from these revolutions?

9. How did Lenin and the Bolsheviks come to power?

10. When and why did the United States enter the war? What did this move mean?

11. What was the intent of the League of Nations? What were the weaknesses of this body?

12. How did the mandate system work in the Middle East? Who profited most from this system?

INQUIRY QUESTIONS

INQUIRY QUESTIONS

1. Was World War I a preventable war, or were the nations of Europe committed to fighting even before the assassination of the Archduke Franz Ferdinand? Can you envision a realistic scenario by which the outbreak of war might have been averted?

2. What were the essential elements of Woodrow Wilson's peace program? Which of his Fourteen Points were included in the final peace treaties? Why was it so difficult to implement his vision?

STUDENT QUIZ

1. By the end of the nineteenth century, nationalistic movements resulted in independent sovereignty for all of the following *except*
   a. Bulgaria.
   b. Germany.
   c. Greece.
   d. Ireland.
   e. Italy.

2. The assassination of Archduke Franz Ferdinand was the catalyst that started World War I because
   a. he was a unifying force between Serbia and the Austro-Hungarian Empire.
   b. his death caused Russia to rush to the defense of Austria.
   c. his death caused Germany to rush to the defense of Serbia.
   d. his death ended plans for national self-determination within the Austro-Hungarian Empire.
   e. his death brought to a head the tensions underlying the alliances in eastern and western Europe.

3. The rivalry between Germany and Britain up to 1914 included
   a. an expensive naval race.
   b. competition for foreign markets.
   c. tariff wars.
   d. competition for colonies in east and southwest Africa.
   e. all of the above.

4. Dreadnoughts were designed primarily
   a. to be quick and agile and slip through an enemy blockade.
   b. to spy on one's enemies.
   c. to protect merchant shipping and conduct high-seas battles.
   d. to launch underwater attacks with unmanned torpedoes.
   e. all of the above.

5. The purpose of alliances such as the Triple Alliance and the Triple Entente was
   a. to create a mutually advantageous free trade association.
   b. to provide mutual defense and support in case of attack.
   c. to cooperatively share resources in African colonies.
   d. to avoid war.
   e. all of the above.

6. The German Schlieffen Plan called for
   a. a quick invasion of Great Britain and destruction of the British navy.
   b. a quick invasion of Russia so that the war would be fought on only one front.
   c. a blockade of France to starve that country into submission.
   d. a swift knockout of France combined with defensive action against Russia.
   e. simultaneous invasions of France, Britain, and Russia with heavy reliance on the navy.

7. Which of the following was *not* a new military technology used for the first time in World War I?
   a. machine guns
   b. armored tanks
   c. airplanes
   d. poisonous gas
   e. nuclear submarines

8. Compared to the western front, fighting on the eastern front was
   a. more fluid, as the Germans made inroads into Russia.
   b. a deadlock, with German and Austrian troops trapped for months in trenches.
   c. more encouraging for the Allies, especially on the Balkan Peninsula.
   d. not as deadly, with far fewer casualties.
   e. over quickly.

9. In World War I, "no man's land" was the
   a. battle line in eastern Europe and the Balkans.
   b. deadly territory between opposing trenches.
   c. killing field around Verdun.
   d. German route of invasion through Belgium.
   e. peninsula of Gallipoli.

10. What effect did World War I have on the status of women?
    a. The demands of total war actually reduced the opportunities for women.
    b. Women engaged in combat for the first time.
    c. Women in many countries received the vote in the years after the war.
    d. Women gained economic status that continued long after the war.
    e. All of the above.

11. The purpose of the Twenty-One Demands was
    a. to demand control of German-held islands in the Pacific.
    b. to reduce China to the status of a Japanese protectorate.
    c. to demand that the British turn over control of Hong Kong.
    d. to reduce Korea to the status of a Japanese protectorate.
    e. all of the above.

12. The Battle of Gallipoli was significant in that
    a. it sounded the death-knell of the Ottoman empire.
    b. it demonstrated that the British navy was no match for German dreadnoughts.
    c. this decisive battle finally broke the stalemate on the western front.
    d. this British-directed debacle cost the lives of many Canadian, Australian, and New Zealand troops.
    e. it demonstrated that, after the arrival of American troops, the Allies would win the war.

13. "Ten days that shook the world" is a reference to
    a. the Paris settlement of the Great War.
    b. the debacle at Gallipoli.
    c. the German thrust toward Paris in August 1914.
    d. the Russian revolution in October 1917.
    e. days in August leading up to the outbreak of the Great War.

14. In addition to fighting off Allied forces, the Ottoman empire faced insurrection from the
    a. Arabs.
    b. Egyptians.
    c. Greeks.
    d. Serbs.
    e. Turks.

15. Tsar Nicholas II was forced to abdicate when
    a. Bolsheviks stormed the Winter Palace.
    b. an assassination attempt revealed that his family was in danger.
    c. troops garrisoned in the capital mutinied.
    d. German forces seized the Ukraine.
    e. all of the above.

16. The provisional government lost the support of many Russians because it
    a. continued to use the police apparatus of the tsar.
    b. continued policies that discriminated against minorities.
    c. denied Russians the right to free speech and free press.
    d. promised to continue the war to victory.
    e. launched an all-out attack on the workers' soviets.

17. Although he called himself a Marxist, Lenin, unlike Marx, believed that
    a. the revolution would be led by rural peasants, not industrial workers.
    b. the revolution would be led by a small, highly disciplined party acting on behalf of the workers.
    c. the revolution would be led by the intelligentsia acting on behalf of all Russia people.
    d. the revolution would not succeed until Russian workers were joined by workers all over the world.
    e. the revolution could not succeed if it alienated the church and the military.

18. A key factor in the U.S. decision to enter World War I was
    a. its long-standing friendship with Great Britain.
    b. the U.S. desire to acquire German colonies in the Pacific.
    c. American prejudice against German immigrants.
    d. the political ambition of Woodrow Wilson.
    e. Germany's resumption of unrestricted submarine warfare against the United States.

19. At the Paris Peace Conference,
    a. the Allies agreed to let ethnic self-determination set the boundaries of the Middle East.
    b. Britain and France were determined to strip Germany of military power.
    c. Russia was forced to cede much of Manchuria to Japan.
    d. Woodrow Wilson gained acceptance of his Fourteen Points.
    e. all of the above.

20. Which of the following statements about the League of Nations is *not* true?
   a. It was conceived by Woodrow Wilson.
   b. It was rejected by the U.S. Congress.
   c. It was designed to solve international disputes through arbitration.
   d. It had no power to enforce its decisions.
   e. It was dominated by the countries of Europe.

MATCHING

Match these figures with the statements that follow.

A. Allied Powers in 1914	G. V. I. Lenin
B. Central Powers in 1914	H. T. E. Lawrence
C. Yugoslavia	I. Mustapha Kemal
D. Bolsheviks	J. Kaiser Wilhelm
E. Franz Ferdinand	K. Leaders of Paris Peace Conference
F. Woodrow Wilson	

1. ___ Serbs, Croats, and Slovenes

2. ___ Britain, France, and Russia

3. ___ Britain, France, and the United States

4. ___ Germany, Austria-Hungary, and the Ottoman Empire

5. ___ Party of radical Russian revolutionaries

6. ___ British adventurer who organized Arab resistance to Ottomans during the war

7. ___ The last German emperor

8. ___ The first Turkish president

9. ___ Idealistic American president who failed to persuade his own Congress to support his vision of a League of Nations to impose collective security

10. ___ Radical leader who engineered the Communist takeover of the Russian revolution

11. ___ Austrian Archduke whose assassination sparked the First World War

SEQUENCING

Place the following clusters of events in chronological order. Consider carefully how one event leads to another, and try to determine the internal logic of each sequence.

A.

____ France mobilizes in defense of its ally, Russia.

____ The heir to the Austrian throne is assassinated by a Serbian nationalist.

____ Germany orders Russia to stand down and, when the tsar refuses, declares war on Russia.

____ Russian forces prepare to come to the defense of Serbia.

____ Germany activates the Schlieffen Plan to invade France by way of Belgium.

____ A system of secret alliances commits the various nations of Europe to come to one another's defense.

____ Not satisfied with the Serbian response, the Austrian government declares war on Serbia.

____ Britain declares war on Germany for violating Belgian neutrality.

B.

____ After storming the headquarters of the provisional government, the Bolsheviks take control of the revolution.

____ The new provisional government provides free speech and free press but does nothing to change the inequities of land distribution or to take Russia out of the war.

____ The Bolsheviks end Russian involvement in World War I by signing a treaty with Germany.

____ By 1917, the Russian people are exhausted by the war effort and are suffering food shortages.

____ A parallel system of government emerges in the revolutionary councils, or soviets, organized by socialists in various cities across Russia.

____ When his own troops mutiny, Tsar Nicholas II is forced to abdicate.

____ Smuggled into Russia by the Germans, Lenin organizes the Bolshevik party, which soon takes over the Petrograd soviet.

C.

_____ American banks make substantial loans and American companies sell considerable supplies to the Allies.

_____ U.S. government declares itself to be officially neutral.

_____ The German government tries to break the stalemate by sinking American supply ships with submarines.

_____ World War I breaks out in Europe.

_____ President Wilson reverses his position, and Congress declares war on Germany.

_____ The long-standing stalemate on the western front suggests that the Allies might not be able to pay off war debts.

QUOTATIONS

For each of the following quotes, identify the speaker, if known, or the point of view. What is the significance of each passage?

1. "The present German submarine warfare against commerce is a warfare against mankind. It is a war against all nations. . . . Our object now, as then, is to vindicate the principles of peace and justice in the life of the world as against selfish and autocratic power. . . . The world must be made safe for democracy."

2. "Peace, Land, Bread."

3. "*Article 231.* The Allied and Associated Governments affirm and Germany accepts the responsibility of Germany and her allies for causing all of the loss and damage to which the Allied and Associated Governments and their [citizens] have been subjected as a consequence of the war imposed upon them by the aggression of Germany and her allies.

   Article 232. . . . The Allied and Associated Governments ... require that [Germany] will make compensation for all damage done to the civilian population of the Allied and Associated Powers and to their property."

4. "I. Open covenants of peace, openly arrived at after which there shall be no private international understandings of any kind but diplomacy shall proceed always frankly and in the public view."

5. "Only in Communist society, when the resistance of the capitalists has been completely crushed, when the capitalists have disappeared, when there are no classes . . . *only* then 'the state ceases to exist.' . . . Only then will there become complete democracy, a democracy without any exceptions whatever."

6. "Men marched asleep. Many had lost their boots
   But limped on, blood-shod. All went lame; all blind;
   Drunk with fatigue; deaf even to the hoots
   Of gas-shells dropping softly behind."

MAP EXERCISES

1. Compare the maps of Europe in 1914, before the war (Map 34.1, page 953 in the textbook), and in 1920, after the war (Map 34.2, page 970). Then answer the following questions.

    *   What new nations appear on the 1920 map that did not exist as sovereign states before the war?
    *   Consider Poland, Czechoslovakia, and Yugoslavia, in particular. Which states had control of these lands before the war? Which states lost the most territory in the peace settlement?
    *   Explain how the 1920 map reflects the triumph of ethnic self-determination over the old multiethnic empires.

2. What interests seem to have directed the restructuring of the Ottoman provinces in southwest Asia after World War I (Map 34.3, page 973), the interests of self-determination or of empire?

CONNECTIONS

In fifty words or less, explain the relationship between each of the following pairs. How does one lead to or foster the other? Be specific in your response.

    *   Submarines and food shortages
    *   Total war and women's suffrage
    *   Pan-Slavism and the Russian revolution
    *   Eastern Rebellion and Ataturk

FILMS

Gallipoli (1981). This riveting war drama traces the experiences of two young Australians, best friends played by Mark Lee and Mel Gibson, who enlist in the British army in World War I. Their journey across half a world brings them to the trenches at Gallipoli.

Reds (1981). A radical American journalist becomes involved with the Communist revolution in Russia (1917) and hopes to bring its spirit and idealism to the United States. Starring Warren Beatty, Diane Keaton, Jack Nicholson.

All Quiet on the Western Front (1979). Based on the classic German antiwar novel by Eric Maria Remarque. Here we see the Great War, both in the trenches and on the home front, from the German perspective.

Nicholas and Alexandra (1971). This three-hour production traces the reign of the last of the Romanovs up through the Revolution and the assassination of the royal family. Particular attention is paid to the domestic life of the tsar and his family, the illness of his son, and the influence of the corrupt monk, Rasputin.

Doctor Zhivago (1965). The story of a Russian doctor, his family, and his lover, caught up in the Bolshevik Revolution and the difficult years that followed. Starring Omar Sharif, Julie Christie, and Alec Guinness.

CHAPTER 35
AN AGE OF ANXIETY

INTRODUCTION

The decades between the two world wars were neither peaceful nor prosperous. These were anxious, uncertain years. Old certainties were shaken; the liberal ideals of the Enlightenment lost their potency. After 1929, a global depression intensified the social and political unrest, and new extreme ideologies gained momentum. Common elements of this "age of anxiety" include

- Disillusionment. The harsh realities of trench warfare shattered the illusions of many young intellectuals. The culture of the 1920s is characterized by uncertainty and experimentation. Old truths in science, art, and religion were challenged. Nothing seemed certain anymore.

- Political extremism. The momentum of the nineteenth century had been toward democracy and greater inclusion of the poor, minorities, and finally women in the political process. In desperate times, many found democracy too inefficient and sought simple solutions in charismatic dictators.

- Extreme nationalism. The Paris peace settlements both aroused and disappointed nationalist hopes, especially in Italy, Japan, and Germany. Nationalists in these countries were frustrated at being denied territory considered rightly theirs. These frustrations were channeled into militaristic parties: the Fascists and the Nazis.

- The communist alternative. The world watched, in horror and fascination, as the communist experiment unfolded in the Soviet Union. In spite of appalling losses through civil war, forced collectivization, and political purges, the Soviet Union did appear to deliver a basic living to all citizens. With capitalist nations slumped in depression, this was an intriguing alternative. Communism was violently attacked in Italy and Germany.

OUTLINE

I. Probing cultural frontiers

  A. Postwar pessimism

    1. The "lost generation"

      a) Term used to describe pessimism of U.S. and European thinkers after the war

      b) Postwar poetry and fiction reflected disillusionment with Western culture

      c) Scholars—Oswald Spengler, Arnold Toynbee—lamented decline of the West

    2. Religious thought reflected uncertainty and pessimism

      a) Karl Barth attacked liberal Christian theology embracing idea of progress

      b) Older concepts of original sin and human depravity were revived

    3. Attacks on the ideal of progress

a) Science tarnished by the technological horrors of World War I

b) Most Western societies granted suffrage to all men and women

c) Many intellectuals disillusioned with democracy

d) Conservatives decried "the rule of inferiors"

B. Revolutions in physics and psychology

1. Albert Einstein's theory of relativity, 1906

a) Space and time relative to the person measuring them

b) Implication: reality or truth merely a set of mental constructions

2. Werner Heisenberg's uncertainty principle, 1927

a) Impossible to state the position and velocity of a subatomic particle at same time

b) Atomic universe indeterminate; can only speak of probabilities

c) Challenged long-held assumptions about truth, cause and effect

3. Freud's psychoanalytic theory, 1896

a) Sought psychological causes of mental illness

b) Conflict between conscious and unconscious mental processes

c) Sexual repression frequent cause of neuroses

d) Freud's ideas shaped psychiatric profession, influenced literature and arts

C. Experimentation in art and architecture

1. Modern painting: when photography can reproduce nature, why should painting?

a) Painters like Pablo Picasso sought freedom of expression, emotional expression

b) Borrowed from artistic traditions of Asia, Pacific, and Africa

c) No widely accepted standards of good or bad art

2. Modern architecture: the Bauhaus school started in Germany, 1920

a) An international style for twentieth-century urban buildings

(1) Walter Gropius: form should follow function; combined engineering and art

(2) Simple shapes, steel frames, and walls of glass

b) International style dominated urban landscapes well after 1930s

II. Global depression

A. The Great Depression

1. The weaknesses of global economy

a) The tangled financial relationships: Germany and Austria borrowed money from United States, used it to pay reparations to Allies, who used the money to pay war debt to United States

b) In 1928 U.S. lenders withdrew capital from Europe; financial system strained

    c) Industrial innovations reduced demand for raw materials—rubber, coal, cotton

    d) Postwar agriculture depressed in Europe, United States, Canada, Argentina, and Australia

2. The crash of 1929

    a) U.S. economic boom prompted many to speculate, invest beyond their means

    b) Black Thursday (24 October 1929): stock prices dropped, investors lost life savings

    c) Lenders called in loans, forcing investors to keep selling

3. Economic contraction in U.S. economy and the world

    a) Overproduction and reduced consumer demand

    b) Widespread business failure and unemployment

    c) By 1932 U.S. industrial production and national income dropped by half

4. Industrial economies felt banking crisis, unemployment

    a) Germany and Japan unable to sell manufactured goods to purchase fuel and food

    b) Germany by 1932: 35 percent unemployment, 50 percent decrease in industrial production

    c) European industrial states and Japan unable to sell to United States because of tariffs

5. Economic nationalism favored over international cooperation

    a) High tariffs, import quotas, and prohibitions to promote economic self-sufficiency

    b) U.S. trade restrictions provoked retaliation by other nations

    c) International trade dropped 66 percent between 1929 and 1932

B. Despair and government action

1. Government policies to reduce female employment, especially of married women

2. Great Depression caused enormous personal suffering

    a) Millions struggled for food, clothing, and shelter

    b) Marriage and birthrates declined, suicide increased

    c) Intensified social divisions and class hatreds

    d) John Steinbeck's *Grapes of Wrath* criticized U.S. policy of "planned scarcity"

C. Economic experimentation

1. John M. Keynes challenged classical economic theory

    a) Classic theory: capitalism self-correcting, operated best if unregulated

    b) Keynes argued the depression was a problem of inadequate demand, not supply

     c) Governments should play active role in stimulating economy, consumer demand

  2. The New Deal of President Franklin Delano Roosevelt paralleled Keynes's ideas

     a) After 1932, protected banking system, massive public works, farm subsidies

     b) Also, legislation established minimum wage, social security, workers' unions

     c) Military spending in WWII ultimately ended the depression in the United States

III. Challenges to the liberal order

A. Communism in Russia

  1. Civil war, 1918–1920, between Bolsheviks and anticommunist forces, or the Whites

     a) The Red Terror: secret police arrested and killed two hundred thousand suspected Whites

     b) Bolsheviks executed Tsar Nicholas II and his entire family, June 1918

     c) Despite some foreign support, the Whites were defeated by Red Army in 1920

     d) Perhaps ten million died during civil war

  2. Lenin's "war communism" transformed economy

     a) Policy included nationalizing banks, industry, and church holdings

     b) Private trade abolished; peasants reduced production

     c) By 1920, industrial output at one-tenth, agricultural at half prewar levels

  3. Lenin's New Economic Policy (NEP), 1921

     a) Reversed war communism, restored market economy

     b) Returned small-scale industries to private ownership

     c) Allowed peasants to sell their surplus at free market

     d) Programs of electrification and technical schools were carried out

     e) Lenin died, 1924; bitter power struggle followed

  4. Joseph Stalin (1879–1953)

     a) "Man of steel": Georgian by birth, Russian nationalist by conviction

     b) Stalin favored "socialism in one country," not international socialism

     c) Eliminated all rivals; by 1928, unchallenged dictator of Soviet Union

  5. First Five-Year Plan, 1928–1932, replaced Lenin's NEP

     a) Set production quotas, central state planning of entire economy

     b) Emphasized heavy industry at expense of consumer goods

  6. Collectivization of agriculture

     a) States seized private farms, created large collective farms

     b) Believed to be more productive, to feed industrial workers

     c) Collectivization strongly resisted by peasants, especially the wealthier *kulaks*

      d)   Half of farms collectivized by 1931; three million peasants killed or starved

  7. As an alternative to capitalism during the depression, Soviet Union offered full employment and cheap housing and food, but few luxuries or consumer goods

  8. The Great Purge, 1935–1938

      a)   Ruthless policy of collectivization led to doubts about Stalin's administration

      b)   Stalin purged two-thirds of Central Committee members and more than half of the army's high-ranking officers

      c)   By 1939, eight million people were in labor camps; three million died during "cleansing"

B. The fascist alternative

  1. Fascism: new political ideology of 1920s

      a)   Started in Italy, then Germany; also found in other countries around the world

      b)   Fascism hostile to liberal democracies and to socialism and communism

      c)   Sought subordination of individuals to the service of state

  2. Emphasized an extreme form of nationalism, often expressed as racism

      a)   Veneration of the state, devotion to charismatic leaders

      b)   Militarism exalted, uniforms, parades

C. Italian Fascism

  1. Benito Mussolini, founder of Italian Fascism, 1919

      a)   Armed Fascist squads called Blackshirts terrorized socialists

      b)   After march on Rome, Mussolini invited by king to be prime minister

  2. The Fascist state in Italy

      a)   All other political parties banned, Italy became a one-party dictatorship

      b)   Supported by business, the party crushed labor unions, prohibited strikes

      c)   Not aggressively anti-Semitic until after alliance with Hitler in 1938

D. Germany's National Socialism

  1. Adolf Hitler and the emergence of the Nazi party

      a)   1923: attempt to take over Weimar Republic failed; Hitler jailed

      b)   Released in 1924, he organized party for a legal takeover, through elections

  2. The struggle for power after 1929

      a)   National Socialism enjoyed broad appeal, especially from lower-middle class

      b)   Public lost faith in democracy: associated with defeat, depression, inflation

      c)   1930–1932, Nazi party became the largest in parliament

      d)   1932, President Hindenburg offered Hitler the chancellorship

3. Rapid consolidation of power, 1933–1935

   a) Nazis created one-party dictatorship; outlawed all other political parties

   b) Took over judiciary, civil service, military

4. Nazi ideology emphasized purity of race

   a) Women praised as wives and mothers; were discouraged from working

   b) Cult of motherhood: propaganda campaign to increase births was unsuccessful

5. Nazi eugenics: deliberate policies to improve the quality of the German "race"

   a) Compulsory sterilization of undesirables: mentally ill, disabled

   b) State-sponsored euthanasia of physically and mentally handicapped

6. Anti-Semitism central to Nazi ideology

   a) 1935, Nuremberg Laws deprived Jews of citizenship, outlawed intermarriage

   b) Jews economically isolated, lost jobs, assets, businesses

   c) 1938, *Kristallnacht:* official attacks on synagogues and Jewish businesses

   d) 250,000 Jews fled to other countries; many others trapped

IDENTIFICATION: PEOPLE

What is the contribution of each of the following individuals to world history? Identification should include answers to the questions *who, what, where, when, how,* and *why is this person important?*

Albert Einstein

Sigmund Freud

Pablo Picasso

John Maynard Keynes

Franklin Delano Roosevelt

Joseph Stalin

Benito Mussolini

Adolf Hitler

IDENTIFICATION: TERMS/CONCEPTS

State in your own words what each of the following terms means and why it is significant to a study of world history. (Terms with an asterisk are defined in the glossary.)

Uncertainty principle

Psychoanalysis

Bauhaus

Smoot-Hawley Tariff

New Deal

New Economic Policy*

Five-Year Plans*

Collectivization*

Fascism*

National Socialism

Weimar Republic

Mein Kampf

Eugenics

Nuremberg Laws

Kristallnacht

STUDY QUESTIONS

1. What are some indications of the "postwar pessimism" of the 1920s? Why did liberal values such as progress and democracy fall under attack at this time?

2. What were some of the economic problems facing the world powers in the 1920s? Specifically, what factors led to the crash of 1929 and the depression that followed?

3. What are some examples of "economic nationalism"? How effective were these measures?

4. What was the impact of the depression on social attitudes? On women and families?

5. What did John Maynard Keynes recommend as a solution to the economic crisis? How did the New Deal of President Roosevelt exemplify this solution?

6. How did Lenin and the Bolsheviks secure their power in Russia? How did Stalin secure his power within the party and within the Soviet Union?

7. What are the defining characteristics of fascism in both Italy and Germany? Consider the organizational structure and symbols that each adopted. To whom did this message appeal?

8. Compare the rise to power and consolidation of power by Benito Mussolini and Adolf Hitler.

9. What was the social vision of the Nazis? What attitudes are expressed in the passage from *Mein Kampf* on page 998 in the textbook? How did this vision impact women, families, and minorities?

INQUIRY QUESTIONS

1. Explain how new discoveries in physics and psychology undermined earlier ideas about reality and knowledge. Why were these new ideas so unsettling? How were these ideas represented in Western art between the wars?

2. Describe and analyze the experience of the Great Depression between the industrial nations and the primary producing nations. What parts of the world were most affected and what parts were least affected? What would be the economic explanation for this difference?

3. Compare the economic strategies embedded in Lenin's war communism, his New Economic Policy, and Stalin's Five-Year Plan. What were the aims of each program? Which was most effective?

STUDENT QUIZ

1. The author of *All Quiet on the Western Front* was
   a. Enrnest Hemingway.
   b. Oswald Spengler.
   c. Erich Maria Remarque.
   d. W. Somerset Maugham.
   e. Arnold Toynbee.

2. In the years after World War I, the idea of progress
   a. gave a sense of hope in the midst of human suffering.
   b. remained the foundation of Asian thought.
   c. became even more popular among liberal Christian thinkers.
   d. was bolstered by the growing popularity of Confucian thought.
   e. was roundly attacked.

3. The notion that space and time are relative to the person measuring them was first articulated in
   a. Heisenberg's uncertainty principle.
   b. Kepler's three principles of interplanetary movementl.
   c. Spengler's *The Decline of the West*.
   d. Einstein's theory of general relativity.
   e. Newton's theory of gravity.

4. John Maynard Keynes
   a. first discussed the uncertainty principle.
   b. made early discoveries in psychoanalysis.
   c. warned that democracy was a threat to the achievements of Western society.
   d. was positive that laissez-faire capitalism would survive forever.
   e. discussed the end of laissez-faire capitalism.

5. The father of psychoanalysis was
   a. Werner Heisenberg.
   b. Oswald Spengler.
   c. Niokolai Berdiaev.
   d. Sigmund Freud.
   e. Albert Einstein.

6. According to Freud, the root of neurotic behavior was
   a. a conflict between conscious and unconscious mental processes.
   b. summed up in the term uncertainty "principle."
   c. the traumatic bloodshed of World War I.
   d. the hostility that young boys feel toward their mothers.
   e. an easily explainable chemical reaction.

7. The spread of photography
   a. led many painters to choose the camera as their instrument of expression.
   b. resulted in a lack of creative artistic expression because of general pessimism.
   c. led to a new artistic genre that tried to produce paintings that were more accurate than photographs.
   d. led many painters to take an almost Luddite-like glee in smashing cameras.
   e. led many painters to believe that the purpose of painting was not to mirror reality but to create it.

8. Which of the following was *not* one of the new artistic movements of the twentieth century?
   a. expressionism
   b. cubism
   c. dadaism
   d. impressionism
   e. surrealism

9. One of the biggest results of the artistic experimentation of the 1920s and 1930s was that
   a. artists learned to adhere to accepted public definitions of reality.
   b. photography was no longer considered a legitimate art form.
   c. generally accepted standards that distinguished between "good" and "bad" art disappeared.
   d. impressionism was recognized as the single best art form.
   e. a set of criteria was established that allowed art students to distinguish between "good" and "bad" art.

10. The work of Walter Gropius
    a. is the best of the post–World War I painting movement known as cubism.
    b. resulted in the spread of the uncertainty principle.
    c. laid the foundation for later achievements in psychoanalysis.
    d. reintroduced photography to an art world fascinated with cubism and Dadaism.
    e. embodied the architectural principle that form should follow function.

11. The term *Bauhaus* is associated with
    a. photography.
    b. physics.
    c. psychology.
    d. painting.
    e. architecture.

12. A troubling economic problem in the 1920s was the depressed state of agriculture caused by
    a. virulent new strains of disease.
    b. the success of several new communist regimes.
    c. overproduction and falling prices.
    d. the collapse of the cotton market in the southern United States.
    e. dangerous underproduction.

13. During the Great Depression, most nations
    a. cooperated globally to fight the problem on a scale never seen before.
    b. dramatically reduced tariffs in an effort to facilitate international trade.
    c. expanded the money supply and undertook public works to provide jobs.
    d. practiced economic nationalism.
    e. pushed for an expansion of trade.

14. In response to the Great Depression, economist John Maynard Keynes
    a. proposed that the government should do nothing and wait out the economic hard times.
    b. was a big supporter of the Smoot-Hawley Tariff.
    c. felt that the government should tighten the money supply.
    d. wrote that capitalism had failed and that it was time for the United States to experiment with communism.
    e. urged the government to expand the money supply and undertake public works to provide jobs.

15. Which of the following was *not* one of the chief actions of Roosevelt's New Deal?
    a. tighten the money supply
    b. give workers the right to organize and bargain collectively
    c. provide social security in old age
    d. guarantee minimum wages
    e. create jobs through public works projects

16. The Russian civil war that broke out after the revolution was between
    a. Utopian socialists and Trotskyites.
    b. Reds and Whites.
    c. Leninists and Stalinists.
    d. Nicholas II's Imperial Army and Lenin's Revolutionary Army.
    e. eastern and western factions.

17. Lenin's New Economic Policy of 1921
    a. pushed the peasants onto large state-run collectives.
    b. stripped all land ownership away from the peasants.
    c. called for a trading alliance with Communist China.
    d. implemented free market reforms.
    e. initiated the First Five-Year Plan.

18. The First Five-Year Plan was initiated by
    a. Lenin.
    b. Mussolini.
    c. Stalin.
    d. Hitler.
    e. Trotsky.

19. The author of *Mein Kampf* was
    a. Benito Mussolini.
    b. Arthur de Gobineau.
    c. Joseph Stalin.
    d. Otto von Bismarck.
    e. Adolf Hitler.

20. The *Kristallnacht* was
    a. a new artistic movement that flourished after World War I.
    b. a Nazi-arranged attack on thousands of Jewish stores.
    c. Hitler's political treatise that expressed his main ideas.
    d. the Russian term for the destructive civil war that followed the revolution.
    e. a German term for the sense of disillusionment that followed World War I.

MATCHING

Match these figures with the statements that follow.

A. Albert Einstein
B. John Maynard Keynes
C. Benito Mussolini
D. Joseph Stalin

E. Pablo Picasso
F. Sigmund Freud
G. Franklin Delano Roosevelt
H. Adolf Hitler

1. ___ Innovative twentieth-century painter who resisted all notions of representative art.

2. ___ Founder of Italian Fascism.

3. ___ Founder of German fascism.

4. ___ British economist who suggested that governments should initiate public works and other spending programs to invigorate the economy after the depression.

5. ___ Party secretary who seized control of the Bolshevik Party after Lenin's death and eventually became absolute dictator of Russia.

6. ___ Austrian physician who explored the landscape of the unconscious mind.

7. ___ American president who launched the New Deal in an effort to turn around the Great Depression.

8. ___ German physicist who challenged the certainties of Newtonian physics by suggesting that time and space were relative.

SEQUENCING

Place the following clusters of events in chronological order. Consider carefully how one event leads to another, and try to determine the internal logic of each sequence.

A.

_____ While in prison, Hitler writes *Mein Kampf,* a blueprint for the Nazi Party.

_____ The Reichstag moves to eliminate rival parties and give Hitler absolute dictatorial power.

_____ The Nazi Party becomes the largest single party in the Reichstag.

_____ Hitler's first attempt to seize power fails, and he is jailed for a year.

_____ Global depression shatters the fragile German economy but strengthens support for the Nazis.

_____ Hitler is appointed chancellor by President Hindenburg.

B.

_____ In order to stimulate production, Lenin launches the New Economic Program that allows individual ownership of farmland and limits free enterprise.

_____ Russian peasants are forced to give up their land and join massive collective farms.

_____ Lenin and the Bolsheviks defeat the White Russians and their western allies in a civil war. The Soviet Union is now under communist control.

_____ Peasants who resisted collectivization are starved into submission: as many as ten million die over the next ten years.

_____ Stalin cancels the NEP and imposes an ambitious five-year plan of industrial development.

C.

_____ Once in power, the Fascists move swiftly to destroy opposition parties and restrict free speech and free press.

_____ As the government breaks down, Mussolini presents himself as the savior of order and protector of property; the king appoints him prime minister.

_____ Benito Mussolini launches a new political movement, intensely nationalistic and hostile to social and liberal democracy.

_____ Postwar Italy is divided politically between conservative Catholics and radical socialists with little consensus.

_____ Mussolini's Blackshirts start harassing Socialists and inciting riots.

QUOTATIONS

For each of the following quotes, identify the speaker, if known, or the point of view. What is the significance of each passage?

1. "And in the eyes of the people there is the failure; and in the eyes of the hungry there is a growing wrath. In the souls of the people the grapes of wrath are filling and growing heavy, growing heavy for the vintage."

2. "All the great civilizations of the past died out because contamination of their blood caused them to become decadent."

3. "Can we advance our socialized industry at an accelerated rate while having to rely on an agricultural base, such as is provided by small peasant farming. . . . ? No we cannot. . . . The solution lies in enlarging the agricultural units, in making agriculture capable of accumulation. . . . The Socialist way, which is to set up collective farms and state farms, the way which leads to the amalgamation of the small peasant farms into large collective farms, technically and scientifically equipped, and to the squeezing out of the capitalist elements from agriculture."

4. "The main targets of attack by the peasants are the local tyrants, the evil gentry and the lawless landlords. . . . With the collapse of the power of the landlords, the peasant associations have now become the sole organs of authority and the popular slogan 'All power to the peasant associations' has become a reality."

CONNECTIONS

In fifty words or less, explain the relationship between each of the following pairs. How does one lead to or foster the other? Be specific in your response.

- Social Darwinism and the Nuremberg Laws
- The New Deal and the Five-Year Plans
- Nicholas's secret police and Stalin's purges
- Heisenberg's uncertainty principle and fascism

FILMS

Stalin (1992). In the title role, Robert Duvall convincingly portrays one of the most brutal dictators of the twentieth century. The film covers the early history of the Russian Revolution and is far more generous to Lenin than most historians today.

1900 (1976). The film recounts the lives of two men, a peasant and a landowner, from 1900 to 1945. Events include the rise of fascism, communism, and the Second World War. Starring Robert DeNiro, Gerard Depardieu, Dominique Sanda.

The Triumph of the Will (1934). German filmmaker Leni Riefenstahl was hired by the Nazis to create a visual record of the party rally in Nuremberg in 1934. The result has long been considered a masterpiece of both documentary film and political propaganda. While chilling to watch, the film helps explain the appeal of fascism. In German with English subtitles.

CHAPTER 36
NATIONALISM AND POLITICAL IDENTITIES IN ASIA, AFRICA, AND LATIN AMERICA

INTRODUCTION

During the 1920s and 1930s, after the Great War and during the Great Depression, intellectuals and political activists in Asia, Africa, and Latin America challenged the ideological and economic underpinnings of European imperialism and neocolonialism, as nationalist and anti-imperialist movements gained strength on each of these continents.

- In Asia, Japan's militarist leaders sought to build national strength through imperial expansion. In China, the Ming dynasty ended, giving rise to a civil war fought between adherents of competing visions of the new Chinese state. Japanese imperial aggression complicated the progress of this war. In India, a strong nationalist movement began to threaten the hold of the British empire on the subcontinent.

- In Africa, European imperialists tightened their control of colonial possessions, as African economic life became more tightly enmeshed in the global economy. With the onset of the Great Depression, European countries that controlled the export of African products experienced dramatic decreases in trade volume and commodity prices and, consequently, African peoples suffered. Meanwhile, African peoples challenged European imperial authority and developed competing visions of national identity and unity that would come to fruition after World War II.

- In Latin America, statesmen and political activists worked to alter the neo-colonialist economic domination of the United States, their "good neighbor" to the north. Neo-colonialism, which often featured military intervention and political interference, compromised the independent political and economic development of Latin American states, but it did not prevent nationalist leaders from developing strategies to counter new forms of imperialism.

OUTLINE

I. Asian paths to autonomy

    A. India's quest for home rule

        1. Indian National Congress and Muslim League

            a) After WWI, both organizations dedicated to achieving independence

            b) Indian nationalists inspired by Wilson's Fourteen Points and the Russian revolution

            c) Frustrated by Paris Peace settlement: no independence for colonies

            d) British responded to nationalist movement with repressive measures

        2. Mohandas K. Gandhi (1869–1948), leader of Indian nationalism

a) Raised as a well-to-do Hindu, studied law in London

b) Spent twenty-five years in South Africa, embraced tolerance and nonviolence

c) Developed technique of passive resistance, followed a simple life

d) Became political and spiritual leader, called the Mahatma ("Great Soul")

e) Opposed to caste system, especially the exclusion of untouchables

f) 1920–1922, led Non-Cooperation Movement; 1930, Civil Disobedience Movement

3. The India Act of 1937

a) In 1919 British massacre at Amritsar killed 379 demonstrators, aroused public

b) Repression failed, so the British offered modified self-rule through the India Act

c) Unsuccessful because India's six hundred princes refused to support

d) Muslims would not cooperate, wanted an independent state

e) Great Depression worsened conflict between Hindus and Muslims

f) Muslims believed Hindus discriminated against them

g) Muhammad Ali Jinnah, head of the Muslim League, proposed two states, one of which would be Pakistan

B. China's search for order

1. The republic, after 1911

a) 1911 revolution did not establish a stable republic; China fell into warlords' rule

b) Through unequal treaties, foreign states still controlled economy of China

2. Growth of Chinese nationalism

a) Chinese intellectuals expected Paris Peace Conference to end treaty system

b) Instead, Paris treaties approved Japanese expansion into China

c) May Fourth Movement: Chinese youths and intellectuals opposed to imperialism

d) Some were attracted to Marxism and Leninism; CCP established in 1921

3. CCP (Chinese Communist Party) and *Guomindang* (The Nationalist Party)

a) CCP leader Mao Zedong advocated women's equality, socialism

b) *Guomindang* leader Sun Yatsen favored democracy and nationalism

c) Two parties formed alliance, assisted by the Soviet Union, against foreigners

4. Civil war after death of Sun Yatsen, 1925

a) Led by Jiang Jieshi, both parties launched Northern Expedition to reunify China

b) Successful, Jiang then turned on his communist allies

c) 1934–1935, CCP retreated to Yan'an on the Long March, 6,215 miles

5. Mao emerged as the leader of CCP, developed Maoist ideology

C. Imperial and imperialist Japan

1. Japan emerged from Great War as a world power

   a) Participated in the League of Nations

   b) Signed treaty with United States guaranteeing China's integrity

2. Japanese economy boosted by war: sold munitions to Allies

   a) Prosperity short-lived; economy slumped during Great Depression

   b) Labor unrest, demands for social reforms

3. Political conflict emerged between internationalists, supporters of Western-style capitalism, and nationalists, hostile to foreign influences

4. The Mukden incident, 1931, in Manchuria

   a) Chinese unification threatened Japanese interests in Manchuria

   b) Japanese troops destroyed tracks on Japanese railroad, claimed Chinese attack

   c) Incident became pretext for Japanese attack against China

5. Military, acting without civilian authority, took all Manchuria by 1932

6. League of Nations called for withdrawal of Japanese troops and restoration of Chinese sovereignty; Japan responded by leaving the League

7. The new militant Japanese national identity helped set the stage for global conflagration

II. Africa under colonial domination

A. Africa and the Great War

1. Many belligerents were colonial powers in Africa; nearly every colony took sides

2. German colonial administration faced combined colonial forces of Great Britain, France, Belgium, Italy, and Portugal

   a) Britain sought to maintain naval supremacy and to secure victor's spoils after war

   b) France sought recovery of territory earlier ceded to Germany

   c) Germans, outnumbered ten to one, could not win but 15,000 troops tied down 60,000 Allied forces until late in the war

3. Large numbers of Africans participated actively in the war as soldiers or carriers

   a) Some volunteered; some were impressed; some were formally conscripted

   b) Greater than 150,000 African soldiers and carriers died and many were injured or disabled

4. During the war, Africans challenged European colonial authority

   a) Colonial subjects noticed that an already thin European presence became even thinner as war channeled colonial personnel elsewhere

b) Africans stage armed revolts, requiring colonial powers to divert military resources to meet these challenges

c) The cause of revolts varied but they included pan-Islamic opposition to war; anti-European and anti-Christian sentiment; and compulsory conscription of Africans

5. Colonial authorities ruthlessly put down all the revolts

B. The colonial economy

1. After the war, Africa was transformed by the pursuit of two economic objectives by colonial powers

a) Ensuring that the costs of colonial administration were borne by the colonized

b) Developing export-oriented economies in which unprocessed raw materials or minimally processed crops were sent abroad

2. Previously self-sufficient African economies were destroyed in favor of colonial economies dependent upon a European-dominated economy

3. During the Great Depression, colonial economies suffered as trade volume and prices fell dramatically

4. Africa's economic integration required infrastructure

a) Port facilities, roads, railways, and telegraph wires were built or installed

b) Infrastructure facilitated conquest and rule, but also linked the agricultural and mineral wealth of the colony to the outside world

c) Europeans and their businesses were the main beneficiaries of modern infrastructure, even though Africans paid for it with labor and taxes

5. Farming and mining were the main enterprises in colonial economies

a) Whites owned the enterprises, and used taxation policies to drive Africans into the labor market

b) Africans became cash crop farmers or wage laborers on plantations or in mines in order to pay taxes levied on land, houses, livestock, and people themselves

c) Large areas of richly productive lands were controlled by Europeans

d) Colonial mining enterprises recruited men from rural areas and paid them minimal wages, which impoverished rural areas

e) Officials resorted to outright forced labor where taxation policies failed to create a suitable native labor force

f) Forced labor essentially a variant of slavery and could be quite brutal, especially among laborers forced to work on road and railway projects, in which many thousands of workers died from starvation, disease, and maltreatment

C. African nationalism

1. After the war, ideas concerning self-determination gained acceptance among a group of African nationalists, giving rise to incipient nationalist movements

2. An emerging class of native urban intellectuals—a new African elite—became heavily involved in these movements offering freedom from colonial rule and new ideas concerning African identity

   a) Members of the elite class were often educated in Europe

   b) The elites included high-ranking civil servants, physicians, lawyers, and writers

   c) Jomo Kenyatta: a good example of this trend

3. African nationalists embraced European concept of the nation-state as the best model for realizing their goals of mobilizing resources, organizing societies, and resisting colonial rule

4. Different opinions prevailed regarding what constituted a people's national identity

   a) Some based identity on ethnicities, religion, and languages of pre-colonial times, and believed that institutions crucial to these identities must be recreated

   b) Some regarded the African race as the foundation for identity, solidarity, and nation-building

   c) Pan-Africanists such as Marcus Garvey called for the unification of all people of African descent into a single African state

   d) Still others looked to an African identity rooted in geography; they would build nations on the basis of borders that defined existing colonial states

5. After World War II, these ideas would be translated into demands for independence from colonial rule

III. Latin American struggles with neocolonialism

A. The impact of the Great War and the Great Depression

1. Having gained independence in the nineteenth century, Latin American nations continued to struggle to achieve stability in the midst of interference from foreign powers

2. Interference usually took the form of neocolonialism: foreign economic domination and, frequently, military intervention and interference in the workings of a nation's political system

3. This new imperial influence emanated from wealthy, industrialized powerhouses such as the United States and Great Britain, not former colonial rulers

4. The Great War and the Great Depression led to a reorientation of political and nationalist ideals in Latin America
   a) Marxism, Lenin's theories on imperialism, and concern for workers shaped the views of many intellectuals and artists
   b) Revolutionary doctrines come to be seen as viable political alternatives to Enlightenment-based liberalism
   c) In the 1920s, inspired by the Mexican and Russian revolutions, university students began to demand reforms such as more representation within the educational system
   d) Students become imbued with Marxist thought and anti-imperialist ideas as universities became training grounds for future political leaders such as Fidel Castro
5. New political parties were formed that openly espoused communism or rebellious agendas for change
   a) In Peru, José Carlos Mariátegui embraced Marxism and in 1928 established the Socialist Party of Peru
   b) Numerous other radical political movements critical of Peru's ruling system emerged during the 1920s and 1930s
   c) Victor Raúl Haya de la Torre, who supported anti-imperialism and workers' rights, influenced the APRA, which advocated a non-communist alternative to existing political arrangements
6. Diego Rivera and his radical artistic visions
   a) This Mexican artist, active in the Mexican Communist Party, blended artistic vision and radical political ideas in large murals created for public buildings, for the appreciation of working people
   b) Rivera's art provoked controversy in the United States, as his paintings, particularly *Imperialism,* visualized the economic dependency and political repressiveness engendered by U.S. neocolonialism
   c) Rivera's art publicized the impact of U.S. imperialism and helped spread political activism in the Americas
B. The evolution of economic imperialism
   1. The export-oriented economies of Latin American states had long been controlled by U.S. and British investors

2. The main trend of neocolonialism of the 1920s was increasing U.S. control of economic affairs of Latin American countries

3. From 1924 to 1929, investments of U.S. banks and businesses grew from $1.5 to $3.5 billion, mostly in mineral extraction and oil drilling enterprises

4. U.S. President Taft argued for substitution of "dollars for bullets" in Latin America, promoting peaceful commerce over expensive military intervention

   a) Critics referred to these policies as "dollar diplomacy"

   b) Such policies illustrate what Latin Americans perceived as "Yankee imperialism"

5. Great Depression halted economic growth as prices for Latin American commodities plummeted

6. Foreign capital investment fell and foreign trade was restricted but domestic manufacturing and internal economic development made important gains, as under the Vargas regime in Brazil, for instance

7. Vargas experimented by implementing protectionist policies, which pleased industrialists and urban workers, and social welfare initiatives to benefit workers

C. Conflicts with a "good neighbor"

1. In late 1920s and 1930s, U.S. reassessed foreign policy in Latin America

   a) Since military intervention expensive and ineffective, rely increasingly on "dollar diplomacy"

   b) Neocolonialism persists in form of "sweetheart treaties" in which U.S. financial interests controlled economies of Latin American states

   c) FDR and "good neighbor policy": pursue cordial relations with Latin American states and have U.S. marines train indigenous police forces to quell unrest

2. Limitations of this policy revealed in Nicaragua where, in the past, widely prevalent U.S. financial interests had engendered U.S. intervention in times of civil unrest

   a) Civil war in mid-to-late 1920s and the insertion of U.S. Marines to restore order provoked nationalist opposition by Augusto César Sandino, who insisted upon removal of Marines from his country

   b) The U.S.-supervised election of 1932 brought Juan Batista Sarcasa to the presidency, and the brutal but effective Anastacio Somoza Garcia installed as commander of the National Guard; the U.S. departed

   c) Somoza's guard troops murdered Sandino in 1934 (making him a martyr) and soon Somoza became president

d) As president, Somoza maintained the loyalty of the National Guard, worked to prove himself a good neighbor of the U.S., built the largest fortune in Nicaragua's history, and established a long-lived political dynasty

3. The nationalization crisis in Mexico under President Lázaro Cárdenas

   a) Cárdenas's 1938 nationalization of the oil industry tested the limits of Roosevelt's more conciliatory approach to Latin American relations

   b) Roosevelt resisted pressure from U.S. and British companies to intervene

   c) Negotiations resulted in foreign companies accepting $24 million in compensation rather than the $260 million originally demanded

4. U.S. desire to cultivate Latin American markets for exports, and to avoid militarist behavior, led to neighborly cultural exchanges reflective of a more conciliatory approach

   a) During and after the Great War, Mexicans migrated to the U.S. in large numbers to serve as agricultural and industrial laborers (but many were deported during the Great Depression)

   b) Hollywood promoted Brazilian singing and dancing sensation Carmen Miranda in order to promote more positive images of Latin America

   c) The United Fruit Company used Miranda's image to sell bananas, which symbolized U.S. economic control of various regions of Latin America

   d) Through its ads, the United Fruit Company gave its neocolonial policies a softer image for consumers in the U.S., which provided a counterpoint to Rivera's *Imperialism*

IDENTIFICATION: PEOPLE

What is the contribution of each of the following individuals to world history? Identification should include answers to the questions *who, what, where, when, how,* and *why is this person important?*

Muhammad Ali Jinnah

Mohandas K. Gandhi

Bal Gangadhar Tilak

Mao Zedong

Jiang Jieshi

Sun Yatsen

Jomo Kenyatta

Marcus Garvey

José Carlos Mariátegui

Victor Raúl Haya de la Torre

Diego Rivera

Getúlio Dornelles Vargas

Augusto César Sandino

Anastacio Somoza Garcia

Lázaro Cárdenas

Carmen Miranda

IDENTIFICATION: TERMS/CONCEPTS

State in your own words what each of the following terms means and why it is significant to a study of world history. (Terms with an asterisk are defined in the glossary.)

Indian National Congress

Ahimsa

India Act

Satyagraha

Chinese Communist Party (CCP)

Long March

Guomindang

Pan-Africa

Mukden incident

Neocolonialism

Popular American Revolutionary Alliance (APRA)

Imperialism*

Good neighbor policy

Dollar diplomacy

Yankee imperialism

United Fruit Company

STUDY QUESTIONS

1. What was the status of India within the British empire after World War I? What were some of the sources of tension in India at this time?

2. Two warring factions emerged in China between the wars: the nationalists and the communists. What values and interests did each represent? What advantages did each have?

3. Two political factions dominated Japanese politics after World War I: the internationalists and the militarists. What values and interests did each represent? What advantages did each have?

4. To what extent was the continent of Africa transformed by the Great War? What circumstances caused changes to occur and what was the nature of those changes?

5. What factors caused Africans to challenge European authority during the Great War?

6. Explain the role of the United States and the financial interests of U.S. businesses in the evolution of economic imperialism in Latin America.

7. Describe the reaction of various Latin American states to neocolonialism.

8. Looking at the careers of artist Diego Rivera and entertainer Carmen Miranda, discuss how popular culture related to international politics and diplomacy between the United States and Latin America during the decades after the Great War.

INQUIRY QUESTIONS

1. Compare and contrast the experiences of Latin America and Africa during the Great Depression.

2. What elements need to be in place for Mohandas Gandhi's strategy of *satyagraha,* or nonviolent resistance, to be an effective vehicle for social change? Explain why each is important and list them in order of their importance.

3. Compare and contrast colonialism and neocolonialism.

4. Describe and analyze the nature of the African colonial economy in the decade following the Great War. Include a discussion of labor practices and patterns of landholding. In particular, how did taxation policies relate to labor recruitment?

5. Describe and analyze the role of European ideas and institutions in the formation of nationalist movements in Asia and Africa, and in anti-imperialist movements in Latin America.

STUDENT QUIZ

1. *Satyagraha* was
   a. Gandhi's philosophy of passive resistance.
   b. the Islamic leader who called for the creation of Pakistan for India's Muslims.
   c. Mao Zedong's adapted philosophy of Chinese communism.
   d. the original name of the Pan-African movement.
   e. the Chinese political party headed by Jiang Jicshi.

2. Gandhi embraced a moral philosophy of tolerance and nonviolence (*ahimsa*) during the twenty-five years he spent in
   a. South Africa.
   b. China.
   c. Morocco.
   d. Great Britain.
   e. Argentina.

3. Gandhi
   a. fought hard to improve the status of the casteless Untouchables.
   b. launched the Non-Cooperation Movement.
   c. began the Civil Disobedience Movement.
   d. worked to secure approval of the Government of India Act.
   e. all of the above.

4. Which of the following was *not* one of the foundations of Gandhi's philosophy?
   a. an attempt to improve the position of the *harijans*
   b. boycotting British goods
   c. heavy industrialization
   d. passive resistance
   e. economic self-sufficiency

5. Muhammad Ali Jinnah called for the creation of
   a. Pakistan.
   b. Iraq.
   c. Palestine.
   d. Saudi Arabia.
   e. Afghanistan.

6. Muhammad Ali Jinnah
   a. led the Civil Disobedience Movement.
   b. was an adherent of values and virtues discussed in the *Bhagavad Gita*.
   c. was Gandhi's main challenger for political leadership of Hindus.
   d. headed the Muslim League.
   e. was the founder of the Indian National Congress.

7. The *Three Principles of the People* summarized the political views of
   a. Mohandas Gandhi.
   b. Jiang Jieshi.
   c. Puyi.
   d. Sun Yatsen.
   e. Mao Zedong.

8. Mao Zedong's main rival after 1925 was
   a. Puyi.
   b. Sun Yatsen.
   c. Jiang Jieshi.
   d. Mohandas Gandhi.
   e. Muhammad Ali Jinnah.

9. The May Fourth Movement
   a. was a significant turning point in the evolution of Marcus Garvey's political efforts.
   b. was a sign of growing Japanese nationalism.
   c. became the pretext for Japan to invade Manchuria.
   d. galvanized the Chinese against foreign influence.
   e. was typical of Gandhi's nonviolent movement.

10. The Long March
    a. destroyed Mao Zedong's credibility with the Chinese.
    b. left Jiang Jieshi in complete control of the Chinese Communist Party.
    c. greatly strengthened Mao Zedong's leadership position.
    d. was the final victory for the Guomindang.
    e. forced Mao Zedong to flee China and hide in the Soviet Union.

11. Who among the following emerged as the leader and principal theoretician of the Chinese Communist movement?
    a. Mao Zedong
    b. Jiang Jieshi
    c. Sun Yatsen
    d. Shanfei
    e. None of the above

12. In the decades following the Great War, the economies of most African colonies were dominated by
    a. the export of unprocessed raw materials or minimally processed cash crops.
    b. light manufacturing.
    c. production of steel.
    d. cattle ranching.
    e. furniture manufacture.

13. Which of the following is *not* true regarding Africa during the decades after the Great War?
    a. Colonial taxation policies were designed to drive Africans into the labor market.
    b. Using African labor and tax monies, Europeans built economic infrastructure.
    c. Europeans promoted rapid, intensive industrialization among their colonial possessions.
    d. The Great Depression exposed the vulnerability of dependent colonial economies.
    e. In areas with extensive white settlement, settler agriculture was most prominent.

14. Who among the following was an artist who blended artistic vision and radical political ideas in large murals that he created for the appreciation of working people?
    a. Carmen Miranda
    b. Lázaro Cárdenas
    c. Victor Raúl Haya de la Torre
    d. Diego Rivera
    e. Anastacio Somoza Garcia

15. Who among the following was noted for his "good neighbor policy"?
    a. Woodrow Wilson
    b. Theodore Roosevelt
    c. Howard Taft
    d. Franklin Delano Roosevelt
    e. Herbert Hoover

16. Marcus Garvey
    a. was a member of the "new elite" of African colonies who became president of Kenya.
    b. was a Jamaican who championed the "Back to Africa" movement.
    c. was a leader of the Mumbo cult.
    d. mobilized Africans to revolt against British rule during the Great War.
    e. none of the above.

17. Each of the following statements about Sun Yatsen is true, *except* that he
    a. was a leading opponent of the Qing dynasty.
    b. proclaimed a Chinese republic in 1912.
    c. authored *Three Principles of the People.*
    d. established the Nationalist People's Party, or *Guomindang.*
    e. led the Chinese in resisting Japanese military aggression.

18. Carmen Miranda
    a. created a famous painting called *Imperialism.*
    b. wore colorful headdresses adorned with fruits, such as bananas, grown in Latin America.
    c. was the popular wife of an Argentine dictator.
    d. served as the model for an ad created by the United Fruit Company.
    e. both b and d.

19. José Carlos Mariátegui
    a. established the Socialist Party of Peru.
    b. had been a protégé of Fidel Castro.
    c. served as president of Mexico.
    d. was a famous Mexican muralist.
    e. was a Brazilian dictator-president.

20. Augusto César Sandino
    a. was the leader of the *Guarda Nacional* in Nicaragua.
    b. played the starring role in the film *Down Argentine Way.*
    c. was assassinated by agents of the United Fruit Company.
    d. led the opposition to the occupation of Nicaragua by U.S. Marines.
    e. served as president of Nicaragua.

MATCHING

Match these figures with the statements that follow.

A. Mohandas Gandhi
B. Diego Rivera
C. Marcus Garvey
D. Jiang Jieshi
E. Muhammad Ali Jinnah

F. Mao Zedong
G. Carmen Miranda
H. Bal Gangadhar Tilak
I. Sun Yatsen
J. Lázaro Cárdenas

1. ___ Driving force behind the Chinese Communist Party.

2. ___ Indian political activist whose slogan was "*Swaraj* (Self Rule) is my birthright."

3. ___ A famed Mexican artist who blended his artistic and political visions in vast murals intended for viewing and appreciation by the masses.

4. ___ President of Mexico who tested the limits of the "good neighbor" policy by nationalizing Mexico's oil industry.

5. ___ Chinese nationalist who joined forces with the Communists to expel foreigners from China, then turned against his former allies.

6. ___ Latin American entertainer who softened representations of Latin America for audiences of the United States.

7. ___ Chinese nationalist whose ideology was summarized in *Three Principles of the People*.

8. ___ Indian nationalist, leader of the Muslim League, who proposed that India be partitioned between Muslims and Hindus.

9. ___ A Jamaican who preached the greatness of the African heritage and championed a "Back to Africa" movement.

10. ___ Indian nationalist who used civil disobedience and passive resistance as weapons against British rule in India.

SEQUENCING

Place the following clusters of events in chronological order. Consider carefully how one event leads to another, and try to determine the internal logic of each sequence.

A.

_____ Government of India Act

_____ Muhammad Ali Jinnah proposes two states in place of India

_____ 379 demonstrators killed in Amritsar

_____ Gandhi becomes active in Indian politics

_____ The Non-Cooperation Movement begins

_____ The Civil Disobedience Movement begins

B.

_____ The Chinese Communist Party is organized

_____ Sun Yatsen proclaims a Chinese Republic

_____ The Long March

_____ The May Fourth Movement

_____ Jiang Jieshi launches the Northern Expedition

_____ The Mukden incident

<u>QUOTATIONS</u>

For each of the following quotes, identify the speaker, if known, or the point of view. What is the significance of each passage?

1. "One fact is that this alien government has ruined the country. . . . Pax Britannica has been established in this country in order that a foreign Government may exploit the country. . . . Your industries are ruined utterly, ruined by foreign rule; your wealth is going out of the country and you are reduced to the lowest level which no human being can occupy. In this state of things, is there any remedy by which you can help yourself? The remedy is not petitioning but boycott."

2. "We have stolen his land. Now we must steal his limbs. Compulsory labor is the corollary to our occupation of the country."

3. "George Washington was not God Almighty. He was a man like any Negro in this building, and if he and his associates were able to make a free America, we too can make a free Africa. . . . Lenin and Trotsky were not Jesus Christs, but they were able to overthrow the despotism of Russia, and today they have given the world a Social Republic, the first of its kind. If Lenin and Trotsky were able to do that for Russia, you and I can do that for Africa. . . . I prefer to die at this moment rather than not to work for the freedom of Africa. . . . It falls to our lot to tear off the shackles that bind Mother Africa. Can you do it?"

<u>MAP EXERCISES</u>

1. On the outline map of Asia, locate and label the following:

    - Countries: China, Japan, Indochina, Korea, Manchuria, Mongolia, Siam, Soviet Union
    - The territories controlled by the Japanese, the Nanjing government, and the Chinese
      Communist Party
    - The route of the Long March, 1934–1936

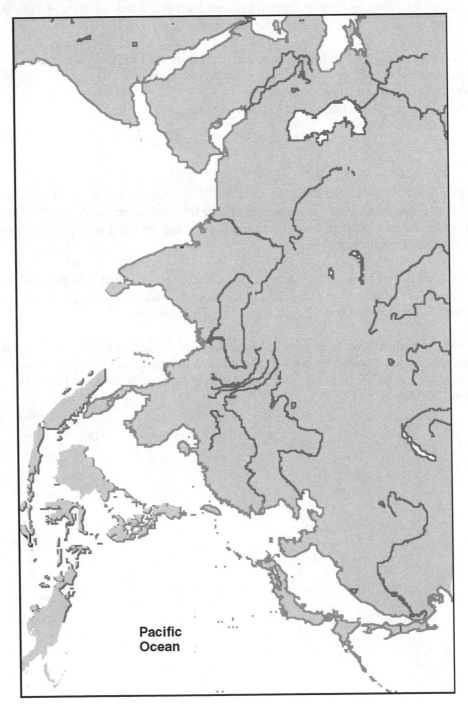

Pacific
Ocean

223

2. Explain the strategic importance of Manchuria to the Japanese, the Soviet Union, and China.

3. To fully appreciate the distances of the Long March, translate this route into comparable distances in North America.

CONNECTIONS

In fifty words or less, explain the relationship between each of the following pairs. How does one lead to or foster the other? Be specific in your response.

- The Mukden incident and Japanese withdrawal from the League of Nations
- The Great War and African self-determination movements
- Neocolonialism and Rivera's *Imperialism*
- The "good neighbor" policy and Carmen Miranda

FILMS

Raise the Red Lantern (1991). Set in China in the 1920s. An impoverished but educated young woman is forced to enter the household of a wealthy nobleman as his fourth wife. Reveals tensions between tradition and modernity and the dangerous politics in such a household. English subtitles.

Passage to India (1984). Tensions between Indians and the colonial British intensify when a white female tourist accuses a young Indian doctor of rape. Based on E. M. Forster's novel. Starring Judy Davis, Peggy Ashcroft, Alec Guinness.

Gandhi (1982). A sympathetic biography of Mohandas Gandhi, Indian lawyer, activist, and spiritual leader, who led the Indian people in a nonviolent and ultimately successful revolt against the British. The film earned Oscars for Best Picture and Best Actor, with Ben Kingsley in the title role.

CHAPTER 37
NEW CONFLAGRATIONS: WORLD WAR II

<u>INTRODUCTION</u>

The Second World War (1939–1945) was indeed a conflagration such as the world had never seen before. There was no precedent for the scale of the devastation, the millions of dead, the unimaginable barbarity. World War II was the defining event of the twentieth century. It determined the global powers, the global alignments, and many of the issues for the next generation. Some aspects of the war to consider as you read:

- Appeascment. The causes of the war are complex but must include the failure of Western democracies to take seriously the threat of fascism. When Japan invaded Manchuria in 1931, when Italy seized Ethiopia in 1935, when Germany claimed first the Sudetenland and then all of Czechoslovakia in 1938: at every turn, world leaders decided to appease the aggressor rather than risk a war.

- Isolationism. Sunk in the depression, Britain, France, and the United States erected walls of tariffs against imports, which only deepened the global depression. Disillusioned with the outcome of World War I, the Western democracies did not maintain their military strength. When the next war came, they were ill prepared.

- Total war. Like the First World War, the second involved whole populations on an unprecedented scale. Women on both sides performed industrial work and joined auxiliary forces. Civilians were targets of war through aerial attacks, blockades, rape, and internment. Civilian casualties were in the tens of millions.

- Genocide. Certainly the most horrifying aspect of the war was the Nazi attempt to methodically exterminate the entire Jewish population of Europe, along with other "undesirable" populations. Nearly six million Jews were killed in the death camps.

- An uneasy alliance. Capitalist and communist states found common cause in the battle against fascism. By keeping up the pressure on two fronts, the Allies eventually crushed the Axis empire. However, by the end of the war, the alliance between Britain, the United States, and the Soviet Union was frayed and unstable.

- Postwar uncertainties. At the Yalta conference of 1945, the Allies agreed that the Soviets could establish temporary governments in eastern Europe and eastern Germany in exchange for Stalin's pledge to help the United States defeat Japan. These puppet states were supposed to be temporary but instead became permanent dependents of the Soviet Union. The postwar conflict between the United States and the Soviet Union was already apparent.

OUTLINE

I. Origins of World War II

A. Japan's war in China

1. Global conflict began with Japanese invasion of Manchuria, 1931

    a) League of Nations condemned action; Japan simply withdrew from league

    b) 1937, Japan launched full-scale invasion of China

2. The Rape of Nanjing characterized war waged against civilians

    a) Aerial bombing of Shanghai

    b) In Nanjing, widespread rape and slaughter

3. Chinese resistance movement

    a) Nationalists and communists formed "united front" against Japanese

    b) Unable to effectively work together, they conducted guerilla attacks

    c) Communists gained popular support throughout war

4. Japan's Tripartite Pact with Germany and Italy, 1940; neutrality pact with Soviet Union, 1941

B. Italian and German aggression

1. Italy after the Great War

    a) Italians felt slighted at the Paris Peace Conference

    b) Italian losses were high in World War I; economy never recovered

    c) Mussolini promised national glory, empire

    d) Annexed Libya; invaded Ethiopia (1935–1936), killed 250,000 Ethiopians

2. Germany: deep resentment at Treaty of Versailles

    a) Harsh terms: reparations, economic restrictions

    b) Former Allies inclined not to object when Hitler violated terms of the treaty

    c) Hitler blamed Jews, communists, liberals for losing the war and accepting the treaty

3. After 1933, Hitler moved to ignore terms of peace settlement

    a) Withdrew from League of Nations, 1933

    b) Rebuilt military, air force; reinstated draft

    c) Took back the Rhineland, 1936, then annexed Austria, 1938

    d) Reclaimed Sudetenland from western Czechoslovakia, 1938

    e) At each step, France and Britain did nothing to stop him

4. The Munich Conference: Peace for our time?

    a) In 1938, Germany "appeased" by taking Sudetenland, promised to stop there

b) Britain and France desperate to avoid war

c) 1939, violating Munich agreement, Hitler seized most of Czechoslovakia

5. Russian-German Treaty of Non-Aggression, 1939, shocked the world

II. Total war: the world under fire

A. *Blitzkrieg:* Germany conquers Europe

1. Strategy of a "lightning war": unannounced, surprise attacks

2. September 1939, Nazi invasion of Poland

a) Poland defeated in one month

b) Divided between Germany and Soviet Union

3. Battle of the Atlantic: German U-boats (submarines) against British ship convoys

4. Spring 1940, the fall of France

a) Nazis swiftly conquered Denmark, Norway, Belgium, Netherlands

b) French signed an armistice in June 1940

c) Italy entered the war on Nazis' side

5. The Battle of Britain

a) Germans' strategy to defeat Britain solely through air attacks

b) Aerial bombing killed forty thousand British civilians; Royal Air Force prevented defeat

c) Summer 1941, Germany also controlled Balkans and North Africa

B. The German invasion of the Soviet Union

1. Operation Barbarossa: German surprise invasion of Soviet Union, June 1941

a) Wanted eastern land on which to resettle Germans

b) Captured Russian heartland; Leningrad under siege; troops outside Moscow

2. *Blitzkrieg* strategies less effective in Russia

a) Soviets drew on tremendous reserves: 360 Soviet divisions against 150 German

b) Hitler underestimated Soviet industrial capacity

c) Stalin quickly moved Soviet industry east of the Ural Mountains

3. Russian winter caught German troops ill-prepared

C. Battles in Asia and the Pacific

1. U.S. support of the Allies before Pearl Harbor

a) Roosevelt sold and then "loaned" arms and war material to the British

b) Later supplied the Soviets and the Chinese

2. Japanese expansion continued into southeast Asia: Indochina, 1940–1941

a) United States responded by freezing Japanese assets, implementing oil embargo

      b) Demanded withdrawal from China and southeast Asia

      c) Prime minister Tojo Hikedi developed plan of attack

  3. 7 December 1941: U.S. naval base at Pearl Harbor attacked by Japanese pilots

      a) U.S. naval power in Pacific devastated

      b) United States declared war on Japan; Germany and Italy declared war on United States

  4. Japanese victories after Pearl Harbor

      a) Japan advanced swiftly in the Pacific and southeast Asia

      b) Conquered Philippines, Dutch East Indies, Indochina, Burma, Singapore

      c) Slogan "Asia for Asians" masked Japanese imperialism against fellow Asians

D. Defeat of the Axis Powers

  1. Impact of Soviet Union and U.S. entry in 1941

      a) Brought vital personnel and industry to Allies

      b) German subs sank 2,452 merchants ships, but U.S. shipyards built more

  2. Allied victories came after 1943

      a) Russians defeated the Germans at Stalingrad, pushed them back

      b) 1944, British-U.S. troops invaded North Africa and then Italy

      c) June 1944, British-U.S. forces invaded northern France at Normandy

      d) Overwhelmed Germans on coast of Normandy, 6 June 1944

      e) Round-the-clock strategic bombing by United States and Britain leveled German cities

      f) Germans surrendered unconditionally 8 May 1945; Hitler committed suicide

  3. Turning the tide in the Pacific

      a) Turning point: the Battle of Midway, June 1942; United States broke Japanese code

      b) Island-hopping strategy: moving to islands close to Japan for air attacks

  4. Savage fighting on islands of Iwo Jima and Okinawa

      a) Japanese used suicide *kamikaze* pilots

      b) Okinawan civilians refused to surrender

      c) U.S. military was convinced that Japan would not surrender

  5. Japanese surrender after devastating assault

      a) U.S. firebombing raids devastated Japanese cities: in Tokyo, one hundred thousand killed

    b) August 1945: atomic bombs on Hiroshima and Nagasaki killed two hundred thousand

    c) The Soviet Union declared war on Japan, 8 August

    d) Japanese emperor surrendered unconditionally 15 August, ending WWII

III. Life during wartime

A. Occupation, collaboration, and resistance

    1. Patterns of occupation varied

        a) Japanese conquests: puppet governments, independent allies, or military control

        b) German conquests: racially "superior" people given greater autonomy

            (1) In northern Europe, civilian governments under German supervision

            (2) In eastern Europe, conquered territories taken over by military

    2. Both Japan and Germany exploited conquered states, resources, and peoples

        a) Slave labor conscripted from conquered populations to work in factories

        b) Labor conscripted from Poles, Soviets, Balkans, also Chinese and Koreans

    3. Many local people accepted, even collaborated with, occupying forces

        a) In Asia, Japanese domination not much different from European domination

        b) Others aided conquerors to gain power in new administration

        c) Anticommunism led some in western Europe to join the Nazi SS troops

    4. Resistance to occupation took many forms

        a) Active resistance: sabotage, assaults, assassination

        b) Passive resistance as well: intelligence gathering, refusing to submit

        c) Resistance in Japan and Germany was dangerous and rare

    5. Occupation forces responded to resistance with atrocities

        a) Brutal reprisals to acts of resistance by both Germans and Japanese

        b) Despite retaliation, resistance movements grew throughout the war

B. The Holocaust

    1. Long history of anti-Semitism created tolerance of Nazis' anti-Jewish measures

        a) At first Nazis encouraged Jewish emigration

        b) Many Jews were unable to leave after Nazis took their wealth

        c) Nazi conquest of Europe brought more Jews under their control

    2. The "final solution"

        a) Began with slaughter of Jews, Roma, and other undesirables in Soviet Union

        b) By end of 1941, German special killing units had killed 1.4 million Jews

        c) By 1942 Nazis decided to evacuate all European Jews to camps in east Poland

        d) In Auschwitz alone at least one million Jews perished

    3. Jewish resistance

        a) Will to resist sapped by prolonged starvation, disease

        b) Uprising of Warsaw ghetto, 1943: sixty thousand Jews rose up against Germans

    4. Altogether, about 5.7 million Jews perished in the Holocaust

C. Women and the war

    1. "It's a Woman's War, Too!"

        a) Over half a million British and 350,000 American women joined auxiliary services

        b) Soviet and Chinese women took up arms and joined resistance groups

        c) Jewish women and girls suffered as much as men and boys

    2. Women's social roles changed dramatically

        a) By taking jobs or heading families, women gained independence and confidence

        b) Changes expected to be temporary, would return to traditional role after war

    3. "Comfort women"

        a) Japanese armies forcibly recruited three hundred thousand women to serve in military brothels

        b) 80 percent of comfort women came from Korea

        c) A comfort woman had to service between twenty and thirty men each day

        d) Many were killed by Japanese soldiers; survivors experienced deep shame

IV. Neither peace nor war

A. Postwar settlements and cold war

    1. Two strongest postwar powers, Soviet Union and United States, vied for nonaligned nations

    2. War left millions of casualties and refugees

        a) At least sixty million people died in WWII; highest number of casualties in Soviet Union and China

        b) Eight million Germans fled west to British, U.S. territories to escape Soviet army

        c) Twelve million Germans and Soviet prisoners of war made their way home

        d) Survivors of camps and three million refugees from the Balkans returned home

    3. The origins of the cold war (1947–1990)

        a) Unlikely alliance between Britain, Soviet Union, and United States held up for duration of war

        b) Not without tensions: Soviet resented U.S.-British delays in European invasion

4. Postwar settlement established at Yalta (February 1945) and Potsdam (July–August)

   a) Each Allied power to occupy and control territories liberated by its armed forces

   b) Stalin agreed to support United States against Japan

   c) Stalin's plans prevailed; Poland and east Europe became communist allies

   d) President Truman took hard line at Potsdam, widened differences

5. Postwar territorial divisions reflected growing schism between United States and Soviet Union

   a) Soviets took east Germany, while United States, Britain, and France took west Germany

   b) Berlin also divided four ways; by 1950 division seemed permanent

   c) Churchill spoke of an "iron curtain" across Europe, separating east and west

   d) Similar division in Korea: Soviets occupied north and United States the south

6. Truman Doctrine, 1947: United States would support "free peoples resisting subjugation"

   a) Perception of world divided between so-called free and enslaved peoples

   b) Interventionist policy, dedicated to "containment" of communism

B. Global reconstruction and the United Nations

   1. The Marshall Plan, 1948: U.S. aid for the recovery of Europe

      a) Idea to rebuild European economies and strengthen capitalism

      b) Soviet response: Council for Mutual Economic Assistance (COMECON) for its satellite nations

   2. NATO and the Warsaw Pact: militarization of the cold war

      a) 1949, United States created NATO, a regional military alliance against Soviet aggression

      b) 1955, Soviets formed the Warsaw Pact in response

      c) Two global superpowers protecting hegemony with alliances

      d) United Nations, established 1945 to maintain international peace and security

IDENTIFICATION: PEOPLE

What is the contribution of each of the following individuals to world history? Identification should include answers to the questions *who, what, where, when, how,* and *why is this person important?*

Winston Churchill

Tojo Hideki

Harry S. Truman

IDENTIFICATION: TERMS/CONCEPTS

State in your own words what each of the following terms means and why it is significant to a study of world history. (Terms with an asterisk are defined in the glossary).

Rape of Nanjing*

Munich Conference

Russian-German Treaty of Nonaggression

Axis Powers

*Blitzkrieg**

Battle of Britain

Operation Barbarossa

*Kamikaze**

The "final solution"

Comfort women

Truman Doctrine*

Marshall Plan*

NATO*

Warsaw Pact*

STUDY QUESTIONS

1. Why were the numerically superior Chinese so easily defeated by the Japanese? Why did the Chinese resistance efforts fail?

2. Note the specific steps taken by Italy and Germany in the 1930s that were in direct violation of the terms of the Treaty of Versailles.

3. Why didn't Britain and France object when Hitler and Mussolini violated the peace treaty? What were the consequences of their policy of appeasement?

4. Describe the strategy of the *Blitzkrieg*. How were the Germans able to overwhelm continental Europe so quickly?

5. What steps did the United States take to support the Allies, both in Asia and in Europe, before Pearl Harbor?

6.   What was Japan's purpose in attacking the United States? What was its long-range plan?

7.   Compare the occupation policies of Germany and Japan during the war.

8.   What factors led to the defeat of the Axis powers in Europe?

9.   What were some of the forms of resistance to occupying forces? How effective were these efforts? Why was resistance so difficult?

10. How did the war affect civilian populations, families, and women on the home front?

INQUIRY QUESTIONS

1.   What factors led to the American decision to drop the atomic bomb on Hiroshima and Nagasaki? What were the results of this decision, both long- and short-term?

2.   How did Nazi policies toward the Jews change over the course of the war? What does the statement by Heinrich Himmler (page 1051 in the textbook) reveal about Nazi attitudes toward the extermination of the Jewish people?

3.   How did U.S.-Soviet relations change over the course of the war, from the lend-lease program in 1941 to the Potsdam Conference in 1945? What were the sources of tensions between the two allies?

WORLD WAR II ALIGNMENTS

Complete the chart below.

NATION	*ALLIED OR AXIS*	*LEADER DURING WWII*
Britain		
China		
France		
Germany		
Italy		
Japan		
Soviet Union		
United States		

1. The height of Japanese atrocity in China was reached at the rape of
   a. Beijing.
   b. Shanghai.
   c. Hong Kong.
   d. Nanjing.
   e. Manchukuo.

2. The Tripartite Pact brought together
   a. England, France, and the Soviet Union.
   b. China, England, and the United States.
   c. Germany, Italy, and Japan.
   d. England, the Soviet Union, and the United States.
   e. Germany, Italy, and Austria.

3. Chinese resistance to the Japanese was
   a. a well-coordinated guerilla movement.
   b. weakened by rivalry between Chinese nationalists and communists.
   c. effectively crushed by the brutality of Japanese occupation.
   d. armed by the Soviet Union.
   e. powerful, overwhelming, and extraordinarily effective.

4. As evidence of the renewed power and glory of Italy, Mussolini
   a. annexed Albania.
   b. annexed Libya.
   c. invaded Ethiopia.
   d. supported militarists in the Spanish Civil War.
   e. all of the above.

5. In 1938 Germany sent troops into what country and forced its leaders to accept the *Anschluss?*
   a. the Rhineland
   b. Poland
   c. France
   d. Austria
   e. Czechoslovakia

6. At the Munich Conference, British Prime Minister Neville Chamberlain
   a. took a hard line with Hitler, threatening military retaliation for any further aggression.
   b. agreed that Hitler could keep lands already taken in exchange for a pledge to end German expansion.
   c. agreed that the Treaty of Versailles had been unfair to the Germans and that their former empire should be restored.
   d. created the regional Allied defense against Hitler's aggression.
   e. made a secret alliance with the Axis powers.

7. The Russian-German Treaty of Nonaggression of 1939
    a. conceded German control over eastern Europe.
    b. conceded Soviet control over eastern Europe.
    c. freed Hitler to pursue a more aggressive policy in western Europe.
    d. pledged Soviet support to Germany in case of war.
    e. brokered critical trade agreements between the two countries.

8. The German *Blitzkrieg* referred to
    a. an elaborate series of concrete bunkers built on the experiences of World War I.
    b. the Nazi plan for a "final solution" to the Jewish question.
    c. the living space in the east that was necessary for an expanding Germany.
    d. a lightning war.
    e. the German representative assembly that voted Hitler into power.

9. Operation Barbarossa in 1941 was code for the
    a. German invasion of France.
    b. German invasion of North Africa.
    c. German invasion of the Soviet Union.
    d. Japanese attack on Pearl Harbor.
    e. Allied invasion of Normandy.

10. All of the following were essential to the Soviet defense against the Nazis *except*
    a. Allied support through the lend-lease program.
    b. German overconfidence of a swift victory, which left them trapped far inside Russia when winter came.
    c. the rapid relocation of Soviet industry to the east.
    d. outrage at the German treatment of Jewish minorities in eastern Europe.
    e. the willingness of the Russian people to fight the "Great Patriotic War."

11. Immediate provocation for the Japanese attack on Pearl Harbor was
    a. the internment of Japanese citizens living in the United States.
    b. an American-led oil embargo against Japan.
    c. resentment over the unequal treaties imposed on Japan in the nineteenth century.
    d. resentment that Japan has not gotten more of the territorial "spoils" at the Paris peace settlements after World War I.
    e. fears of an American attack on the Japanese homeland.

12. The key to Allied victory in Europe was the
    a. success of resistance movements at undermining German authority.
    b. vast personnel and industrial capacity of the United States and Soviet Union.
    c. lack of commitment of Italian forces to the Axis cause.
    d. development of the atomic bomb.
    e. leadership of Harry Truman after the death of Franklin D. Roosevelt.

13. A key factor in the Allied victory in the Pacific was
    a. the island-hopping strategy that positioned U.S. troops within striking range of Japan.
    b. massive aerial bombing of key Japanese cities.
    c. the development of the atomic bomb.
    d. the declaration of war by the Soviet government against Japan.
    e. all of the above.

14. At the height of their expansion, the Japanese had established either direct or indirect control over all of the following *except*
    a. Dutch East Indies.
    b. Indochina.
    c. Philippines.
    d. Singapore.
    e. Thailand.

15. The Japanese finally surrendered in 1945
    a. in response to the surrender of Germany.
    b. after the emperor resigned and a republic was established.
    c. after the atomic bombing of Hiroshima and Nagasaki.
    d. after the American landing at Kyushu.
    e. after the Soviet landing at Okinawa.

16. At the Wannsee Conference in 1942, Nazi leaders decided to
    a. invade Poland.
    b. invade the Soviet Union.
    c. eliminate undesirable minorities in conquered territories in the Soviet Union.
    d. deport all European Jews to concentration camps in Poland for extermination.
    e. create the *SS Einsatzgruppen*.

17. Women in the United States and Britain performed all the following wartime activities *except*
    a. direct combat.
    b. industrial work.
    c. frontline support.
    d. training and transport piloting.
    e. ambulance and hospital work.

18. The highest casualties in World War II were suffered by
    a. Britain and the United States.
    b. China and the Soviet Union.
    c. Germany and Italy.
    d. Germany and Japan.
    e. Japan and the United States.

19. As the end of the war approached, Allied leaders agreed that each power would have control over
    a. those territories liberated by their own armed forces.
    b. lands evenly divided among the three main Allies according to a secret treaty.
    c. only those lands illegally seized by the Axis.
    d. different sectors of Italy.
    e. only the defeated territories in Asia.

20. The Truman Doctrine pledged that
    a. Soviet aggression would be met with American force.
    b. the United States would help rebuild Europe and Japan.
    c. the United States would support free people resisting subjugation by insurrection or outside interference.
    d. the United States would never again resort to atomic weapons.
    e. the United States would participate in the United Nations.

21. The Marshall Plan was
    a. the U.S. plan for the final defeat of Germany through an invasion at Normandy.
    b. the code name for the German invasion of the Soviet Union in 1941.
    c. the secret United States code during World War II.
    d. a U.S. financial plan to rebuild Europe and stop Soviet expansion.
    e. the official name for the "final solution."

SEQUENCING

Place the following clusters of events in chronological order. Consider carefully how one event leads to another, and try to determine the internal logic of each sequence.

A.   The Japanese:

_____   attack on Pearl Harbor

_____   Rape of Nanjing

_____   capture of Singapore

_____   invasion of Manchuria

_____   invasion of Borneo, Burma, and Dutch East Indies

B.   The German invasion and occupation of:

_____   the Sudetenland

_____   France

_____   Austria

_____   Soviet Union

_____   Poland

237

C.

_____ Germany and Italy declare war on the United States.

_____ Under the lend-lease program, the United States loans destroyers and warplanes to the British and the Soviets.

_____ The U.S. government sponsors the Kellogg-Briand Pact, renouncing war as an instrument of national policy.

_____ The U.S. government cautiously permits a cash-and-carry policy whereby the British pay cash and carry materials on their own ships.

_____ Japanese bombers attack the U.S. Pacific fleet at Pearl Harbor. The United States declares war on Japan.

QUOTATIONS

For each of the following quotes, identify the speaker, if known, or the point of view. What is the significance of each passage?

1. "Now it is impossible for us to lose the war: We now have an ally who has never been vanquished in three thousand years."

2. "I believe it must be the policy of the United States to support free peoples who are resisting attempted subjugation by armed minorities or by outside pressures."

3. "From Stettin in the Baltic to Trieste in the Adriatic an iron curtain has descended across the Continent."

4. "We, the German Führer and Chancellor and the British Prime Minister, have had a further meeting today and are agreed in recognizing that the question of Anglo-German relations is of the first importance for the two countries and for Europe."

5. "The establishment of order in Europe and the rebuilding of national economic life must be achieved by processes which will enable the liberated peoples to destroy the last vestiges of Nazism and Fascism and to create democratic institutions of their own choice. . . . [Therefore] the three governments . . . [are] pledged to the earliest possible establishment through free elections of Governments responsive to the will of the people."

6. "Most of you men know what it is like to see 100 corpses side by side, or 500 or 1,000. To have stood fast through this and—except for cases of human weakness—to have stayed decent, that has made us hard."

1. Determine the status of the following European states, whether Neutral (N), Axis (X), Axis-occupied (XO), Axis-ally (XA), or an Allied state (A), using Map 37.1 (page 1043 in the textbook).

    -   Austria, Belgium, Britain, Czechoslovakia, Denmark, Finland, France, Germany, Greece, Hungary, Ireland, Italy, Netherlands, Norway, Poland, Portugal, Soviet Union, Spain, Sweden, Switzerland, Turkey, Yugoslavia.
    -   Consider the neutral states. What would neutrality have meant in the context of World War II?
    -   What was the distinction between an Axis-ally and an Axis-occupied nation? What would this distinction have meant to the people of those nations?
    -   What does the map on page 1043 indicate about the Allied position in 1942 and 1943?

2. Locate and label the following on the outline map (see Map 37.2 on page 1046).

- States: Australia, Borneo, Burma, China, Japan, Indochina, Korea, Manchuria, Philippines, Taiwan, Thailand
- Cities: Beijing, Hong Kong, Hiroshima, Manila, Nagasaki, Nanjing, Singapore
- Other features: Aleutian Islands, Hawaiian Islands, Midway Islands, Okinawa
- Indicate the territory controlled by the Japanese in 1942, at the point of their farthest advance.
- Indicate the territory controlled by August 1945, when the Japanese surrendered.
- Use this map to explain the American strategy of island-hopping.

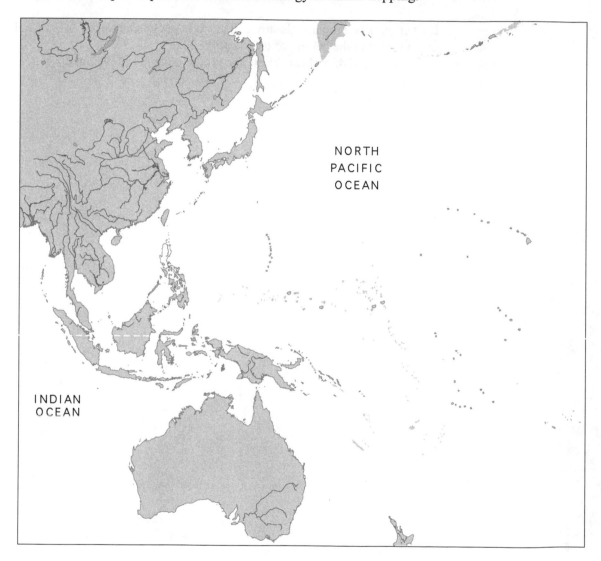

<u>CONNECTIONS</u>

In fifty words or less, explain the relationship between each of the following pairs. How does one lead to or foster the other? Be specific in your response.

- Treaty of Versailles and the Munich Conference
- "Asia for Asians" and comfort women
- Stalingrad and the Warsaw Pact
- Reparations and the Marshall Plan

<u>FILMS</u>

Saving Private Ryan (1998). Arguably the finest combat picture ever made. The action begins with the Allied invasion of Normandy in 1944 and follows a group of American soldiers as they move inland. Directed by Steven Spielberg. Starring Tom Hanks, Matt Damon.

Schindler's List (1993). Oskar Schindler was an unheroic, German war profiteer who nevertheless risked his life and his fortune to rescue more than one thousand Jews from the concentration camps. Directed by Steven Spielberg. Starring Liam Neesen.

Empire of the Sun (1987). Jim was a sheltered child, living comfortably in the British quarters of Singapore at the outbreak of the war. In the confusion of the Japanese invasion, he was separated from his family and had to survive in a prison camp. Directly by Steven Spielberg. Starring Christian Bale.

Das Boot ("*The Boat*") (1981). A powerful—often claustrophobic—German production about the crew of a U-boat in the Battle of the Atlantic. Widely acclaimed both for the gripping story and for the empathy with the subject. With English subtitles.

Tora, Tora, Tora (1970). In this unusual American-Japanese coproduction, the Japanese attack on Pearl Harbor is presented from both perspectives. The film builds from the breakdown of diplomacy to military planning and climaxes with the battle itself.

CHAPTER 38
THE BIPOLAR WORLD

INTRODUCTION

Two superpowers emerged from the ashes of the Second World War, the United States and the Soviet Union. Former allies, the two were now actively hostile, but they repeatedly stopped short of a full-out war. The prospect of a nuclear confrontation was too awful to contemplate. The cold war was characterized by the following:

- The arms race. The logic of the cold war drove both superpowers to stockpile nuclear weapons in order to match one another's destructive capabilities. The two powers were evenly matched in the 1960s, but by the 1980s the effort had severely strained the Soviet economy.

- Bipolar alliances. The cold war saw new defensive alliances, NATO in the west and the Warsaw Pact of the Soviet satellites. The world was divided into two camps, and the "third world" nations were courted and pressured to join one or the other. Some states, such as France and Yugoslavia, demonstrated that it was possible to avoid such entanglements. The People's Republic of China turned briefly to the Soviet Union for support, but broke free after 1964.

- Aggressive saber-rattling. Although the superpowers avoided direct and full-scale war, a number of minor conflicts sapped their energies and resources: Berlin, Korea, Hungary, Cuba, and Czechoslovakia. The United States fought a long and ultimately futile war in Vietnam. The Soviet Union was likewise drawn into a civil war in Afghanistan. Both of these campaigns failed.

- The failure of communism. As an economic system, Soviet communism provided a shabby equality for all, with few consumer goods and limited opportunities. In contrast, the postwar decades saw unprecedented prosperity in the United States, Europe, and Japan. Overall the standard of living in the capitalist societies improved dramatically, although there were greater extremes of wealth and poverty.

- The collapse of the Soviet Union. The breakdown of the Soviet Union, while a long time coming, was swift and unexpected when it came. Between 1989 and 1991, the Soviet Empire completely unraveled, and the cold war ended.

OUTLINE

I. The formation of a bipolar world

    A. The cold war in Europe

        1. Postwar Europe divided into competing political, military, economic blocs

           a) Western Europe U.S. allies: parliamentary governments, capitalist economies

           b) Eastern Europe dominated by Soviet Union, communist governments

2. Germany divided east and west in 1949

   a) Soviets refused to withdraw from eastern Germany after World War II

   b) Allied sectors reunited 1947–1948, Berlin remained divided as well

3. Berlin blockade and airlift, 1948–1949

   a) Soviet closed roads, trains, tried to strangle West Berlin into submission

   b) Britain and United States kept city supplied with round-the-clock airlift

   c) After embargo against Soviet satellites, Soviets backed down and ended blockade

4. The Berlin Wall, 1961

   a) 1949–1961, flood of refugees from East to West Germany, East to West Berlin

   b) Soviet solution: a wall of barbed wire through the city fortified the border

   c) Former Allied nations objected but did not risk a full conflict over the wall

5. Nuclear arms race: terrifying proliferation of nuclear weapons by both sides

   a) NATO and Warsaw Treaty Organization amassed huge weapons stockpiles

   b) By 1960s USSR reached military parity with United States

   c) By 1970 both superpowers acquired MAD, "mutually assured destruction"

B. Confrontations in Korea and Cuba

1. The Korea War, 1951–1953

   a) Korea divided at thirty-eighth parallel in 1948; U.S. ally in south, Soviet ally in north

   b) North Korean troops crossed the thirty-eighth parallel and captured Seoul, June 1950

   c) U.S. and UN troops pushed back North Korean troops to Chinese border

   d) Chinese troops came in, pushed U.S. forces and their allies back in the south

   e) Both sides agreed to a cease-fire in July 1953, again at thirty-eighth parallel

2. Globalization of containment

   a) Western fears of an international communist conspiracy, which must be contained

   b) Creation of SEATO, an Asian counterpart of NATO

   c) The "domino theory": if one country falls to communism, others will follow

3. Cuba: nuclear flashpoint

   a) Castro's revolutionary force overthrew dictator Batista in 1959

   b) Castro seized foreign properties (mostly U.S.), and killed or exiled thousands of political opponents

   c) United States cut off Cuban sugar imports, imposed export embargo

      d) Castro accepted Soviet massive economic aid and arms shipments, fueling U.S. fears about his communist leanings

   4. Bay of Pigs fiasco, April 1961

      a) CIA-sponsored invasion of Cuba failed

      b) Diminished U.S. prestige in Latin America and strengthened Castro's commitment to communism

      c) U.S. instituted Operation Mongoose, a clandestine effort to destabilize Cuba

   5. Cuban missile crisis, October 1962

      a) Soviet deployed nuclear missiles in Cuba, aimed at United States; claimed Cuban defense

      b) Kennedy blockaded Cuba, demanded removal; two tense weeks

      c) Khrushchev backed down; Kennedy pledged not to invade Cuba, and U.S missiles in Turkey would be removed

      d) Global tensions begin to ebb

C. Cold war societies

   1. Domestic containment

      a) U.S. leaders held families to be best defense against communism

      b) Women discouraged from working, should stay home and raise kids

      c) Senator McCarthy led attack against suspected communists in United States

      d) Increasing pressure to conform, retreat to home and family

   2. Female liberation movement a reaction to postwar domesticity

      a) Working women unhappy with new cult of domesticity

      b) Writers Simone de Beauvoir and Betty Friedan reflected women's dissatisfaction

      c) Some feminists used Marxist language, argued for "women's liberation"

   3. Black nationalism in United States, Caribbean, and emerging states of Africa

      a) Influenced by Jamaicans, singer Bob Marley, nationalist Marcus Garvey

      b) Martin Luther King Jr. inspired by Gandhi's nonviolent methods

   4. The U.S. civil rights movement emerged from cold war

      a) USSR critical of United States for treatment of African-Americans

      b) African-Americans organized in protest of southern segregation

      c) 1954, U.S. Supreme Court ruled that segregated education was unconstitutional

      d) Rosa Parks started boycott of Montgomery buses, led by M. L. King, 1955

   5. Cold war consumerism

    a) Socialist countries could not match United States in material wealth, consumer goods

    b) Stark contrasts between economies of western and eastern Europe

    c) Marshall Plan infused western Europe with aid, increased standard of living

6. The space race exemplified U.S.-Soviet competition in science and technology

    a) Soviets gained nuclear weapons, then intercontinental ballistic missiles (ICBM)

    b) Soviets launched *Sputnik*, first satellite, 1957

    c) Soviet cosmonaut, Yuri Gagarin, first man to orbit the earth, 1961

    d) American space program followed; John Glenn orbited, 1962

    e) President Kennedy established NASA; United States put man on the moon, 1969

7. "Peaceful coexistence" begins after Stalin's death, 1953

    a) Slight relaxation of censorship under Khrushchev

    b) Both sides feared nuclear confrontation

    c) Khrushchev visited United States in 1959, put a human face on communism

II. Challenges to superpower hegemony

A. Defiance, dissent, and intervention in Europe

1. France under de Gaulle

    a) Charles de Gaulle wanted Europe free from superpower domination

    b) French government refused to ban nuclear tests in 1963, tested bomb in 1964

    c) Other European states not persuaded to leave U.S. protection

2. Tito's Yugoslavia, an independent communist state

    a) Marshall Tito (Josip Broz) resisted Soviet control of Yugoslavia

    b) Stalin expelled Yugoslavia from Soviet bloc, 1948

    c) Remained nonaligned throughout cold war

3. De-Stalinization following death of Stalin, 1953

    a) 1956, Khrushchev denounced Stalin's rule of terror

    b) Millions of political prisoners released from work camps

    c) Brief "thaw" in Soviet culture from 1956 to 1964, easing censorship

4. Hungarian challenge, 1956

    a) De-Stalinization led to pro-democracy movement in Hungary

    b) New government announced neutrality, withdrew from Warsaw Pact

    c) Soviet tanks crushed Hungarian uprising, 1956

5. Prague Spring, Czechoslovakia, 1968

    a) Liberal movement led by Dubček sought "socialism with a human face"

      b) Soviet and east European forces crushed Prague liberal communism

      c) Soviet Premier Brezhnev justified invasion by Doctrine of Limited Sovereignty

B. The People's Republic of China

  1. Origins of Communist China

      a) Civil war between nationalists and communists resumed, 1945

      b) Outmaneuvered, the nationalists under Jiang Jieshi fled to Taiwan in 1948

      c) Mao Zedong proclaimed People's Republic of China, 1949

  2. Social and economic transformation of China

      a) Political reorganization dominated by Communist Party, Chairman Mao

      b) Suspected nationalists were executed or sent to forced labor camps

      c) Five-Year Plan stressed heavy industry

      d) Massive land redistribution at village level

      e) Collective farms with basic health and primary education

      f) Emancipation of women: footbinding ended; divorce, abortion allowed

  3. Fraternal cooperation between China and Soviet Union

      a) Both communist; shared common enemy, the United States

      b) Alarmed by U.S. support of Japan, South Korea, and Taiwan

      c) Beijing accepted direction from Moscow in early 1950s

      d) USSR gave military-economic aid, helped seat China in UN

  4. Cracks in alliance began in late 1950s

      a) USSR gave more economic support to noncommunist countries

      b) Both nations openly competed for influence in Africa and Asia

      c) Rift between the two nations was public by the end, 1964

C. Détente and the decline of superpower influence

  1. Era of cooperation

      a) Leaders of both superpowers agreed on policy of détente, late 1960s

      b) Exchanged visits and signed agreements calling for cooperation, 1972, 1974

      c) Concluded Strategic Arms Limitations Talks (SALT), 1972, again 1979

  2. Demise of détente

      a) Full U.S.-China diplomatic relations in 1979 created U.S.-USSR strain

      b) U.S. weapons sale to China in 1981 undermined U.S.-Soviet cooperation

      c) 1980 Soviet intervention in Afghanistan prompted U.S. economic sanctions

  3. U.S. defeat in Vietnam

a) 1950s, United States committed to support noncommunist government in South Vietnam

b) U.S. involvement escalated through 1960s

c) United States and allies unable to defeat North and South Vietnamese communists

d) President Nixon pledged in 1968 to end war with Vietnam

e) U.S. troops gradually withdrew; U.S. phase of war ended in 1973

f) North Vietnam continued war effort, unified the nation in 1976

4. Soviet setbacks in Afghanistan

a) Afghanistan had been a nonaligned nation until 1978, pro-Soviet coup

b) PDPA's radical reforms in 1978 prompted backlash

c) Islamic leaders objected to radical social change, led armed resistance

d) 1979, rebels controlled much of Afghan countryside; USSR intervened

e) United States and other nations supported anti-PDPA rebels; struggle lasted nine years

f) 1989 cease-fire negotiation by UN led to full Soviet withdrawal

g) Taliban forces captured Kabul and declared Afghanistan a strict Islamic state, 1996

5. Cold war countercultural protests in 1960s and 1970s

a) Cultural criticism of cold war as seen in film *Dr. Strangelove,* 1964

b) European and U.S. students agitated for peace, end to arms race, Vietnam war

c) Rock and roll music expressed student discontent

6. Watergate scandal brought down U.S. president Nixon, fed disillusionment

III. The end of the cold war

A. Revolutions in eastern and central Europe

1. 1980s, Ronald Reagan advocated massive military spending, opposed "evil empire"

2. Moscow's legacies

a) After World War II, Soviets had credibility for defeating Nazis

b) Communism unable to satisfy nationalism in eastern and central Europe

c) Soviet-backed governments lacked support and legitimacy

d) Soviet interventions in 1956 and 1968 dashed hopes of a humane socialism

3. Mikhail Gorbachev, Soviet leader 1985–1991

a) 1989, Gorbachev announced restructuring of USSR, withdrawal from cold war

b) Satellites states informed that each was on its own, without Soviet support

4. Rapid collapse of communist regimes across eastern and central Europe, 1989

    a) In Poland, Solidarity leader Lech Walesa won election of 1990

    b) Communism overthrown in Bulgaria and Hungary

    c) Czechoslovakia's "velvet revolution" ended communism in 1990, divided into Czech Republic and Slovakia in 1993

    d) Only violent revolution was in Romania; ended with death of communist dictator

    e) East Germany opened Berlin Wall in 1989; two Germanies were united in 1990

B. The collapse of the Soviet Union

  1. Gorbachev's reforms

    a) Gorbachev hoped for economic reform within political and economic system

    b) Centralized economy inefficient, military spending excessive

    c) Declining standard of living, food shortages, shoddy goods

  2. *Perestroika:* "restructuring" the economy

    a) Tried decentralizing economy, market system, profit motive

    b) Alienated those in positions of power, military leaders

  3. *Glasnost:* "openness" to public criticism, admitting past mistakes

    a) Opened door to widespread criticism of party and government

    b) Ethnic minorities, especially Baltic peoples, declared independence from USSR

    c) Russian Republic, led by Boris Yeltsin, also demanded independence

  4. Collapse of the Soviet Union, December 1991

    a) In 1991, conservatives attempted coup; wished to restore communism

    b) With help of loyal Red Amy units, Boris Yeltsin crushed the coup

    c) Yeltsin dismantled Communist party, led market-oriented economic reforms

    d) Regions of ethnic groups became independent; Soviet Union ceased to exist

C. Toward an uncertain future

  1. Ideological contest of the cold war ended in 1991 after defining the world for fifty years

  2. NATO and Warsaw Pact provided an uneasy security; now, lack of certainty

  3. Communism remained only in a few states in the world

IDENTIFICATION: PEOPLE

What is the contribution of each of the following individuals to world history? Identification should include answers to the questions *who, what, where, when, how,* and *why is this person important?*

Nikita Khrushchev

Fidel Castro

John F. Kennedy

Joseph McCarthy

Martin Luther King Jr.

Charles de Gaulle

Marshal Tito

Richard Nixon

Ronald Reagan

Mikhail Gorbachev

Lech Walesa

Boris Yeltsin

IDENTIFICATION: TERMS/CONCEPTS

State in your own words what each of the following terms means and why it is significant to a study of world history. (Terms with an asterisk are defined in the glossary.)

Berlin blockade

Berlin Wall

Mutually assured destruction (MAD)

Korean War

Containment*

Bay of Pigs

Cuban missile crisis

Sputnik

De-Stalinization

"Prague spring"

Détente*

Counterculture

*Perestroika**

*Glasnost**

STUDY QUESTIONS

1. What factors led to the division of Germany and Berlin at the end of World War II?

2. What factors led to the Korean War and how was that conflict resolved?

3. What were some of the concerns of modern feminists? In what ways did Western feminists take inspiration from other revolutionary movements?

4. How did fears of communist infiltration affect American culture in the 1950s and early 1960s?

5. What factors led to the postwar civil rights movement in the United States? How did this movement reflect global events and concerns at the same time?

6. What technological achievements can be attributed to the rivalry of the cold war?

7. How did France and Yugoslavia escape from the bipolar alliances of the cold war?

8. In what specific ways did the Chinese Communist Party mount "a frontal attack on Chinese traditions" after 1949? What aspects of Chinese society were most dramatically affected?

9. Why were the two communist giants, China and the Soviet Union, unable to sustain an alliance?

10. Compare the American defeat in Vietnam with the Soviet defeat in Afghanistan. In what ways did each conflict reflect the limits of cold war bipolarism?

11. Why did communism fail to connect with nationalism? How did this failure lead to the collapse of the Soviet empire?

12. Discuss the efforts of Mikhail Gorbachev to restructure the Soviet economy. Why did these reforms fail?

INQUIRY QUESTIONS

1. Compare the official American responses to the Hungarian revolution, the Berlin Wall, and the Cuban missile crisis. Why did the situation in Cuba provoke such a strong reaction and not the others?

2. Explain how the concept of containment shaped American foreign policy after 1945, with specific reference to Korea and Vietnam. How successful was this policy?

3. Explain the differences between American capitalism and Soviet communism in terms of the daily life, work, and choices of average citizens. How did the life of a typical Soviet citizen change between the 1920s and the 1950s? How did the life of a typical American or European citizen change in the same period?

STUDENT QUIZ

1. Ideologically, the two competing sides in the cold war were
    a. socialism and communism.
    b. communism and fascism.
    c. capitalism and communism.
    d. republican and democrat.
    e. fascism and capitalism.

2. The Berlin blockade clearly demonstrated that
    a. the Western allies were afraid of a nuclear war.
    b. the Soviet Union lacked the will to confront the West.
    c. Britain and the United States would not be intimidated into abandoning Berlin.
    d. Berlin could survive without outside support.
    e. all of the above.

3. As a result of the Korean War,
    a. the border between North and South Korea was restored at the thirty-eighth parallel.
    b. the Korean Peninsula became the site of prolonged, unresolved tensions.
    c. the United Nations sponsored military action to restore the sovereignty of South Korea.
    d. China intervened when provoked by American troops on its border.
    e. all of the above.

4. Which of the following would *not* be an example of the U.S. policy of containment?
    a. the Korean War
    b. the Berlin airlift
    c. the Vietnam War
    d. NATO
    e. the Warsaw Pact

5. The United States tentatively supported a failed invasion of Cuba at
   a. Havana.
   b. the Bay of Pigs.
   c. Hukbalahap.
   d. Sukarno.
   e. Guantánamo.

6. At the Bay of Pigs in 1961,
   a. invading anti-Castro Cuban forces were overwhelmed by Cuban troops.
   b. American special forces were defeated by Cuban troops.
   c. anti-Castro Cuban forces defeated Cuban forces on the beach but failed to spark an uprising against Castro.
   d. an American naval blockade turned back Soviet supply ships.
   e. the Soviet Union set up nuclear missiles aimed at the United States.

7. The Cuban missile crisis ended when
   a. the United States invaded Cuba and overthrew Batista.
   b. the Soviets agreed to withdraw their missiles in exchange for Kennedy's pledge not to invade Cuba and his agreement to withdraw U.S. missiles from Turkey.
   c. Khruschev agreed to end the blockade of Berlin.
   d. the United States threatened to impose a strict embargo on all Cuban exports.
   e. none of the above.

8. The expression "domestic containment" refers to
   a. the public hearings to expose spies and communists in the United States in the 1950s.
   b. strict immigration quotas imposed against people from communist countries.
   c. efforts to keep communism from taking hold in the western hemisphere.
   d. the popular retreat to the home and family to escape from the anxieties of the cold war.
   e. volunteer activities of U.S. housewives to showcase the American way of life.

9. Despite the prosperity of the postwar years, many groups expressed dissatisfaction, including
   a. middle-class housewives, who felt lonely and unfulfilled with domestic life.
   b. African-Americans, who organized to protest institutional segregation.
   c. college students, who organized to protest American involvement in Vietnam.
   d. political radicals, who expressed their unhappiness with national policies through rock and roll.
   e. all of the above.

10. The Soviet Union dominated the foreign affairs of all the following countries *except*
    a. East Germany.
    b. Czechoslovakia.
    c. Hungary.
    d. Poland.
    e. Yugoslavia.

11. The reorganization of China under communism included all of the following *except*
    a. incentives to individual farmers to increase productivity.
    b. a Five-Year Plan that emphasized heavy industry over consumer goods.
    c. collective farming to replace individual farming.
    d. full legal equality for women.
    e. health and public education provided through local collectives.

12. Tensions developed between China and the Soviet Union after
    a. the Soviets refused to buy any Chinese goods.
    b. the two countries disagreed over who should get control of Tibet.
    c. the Soviets tried to prevent the Chinese from developing nuclear weapons.
    d. the Soviets refused to support China against India and stinted China on foreign aid.
    e. all of the above.

13. President Richard Nixon sought to end the conflict in Vietnam by all the following strategies *except*
    a. heavily bombing North Vietnam.
    b. negotiating a peace settlement with the North Vietnamese.
    c. expanding the war into Cambodia and Laos, where guerillas were thought to be hiding.
    d. threatening to use nuclear weapons against the North Vietnamese.
    e. arming and training the South Vietnamese and then letting them conduct the war.

14. The Soviet Union failed to impose a communist government in Afghanistan because
    a. Islamic leaders objected to radical social reforms.
    b. the PDPA was brutal and unpopular.
    c. the Soviet people grew tired of the war after several futile years.
    d. the CIA supplied the mujahideen with arms for their resistance.
    e. all of the above.

15. Which of the following would *not* be an example of the popular youth movements of the 1960s and 1970s?
    a. antiwar protests in American universities
    b. political satire like *Dr. Strangelove*
    c. the Red Guard of the Chinese Cultural Revolution
    d. student riots in Paris
    e. the Berkeley free speech movement

16. The Watergate scandal demonstrated that
    a. the United States could not win the war in Vietnam.
    b. Richard Nixon had stolen the election of 1972.
    c. Nixon had launched unauthorized bombing of Cambodia.
    d. Nixon had supported a massive cover-up of crimes committed by his staff.
    e. all of the above.

17. Gorbachev
    a. intended from the very beginning to tear down the Soviet system.
    b. was informed by the economic reforms of Deng Xiaoping.
    c. was mainly inspired by Leonid Brezhnev.
    d. never intended to abolish the existing Soviet political and economic system.
    e. had been a capitalist reformer since his college education in London.

18. The end of communism in east and central Europe was peaceful in every state except
    a. Bulgaria.
    b. Czechoslovakia.
    c. Hungary.
    d. Poland.
    e. Romania.

19. The greatest resistance to Gorbachev's economic reforms came from
    a. party leaders who refused to relinquish control over economic planning.
    b. military leaders who feared that any changes would mean less for them.
    c. Russian consumers who feared that changes would mean more hardship for them.
    d. other communist states that counted on the economic support of the Soviet Union.
    e. Boris Yeltsin, president of the Russian Republic, fearing that Russia might lose its central position.

20. Gorbachev was rescued from an unsuccessful coup by
    a. the United States.
    b. a unified force of eastern European nations who owed their own independence to Gorbachev's reforms.
    c. British paratroopers.
    d. the French Navy.
    e. Boris Yeltsin and some loyal Red Army units.

MATCHING

Match these figures with the statements that follow.

A.	John F. Kennedy	G.	Boris Yeltsin
B.	Joseph McCarthy	H.	Martin Luther King Jr.
C.	Charles de Gaulle	I.	Marshal Tito
D.	Nikita Khrushchev	J.	Fidel Castro
E.	Mikhail Gorbachev	K.	Lech Walesa
F.	Richard Nixon	L.	Ronald Reagan

1. ___ French president who resisted U.S. hegemony and insisted that France develop its own nuclear capability.

2. ___ Leader under whom Soviet censorship eased and criticism of Stalinism was permitted but also under whom the two superpowers came perilously close to a nuclear confrontation.

3. ___ Leader whose strategy for ending the war in Vietnam was to increase aerial bombing of North Vietnam.

4. ___ President whose massive military spending ultimately contributed to the economic collapse of the Soviet Union.

5. ___ U.S. senator who led attacks on suspected American communists; his name has become synonymous with cold war paranoia.

6. ___ Revolutionary leader who overthrew a dictatorship and established a communist government in the western hemisphere.

7. ___ Soviet leader whose commitment to economic and political reform eventually led to the dissolution of the Warsaw Pact and the Soviet Union.

8. ___ Dockworker, union organizer, political dissident, and the first democratically elected president of Poland after the collapse of communism.

9. ___ American civil rights leader who adopted Gandhi's strategy of nonviolent, passive resistance to injustice.

10. ___ Leader of the only communist state in eastern Europe to escape domination by the Soviet Union.

11. ___ American president who refused to back down over the presence of nuclear warheads in Cuba until "the other guy blinked."

12. ___ President of the Russian Republic who thwarted an attempted coup by hard-line communists; the withdrawal of Russia under his leadership signaled the end of the Soviet Union.

SEQUENCING

Place the following clusters of events in chronological order. Consider carefully how one event leads to another, and try to determine the internal logic of each sequence.

A.

____ Economic recovery of western Europe

____ The construction of the Berlin Wall

____ Thousands defect from East Germany to West Germany

____ Victory in Europe

____ The Marshall Plan

B.

____ Nikita Khrushchev

____ Joseph Stalin

____ V. I. Lenin

____ Boris Yeltsin

____ Mikhail Gorbachev

C.

____ Richard Nixon

____ Ronald Reagan

____ Dwight D. Eisenhower

____ Franklin D. Roosevelt

____ John F. Kennedy

D.

____ United States sends military "advisers" to support anticommunist South Vietnamese government.

____ Vietnam is divided into north and south until elections can be held.

____ President Nixon begins bombing North Vietnam in hopes of forcing a negotiated settlement.

____ Vietnam reunites under a communist government.

____ North and South Vietnamese communists conduct a successful guerilla campaign against American forces.

____ American troops withdraw from Vietnam.

<u>QUOTATIONS</u>

For each of the following quotes, identify the speaker, if known, or the point of view. What is the significance of each passage?

1. "I have been a Marxist-Leninist all along, and will remain one until I die."

2. "In the course of the peaceful competition of the two systems capitalism has suffered a profound moral defeat in the eyes of all peoples. The common people are daily convinced that capitalism is incapable of solving a single one of the urgent problems confronting mankind. . . . Faith in the capitalist system and the capitalist path of development is dwindling. . . . We have long proposed to the capitalist world that we compete not in an arms race but in improving people's lives. We are confident that capitalism cannot stand up under that kind of competition!"

<u>MAP EXERCISES</u>

1. Consider how the borders of Germany have changed over time. Study the boundaries of the German Empire in 1871 (Map 29.4, page 809 in the textbook), at the end of World War I (Map 34.2, page 970), and finally, the partition of Germany at the end of World War II (Map 38.1, page 1066). What changes do you see to the western border between Germany and France and the eastern border between Germany and Poland?

2. Locate and label the following on the outline map on the next page:
   - Pacific Ocean, Indian Ocean, Atlantic Ocean
   - North America, South America, Africa, Asia, Europe
   - Cuba, Mexico, Guatemala, United States, Canada, USSR, China, Korea, Japan, Philippines, Indonesia, Vietnam, Pakistan, India, Iran, Iraq, Turkey, Yugoslavia
   - NATO nations and other U.S. allies; Warsaw Pact nations and other USSR allies

259

3. Consider the global alignments of the cold war as represented by Map 38.2 on page 1071. Summarize those alignments in terms of major world regions (Europe, Asia, etc). From the map, what would appear to be the global hot spots?

4. Consider the map of the former Soviet Empire after 1991 (Map 38.3, page 1089).
   - List the former Soviet republics that had become sovereign states in the 1990s.
   - Which of these new states would seem to have the most geographic advantages such as land, access, and resources?
   - Which of these new states have the least advantages?

CONNECTIONS

In fifty words or less, explain the relationship between each of the following pairs. How does one lead to or foster the other? Be specific in your response.

   - Yalta conference and the Berlin Wall
   - Truman Doctrine and the Hungarian revolution
   - NATO and the Cuban missile crisis
   - MAD and *Sputnik*
   - Domino theory and Joseph McCarthy

FILMS

Thirteen Days (2001). Date: October, 1962. Place: Kennedy White House. The tense standoff between the United States and the Soviet Union over Soviet missiles installed in Cuba is shown here through the eyes of a presidential aide, played by Kevin Costner.

The Fireman's Ball (1967). Before the "Prague Spring" was crushed by the Soviets, the Czech film industry gained international recognition. This dark comedy is a thinly veiled parody of Stalinism and petty authority in a small town. Directed by Milos Forman. In Czech with English subtitles.

The Spy Who Came in From the Cold (1965). In this gritty, unglamorous tale of cold war espionage, Richard Burton plays Alex Leamas, a British agent posing as a defector. Based on a novel by spymaster John Le Carré with an exciting climax at the Berlin Wall.

Failsafe (1965). This movie imagines what might happen if an American nuclear bomber were accidentally sent to Moscow and could not be recalled. The film reflects cold war anxieties about nuclear war and technology in general. With Henry Fonda as President.

Dr. Strangelove, or How I Learned to Stop Worrying and Love the Bomb (1964). Stanley Kubrick's brilliant satire of the insane logic of the nuclear arms race. A parody of cold war militarism and containment politics, *Dr. Strangelove* (a direct translation of the German for "Dr. Pervert") beautifully anticipates the protests of the late 1960s.

The Manchurian Candidate (1962). A veteran of the Korean War has been brainwashed by the Chinese as a political assassin; a fellow soldier suspects the truth. True to the paranoia of the cold war, people are not as they seem, and heroes cannot be trusted. With Frank Sinatra, Lawrence Harvey, and Angela Lansbury.

CHAPTER 39
THE END OF EMPIRE

INTRODUCTION

One of the most dramatic developments of the postwar era was the rapid breakup of the colonial empires that had dominated the world at the beginning of the century. Between 1945 and 1975, most of the former colonies of Africa and Asia became independent states. (Namibia was the last, in 1990). A number of forces contributed to the process of decolonialism and helped shape postcolonial societies, including

- Wars of liberation. The road to independence was sometimes amicable, as in Ghana and Morocco, but was often fiercely contested, as in Kenya and Algeria. Colonial powers fought to recover the empires that once attested to their world dominance. Concern for local settler populations also contributed to their resistance. In Vietnam the struggle for national liberation began with resistance to the Japanese during the war and continued afterward against the French.

- Cold war politics. In the global conflict between the United States and the Soviet Union (discussed in Chapter 38), new states were pressured to choose between the superpowers. Foreign aid and military support were often contingent on an alliance. Stronger nations like India presented a third alternative, nonalignment, with limited success.

- Ethnic and religious conflicts. Nationalism was a powerful force in postwar independence movements. In states where the national identity was defined by religion or ethnicity, however, this force could lead to internal and regional conflicts. The partition of India into Muslim and Hindu states did little to ease tensions in that region. The Iran-Iraq war was fueled by both religious and ethnic differences. In sub-Saharan Africa, where national boundaries bore little relation to tribal lands, each new nation was a potential hothouse for ethnic conflict.

- Fragile new democracies. Many of the new states were ill-prepared for self-government, lacking both the institutions and traditions that support democracy. In sub-Saharan Africa, democratic governments were soon taken over by military dictators, and those states often plunged into prolonged civil wars. South Africa was technically a democracy but, until 1990, only for a small white ruling class. Likewise in east Asia, new states were governed by military regimes until the late 1980s. Notable exceptions to this global retreat from democracy are Mexico and India, both relatively stable and continuous democracies.

- Creation of Israel. The creation of a new Jewish state in previously Muslim Palestine eased western guilt over the atrocities of the Second World War. The achievements of modern Israel are undeniable. Lacking significant oil or mineral resources, Israel is nonetheless the most prosperous and democratic state in the region. Unresolved tensions over the status of Muslim Palestinians and the future of the Occupied Territories continue to threaten the region and hamper efforts to find a peaceful resolution.

OUTLINE

I. Independence in Asia

    A. India's partitioned independence

        1. Indian self-rule

            a) 1930s: Great Britain grants numerous reforms in response to campaigns of Gandhi and Congress Party and Muhammad Ali Jinnah and the Muslim League

            b) Trend toward self-rule complicated by call for independent but separate Hindu and Muslim states

            c) British finally willing to consider independence after WWII

            d) Muslim separatism grew; feared domination by Hindus

            e) Muslim League called a Day of Direct Action in 1946; rioting left six thousand dead

        2. Partition of India and ensuing violence

            a) Gandhi condemned division of India as a "vivisection"

            b) Independent India, 1947, divided into Muslim Pakistan and Hindu India

            c) Ten million refugees moved to either India or Pakistan; one million died in migration

            d) Gandhi assassinated by a Hindu extremist, 30 January 1948

        3. Conflicts between India and Pakistan

            a) 1947, fought over province of Kashmir; Pakistan lost

            b) Pakistan allied with United States; India accepted aid from both superpowers

            c) India and Pakistan stayed in British Commonwealth; English was official language

        4. Nonalignment emerged as attractive alternative to a cold war alliance

            a) Indian prime minister Nehru favored policy of nonalignment, the "third path"

            b) At Bandung Conference in Indonesia, 1955, twenty-nine nonaligned nations met

            c) Movement lacked unity; many members sought aid from the United States or USSR

    B. Nationalist struggles in Vietnam

        1. Fighting the French

            a) Japan's invasion ended French rule; Ho Chi Minh declared independence

            b) France reasserted colonial rule, recaptured Saigon and south Vietnam, 1945

            c) Retook north by bombing Hanoi and Haiphong; killed at least ten thousand civilians

            d) Ho and followers (Viet Minh) conducted guerrilla warfare from the countryside e)　Aided by Communist China, Viet Minh defeated the French in 1954

　　2.　Geneva Conference and partial independence, 1954

　　　　a)　Vietnam temporarily divided, north and south, at seventeenth parallel

　　　　b)　South Vietnam's leaders delayed elections, feared communist victory

　　　　c)　United States supported first the French, then the unpopular government of South Vietnam

　　　　d)　North Vietnam received assistance from USSR and China

　　3.　Cold war stalemate

　　　　a)　Nationalist-communist (Viet Cong) attacks on government of South Vietnam

　　　　b)　President Johnson launched bombing campaign, sent ground troops in 1965

　　　　c)　U.S. troops were trapped in a quagmire; dragged on until 1973

C.　Arab national states and the problem of Palestine

　　1.　Arab states, except Palestine, gained independence after World War II

　　2.　Zionist dream of a Jewish state in Palestine

　　　　a)　Zionism affirmed by Balfour Declaration, 1917, and Paris peace talks

　　　　b)　Britain supported Zionist effort, but limited Jewish migrants to Palestine

　　3.　Conflicts between Arab Palestinians and Jewish settlers, 1920s and 1930s

　　　　a)　Arab Palestinians resisted both British rule and Jewish settlement violently

　　　　b)　Increased Jewish migration to escape Nazis; armed for self-protection

　　　　c)　Independent Arab states opposed a Jewish state

　　4.　Creation of Israel

　　　　a)　Unable to resolve conflict, Britain turned Palestine question over to UN, 1947

　　　　b)　UN proposed dividing into two states, Palestine and Israel; Arabs opposed

　　　　c)　1947, British withdrew, civil war broke out, Jews proclaimed the state of Israel

　　　　d)　Egypt, Jordan, Syria, and Iraq declared war on Israel

　　　　e)　Israel achieved victory in 1949; claimed territories larger than had been granted by UN plan

　　5.　Egypt and Arab nationalism

　　　　a)　Military leaders under Gamal A. Nasser seized power in 1952

　　　　b)　Nasser became prime minister, a leader of pan-Arab nationalism

　　　　c)　Egypt neutral in cold war, accepted aid from both powers

　　　　d)　Nasser dedicated to ending imperialism and destroying state of Israel

　　6.　Suez crisis, 1956, greatly enhanced Nasser's prestige

　　　　a)　Canal controlled by Britain; Nasser nationalized it to build Egypt's economy

b) Attacked by British, French, and Israeli forces, which retook canal

c) Both superpowers condemned military action, forced them to withdraw

d) Suez crisis divided United States and its allies in western Europe

II. Decolonization in Africa

A. Forcing the French out of north Africa

1. France in Africa

a) 1950s and 1960s, French granted independence to all its African colonies except Algeria

b) Two million French settlers in Algeria

c) Revolt of May 1954 was repressed by French; eight thousand Algerian Muslims died

2. War in Algeria, 1954–1962

a) Algerian nationalists pursued guerrilla warfare against French rule

b) By 1958, a half-million French soldiers were committed to the conflict

c) Atrocities on both sides; heavy civilian casualties; Algerian independence, 1962

3. Revolutionary writer Franz Fanon urged violence as weapon against colonial racism

B. Black African nationalism and independence

1. Growth of African nationalism

a) Began as grassroots protest against European imperialism

b) African nationalism celebrated *Négritude* (blackness), African roots

2. Obstacles to African independence

a) Imperial powers assumed Africans were not ready for self-government

b) White settlers opposed black independence

c) Anticommunist fears justified interference in African politics

d) Economic and political instability often hampered post-independent Africa

C. Freedom and conflict in sub-Sahara Africa

1. Ghana (Gold Coast) first to gain independence, 1957

a) Kwame Nkrumah, nationalist leader, jailed and censored for political actions

b) Eventually released, Nkrumah became Ghana's first president, 1957

c) Side-by-side posters presented Queen Elizabeth and Nkrumah as equals, 1961

2. Anticolonial rebellion in Kenya

a) Violent clashes between native Kikuyu (Mau Mau) and European settlers after 1947

b) 1930s and 1940s, Kikuyu pushed off farm lands, reduced to wage laborers

    c) Labeling Mau Mau as communist subversives, Britain gained U.S. support

    d) Kikuyu uprising crushed by superior arms in 1955; twelve thousand Africans killed

    e) Political parties legalized, 1959; Kenya gained independence, 1963

III. After independence: long-term struggles in the postcolonial era

  A. Communism and democracy in Asia

    1. Mao reunified China under communism

      a) Great Leap Forward (1958–1961) was an effort to catch up with industrial nations

      b) All land collectivized; farming and industry became communal

      c) Agricultural disaster; great famine followed, 1959–1962

    2. Great proletarian cultural revolution, 1966–1976

      a) To root out "revisionism," revitalize the revolutionary fervor

      b) Millions subjected to humiliation, persecution, and death

      c) Educated elites targeted; setback for Chinese education and science

      d) Died out after Mao's death in 1976

    3. Deng's revolution

      a) Deng Xiaoping regained power in 1981; opened China to foreign influence

      b) Welcomed economic, market reforms; remained politically authoritarian

      c) Crushed pro-democracy student demonstration in Tiananmen Square, 1989

      d) Hong Kong reverted to China in 1997: how to absorb democratic city into China?

    4. Stable Indian democracy was exception to Asian pattern of authoritarian rule

      a) Nehru's daughter, Indira Gandhi, was prime minister of India, 1966–1977, 1980–1984

      b) "Green revolution" dramatically increased agricultural yields

      c) Adopted harsh policy of birth control: involuntary sterilization; voted out in 1977

      d) Reelected in 1980, but faced strong opposition from religious and ethnic groups

      e) Crushed uprising of Sikhs; was assassinated by her Sikh bodyguards in 1984

      f) Her son Rajiv Gandhi was elected in 1985, but was assassinated in 1991

  B. Islamic resurgence in southwest Asia and north Africa

    1. Muslim revival and Arab disunity

      a) Cold war split Arab-Muslim world; pan-Arab unity did not materialize

      b) Israel became a staunch ally of United States; many Arab-Islamic states allied with USSR

c) Israel defeated Egypt and Syria in 1967 and in 1973

d) Egypt's president, Anwar Sadat, ended alliance with USSR in 1976

e) Sadat signed peace treaty with Israel in 1980; was assassinated, 1981

f) Palestine Liberation Organization leader Yasser Arafat and Israeli prime minister Yitzhak Rabin signed peace treaties in 1993–1995

2. Islamism: revival of Muslim traditions

a) Reasserting Islamic values in Muslim politics

b) Resentment at European and American societies

c) Extremists embraced *jihad,* or duty to defend Islam from attack; justified terrorism

3. The Iranian revolution, 1979

a) CIA helped anticommunist Shah Mohammed Pahlavi gain power, 1953

b) Repressive rule overthrown by Islamist followers of Ayatollah Khomeini, 1979

c) Khomeini attacked United States for support of the shah

d) Militants held sixty-nine Americans hostage for 444 days; shut down U.S. military bases

e) Movement encouraged other Muslims to undertake terrorist actions

4. Iran-Iraq war, 1980–1988

a) Iraqi president Saddam Hussein launched attack on Iran in 1980

b) War dragged on until 1988; killed one million soldiers

c) Next, Iraqis invaded Kuwait in 1990, inciting Gulf War, 1991

d) In wake of 11 September 2001 terrorist attacks, U.S. attacked Iraq as part of war on terror

e) Saddam Hussein captured in December 2003

C. Politics and economics in Latin America

1. Argentina: return to military rule

a) Leader of Latin American struggle against U.S. and European intervention

b) Gradual shift to free elections, but often reverted to military rulers

c) Militarist Juan Perón was elected president, 1946; immensely popular

d) His wife, Eva Perón, was national heroine for her service to the poor

e) Perón ousted in 1955; three decades of military dictators followed

f) Late 1970s, death squads conducted "dirty war" against dissidents

2. Guatemala: destabilized

a) Cold war shaped U.S. policies in Central America

    b) Guatemalan president Arbenz nationalized land held by United Fruit Co., 1953

    c) CIA engineered overthrow of Arbenz and armed Colonel Castillo Armas

    d) Castillo Armas established brutal military dictatorship; was assassinated, 1957

3. Nicaragua: American interference

    a) Somoza regime (1934–1980), brutal dictators but anticommunist U.S. ally

    b) Overthrown by Marxist Sandinistas in 1980

    c) Carter administration did not interfere, restored Panama Canal to Panama

    d) Reagan reversed policy; supported Contras, rebels opposed to the Sandinistas

    e) Costa Rican president negotiated end to Contra war, new coalition government

4. Patterns of economic dependence in Latin America

    a) Need to reorient economies from export to internal development

    b) Raul Prebisch, Argentine economist, crafted theory of "economic dependency"

        (1) developed nations controlled world economy at expense of undeveloped ones

        (2) developing nations needed to protect domestic industries

D. War and peace in sub-Saharan Africa

1. Aftermath of decolonization

    a) Organization of African Unity was created in 1963 to maintain peace

    b) Artificial boundaries imposed by colonialism were ruled inviolable

    c) Ghana and many other states became one-party dictatorships

2. Transformation of South Africa

    a) Gained independence in 1901, but denied civil rights to black population

    b) South African economy strong, both mining and industry; prospered during WWII

    c) Black workers demanded political change

3. Apartheid: harsh legal system imposed in 1948, designed to keep races separate

    a) 87 percent of South African land was for white residents, others classified by race

    b) African National Congress, led by Nelson Mandela, launched campaign to protest apartheid

    c) Severe government repression provoked international opposition after 1960

    d) Black agitation and international sanctions brought end to apartheid in 1989

    e) 1994, under new constitution, Mandela won free election as first black president

4. Democratic Republic of Congo (Zaire)

    a) First prime minister, a Marxist, killed in a CIA-backed coup, 1961

b) Dictator Mobutu ruled from 1965 to 1997; plundered Zaire's economy

c) Mobutu ruled Zaire in dictatorial fashion and amassed huge personal fortune

d) Laurent Kabila ousted Mobutu in 1997, changed country's name back to the Congo

e) Kabila killed, 2001; replaced by his son Joseph; no elections yet

5. Developing economies of Africa

a) Africa has 10 percent of world's population but less than 1 percent of industrial output

b) Rich in minerals, raw materials, agricultural resources

c) Lacking in capital, technology, foreign markets, and managerial class

d) Rapid population growth compounds problems

IDENTIFICATION: PEOPLE

What is the contribution of each of the following individuals to world history? Identification should include answers to the questions *who, what, where, when, how,* and *why is this person important?*

Jawaharlal Nehru

Ho Chi Minh

Gamal Abdel Nasser

Kwame Nkrumah

Jomo Kenyatta

Deng Xiaoping

Indira Gandhi

Anwar Sadat

Yasser Arafat

Ayatollah Khomeini

Saddam Hussein

Juan Perón

Jimmy Carter

Nelson Mandela

IDENTIFICATION: TERMS/CONCEPTS

State in your own words what each of the following terms means and why it is significant to a study of world history. (Terms with an asterisk are defined in the glossary.)

Decolonization*

Bandung Conference

Balfour Declaration

Suez crisis

Kikuyu

Great Leap Forward

Cultural Revolution

Tiananmen Square

Palestine Liberation Organization (PLO)*

Islamism

Jihad

Iran-Iraq war

Institutional Revolutionary Party (PRI)

Sandinistas

Liberation theology

Dependency theory

Organization of African Unity (OAU)*

Apartheid*

African National Congress (ANC)

STUDY QUESTIONS

1. What factors led to the partition of India? What kinds of states emerged?

2. What were the goals of the nonaligned movement? How successful was this effort? What were some of the obstacles to nonalignment?

3. Trace the Arab-Israeli conflict from 1947 to 1980. Why has this conflict been so difficult to resolve?

4. What factors have tended to unite the Arab nations since independence? What factors have divided them?

5. Compare the process of independence for both Ghana and Kenya. What factors might account for the differences?

6. What steps did the Chinese Communist Party take to transform the economy of China after the revolution? What were the results of these measures?

7. What have been the greatest challenges confronting the new Indian democracy after independence in 1947? How has India managed to survive as a democracy while other nations of east Asia have not?

8. What are the goals and concerns of the modern Islamist movement? What specific policies and actions have emerged from this movement?

9. Compare the recent political history of Mexico and Argentina. What factors might account for the differences?

10. What factors led the Reagan administration to support the Contra rebels of Nicaragua? What was the outcome of this policy?

11. What kind of society emerged in South Africa under apartheid? What factors led to the end of apartheid?

INQUIRY QUESTIONS

1. Would the Vietnam War be more accurately described as a cold war engagement or a struggle against colonialism? What facts would argue for each description?

2. Why did the French fight so tenaciously to hold on to Vietnam and Algeria, when other French colonies gained their independence with relative ease? What did these struggles cost France?

3. How did the logic of the cold war shape American foreign policy in Central America? What kinds of regimes were supported because of this policy? With what results?

1. Mohandas Gandhi was assassinated by a
    a. Muslim extremist.
    b. Hindu extremist.
    c. British nationalist.
    d. disgruntled follower.
    e. Brahmin.

2. Gandhi and Nehru opposed the partition of India because
    a. it would leave Hindu India surrounded by Muslim states.
    b. it would deprive India of some of its most valuable land.
    c. they mistrusted Muhammad Ali and the Muslim League.
    d. they believed that India could be a successful multicultural state.
    e. all of the above.

3. In 1947, India and Pakistan went to war over
    a. Bangladesh.
    b. Bengal.
    c. Kashmir.
    d. the Punjab.
    e. the Indus River Valley.

4. The nonalignment movement remained weak because
    a. of a lack of vision or leadership among member states.
    b. too few states attended the Bandung Conference to achieve consensus.
    c. many nonaligned states needed and accepted aid from either the United States or Soviet Union.
    d. many new states were afraid to alienate the United States.
    e. all of the above.

5. A Geneva peace conference regarding Vietnam in 1954
    a. followed the defeat of France at Dienbienphu.
    b. determined that Vietnam would be temporarily divided at the seventeenth parallel.
    c. determined that Ho Chi Minh and the communists would have control of North Vietnam.
    d. determined that democratic elections would be held as soon as possible.
    e. all of the above.

6. The Balfour Declaration of 1917 promised that Palestine would
    a. become a homeland for immigrant Jews.
    b. continue as a homeland to the resident Arab Muslims.
    c. remain a British protectorate indefinitely.
    d. be partitioned into distinct Arab and Jewish zones.
    e. have elections to determine its future.

7. Britain withdrew from Palestine in 1947 because
    a. its mandate had ended.
    b. it could not resolve the conflict between Palestinians and Jews.
    c. the United Nations demanded that it leave.
    d. the Arab states demanded that it leave.
    e. all of the above.

8. Israel has fought and defeated all of the following neighboring states *except*
   a. Egypt.
   b. Iraq.
   c. Jordan.
   d. Syria.
   e. Israel has defeated all of the above.

9. Egyptian president Gamel Abdel Nasser gained great international prestige when he
   a. negotiated a peace settlement with Israel.
   b. succeeded in retaking the Suez Canal from the British.
   c. aligned Egypt with the United States.
   d. aligned Egypt with the Soviet Union.
   e. reclaimed the Sinai Peninsula from Israel.

10. The French fought to retain Algeria because
    a. they refused to be intimidated by terrorists.
    b. Algeria provided valuable mineral resources.
    c. there were two million French settlers in Algeria.
    d. President Charles de Gaulle had dreams of a restored French empire.
    e. all of the above.

11. In *The Wretched of the Earth,* Franz Fanon
    a. suggested that the suffering of the Africans was a result of their own sin.
    b. detailed the horrible conditions in Indian cities.
    c. stated that France was meant to rule over Africa because of the civilizing role of the Europeans.
    d. passionately defended the United States as the only country powerful enough to end world hunger.
    e. urged the use of violence against colonial oppressors.

12. Conflicts between native Kikuyu and British settlers intensified in Kenya after World War II because
    a. white settlers had seized the best farmlands for years.
    b. Kikuyu had been crowded onto tribal reserves.
    c. Kikuyu had been reduced to the status of wage laborers.
    d. all of the above.
    e. none of the above.

13. As a result of the Cultural Revolution in China,
    a. the educated elite were persecuted, and China was deprived of their talent.
    b. peasant farmers killed so many sparrows that the ecological balance was thrown off.
    c. student demonstrators in Tiananmen Square were crushed by government troops.
    d. the nation achieved industrialization within a generation.
    e. the Red Guard was discredited.

14. Den Xiaoping
    a. masterminded the Great Leap Forward.
    b. was the driving force behind the Great Proletarian Cultural Revolution.
    c. was the leader of Taiwan who helped bring about tremendous economic expansion.
    d. fled to Taiwan after the Chinese Civil War.
    e. brought free market reforms to China.

15. Indian Prime Minister Indira Gandhi was assassinated because she
    a. pursued aggressive birth control policies.
    b. permitted an attack on Sikh extremists at the sacred Golden Temple.
    c. refused to consider the partition of Kashmir.
    d. insisted that untouchables be fully integrated into Indian society.
    e. suspended the constitution for two years and ruled without being elected.

16. Which of the following is *not* a reason that Arab nationalism failed to materialize?
    a. Some Arabs are Shia and some Sunni Muslims.
    b. Some Arab states aligned with the United States and some with the Soviet Union.
    c. They did not all agree on the status of Israel.
    d. They did not share a common language and culture.
    e. all the above *were* reasons for the failure of Arab nationalism.

17. The regime of the Iranian Shah Mohammed Reza Pahlazi was overthrown because
    a. he alienated conservative Shia Muslims with his secular reforms.
    b. his repressive policies alienated leftist politicians.
    c. he allowed U.S. corporations to heavily influence the economy.
    d. all of the above.
    e. both a and b.

18. Argentina in the late 1970s and early 1980s
    a. moved steadily toward a multiparty system.
    b. was ruled by military dictators who caused the "disappearance" of thousands.
    c. experimented briefly with a communist system.
    d. was invaded and briefly ruled by a Chilean puppet dictator.
    e. became a puppet state of the United States.

19. In both Guatemala and Nicaragua in the 1950s and 1960s,
    a. American aid resulted in widespread popular support for the United States.
    b. the United States supported liberal revolutions against military dictatorships.
    c. the United States supported military dictatorships that were anticommunist.
    d. the United States insisted on human rights as a precondition for aid.
    e. the United States conducted an anti-drug war.

20. Apartheid ended in South Africa because
    a. the Sharpeville massacre instituted a new era of radical activism against it.
    b. the international community imposed economic sanctions against South Africa.
    c. President de Klerk convinced his party to dismantle the system and hold free elections.
    d. the African National Congress provided a vehicle for resistance.
    e. all of the above.

MATCHING

Match these figures with the statements that follow.

A. Kwame Nkrumah   H. Jomo Kenyatta
B. Deng Xiaoping   I. Indira Gandhi
C. Anwar Sadat   J. Yasser Arafat
D. Jawaharlal Nehru   K. Jimmy Carter
E. Ayatollah Khomeini   L. Saddam Hussein
F. Juan Perón   M. Nelson Mandela
G. Gamal Abdel Nasser N. Ho Chi Minh

1. ___ Military dictator of Iraq, a frequent aggressor in the region.

2. ___ Nationalist president of Argentina who had tremendous popular support.

3. ___ U.S. president who made foreign aid contingent on respect for human rights.

4. ___ Leader of the African National Congress and the first black president of South Africa.

5. ___ Communist leader who opened China up to foreign trade.

6. ___ The first president of independent India and a leader in the nonalignment movement.

7. ___ Leader of the Palestine Liberation Organization 1964–2004.

8. ___ Leader of the Vietnamese communists in their guerilla campaigns against first the Japanese, then the French, and finally the Americans.

9. ___ First president of independent Kenya.

10. ___ Military dictator of Egypt in the 1950s who gained tremendous support in the Arab world by asserting Egypt's right to the Suez Canal.

11. ___ Indian president who was widely criticized both for her aggressive birth control policies and for her harsh treatment of Sikh extremists.

12. ___ First president of independent Ghana and a voice for African unity.

13. ___ Militant Islamic cleric who denounced the United States as the "Great Satan" and encouraged his countrymen to seize American property and hold American embassy workers hostage.

14. ___ Egyptian president who shifted from aggression toward Israel to a peace settlement.

SEQUENCING

Place the following clusters of events in chronological order. Consider carefully how one event leads to another, and try to determine the internal logic of each sequence.

A.

_____ The Great Leap Forward

_____ Pro-democracy movement is crushed in Tiananmen Square

_____ The Communists seize control of China

_____ Mao Zedong dies

_____ The Cultural Revolution

_____ Economic reforms take place in China

B.

_____ Assassination of Yitzhak Rabin

_____ British withdrawal from Palestine, which leads to civil war

_____ The Balfour Declaration

_____ Proclamation of the independent state of Israel

_____ The 1967 Arab-Israeli War

C.

_____ The people of Iran overthrow the shah and establish an Islamist state under the direction of the Ayatollah Khomeini.

_____ With help from the CIA, the Shah Mohammed Reza Pahlavi seizes power in Iran.

_____ His secular reforms and repressive military rule alienate much of the conservative Shiite Muslim population.

_____ After the shah seeks refuge in the United States, Iranian militants seize the U.S. embassy and hold all personnel hostage for 444 days.

_____ Under the shah's rule, Iran provides cheap oil to the United States and serves as a strong anticommunist ally in the Middle East.

QUOTATIONS

For each of the following quotes, identify the speaker, if known, or the point of view. What is the significance of each passage?

1. "If I am to die by the bullet of a mad man, I must do so smiling. There must be no anger within me. God must be in my heart and on my lips."

2. "The greatest contribution that Africa can make to the peace of the world is to avoid all the dangers inherent in its success, by creating a political union which will also by its success, stand as an example to a divided world. . . . [A union of African states] will command respect from a world that has regard only for size and influence."

3. "Nonalignment does not mean passivity of mind or action, lack of faith or conviction. It does not mean submission to what we consider evil. . . . We believe that each country has not only the right to freedom, but also to decide its own policy and way of life."

4. "His Majesty's Government view with favour the establishment in Palestine of a national home for the Jewish people, and will use their best endeavours to facilitate the achievement of this object, it being clearly understood that nothing shall be done which may prejudice the civil and religious rights of existing non-Jewish communities in Palestine."

5. "The Hindus and Muslims belong to two different religious philosophies, social customs, literatures. They neither intermarry nor interdine together and, indeed, they belong to two different civilizations which are based mainly on conflicting ideas and conceptions. Their aspects of life and of life are different. . . . Muslim India cannot accept any constitution which must necessarily result in a Hindu majority government."

6. "I have cherished the ideal of a democratic and free society in which all persons live together in harmony and with equal opportunities. It is an ideal which I hope to live for and to achieve. But if needs be, it is an ideal for which I am prepared to die."

MAP EXERCISES

1. On the outline map of Asia, locate and label the following states:

    • Australia, Bangladesh, Brunei, Cambodia, India, Indonesia, Japan, Laos, Kazakhstan,
      Kyrgyzstan, Malaysia, Myanmar (Burma), North Korea, Pakistan, Philippines, Russia,
      Singapore, South Korea, Sri Lanka, Tajikistan, Thailand, Vietnam
    • Note the date of independence for each of these states.
    • Which colonial empire was the first to grant independence to its Asian colonies? Which
      was the last? What factors might account for these differences?

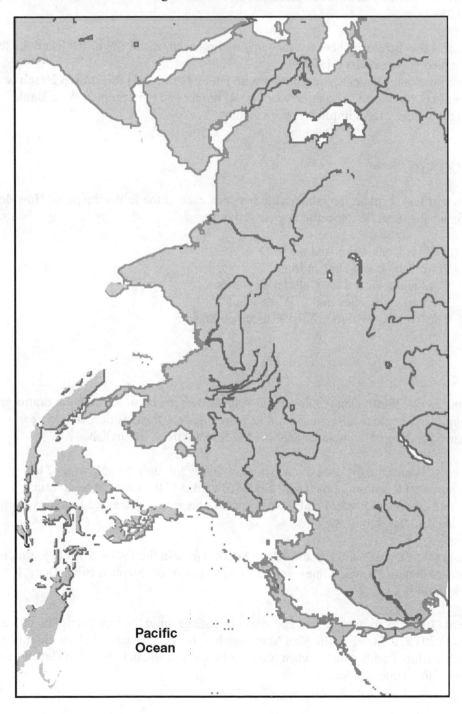

2. Consider the map of the decolonization of Africa (Map 39.3, page 1110).

   - How many countries were formed from the former colonies of French West Africa and French Equatorial Africa? (See Map 33.2 on page 923 for the boundaries of those colonies.)
   - Which colonial empire was the first to grant independence to its African colonies? Which was the last? What factors might account for these differences?
   - Why was 1960 known as "the year of Africa"?

3. Note how the territory claimed by Israel has shifted between 1947 and the present (Map 39.2, page 1105).

   - What is the difference between the territory proposed by the UN in 1947 and the territory occupied by Israel since 1973?
   - Note how many states share a border with Israel. How might this impact Israeli security?
   - Note in particular the border between Israel proper and the occupied West Bank. What are the security risks implicit in such a border?

CONNECTIONS

In fifty words or less, explain the relationship between each of the following pairs. How does one lead to or foster the other? Be specific in your response.

   - Balfour Declaration and the PLO
   - Franz Fanon and Ho Chi Minh
   - Confucianism and the Cultural Revolution
   - Mikhail Gorbachev and F. W. de Klerk
   - The "velvet revolution" and Tiananmen Square

FILMS

Boesnam and Lena (2000). Danny Glover and Angela Bassett star in this moving drama about a couple's struggle to survive and not let hatred destroy them as they live a life of constant turmoil and oppression under apartheid in South Africa. In English.

To Live (1994). Traces the fortunes of one Chinese family through the upheaval of the Communist Revolution, the Great Leap Forward, and the Cultural Revolution. Beautifully photographed and superbly acted, this film was banned for many years in China. English subtitles.

Cry Freedom (1987). Against the upheavals in South Africa in the 1960s, a white journalist, Donald Woods (Kevin Kline), befriends a black activist, Stephen Biko (Denzel Washington).

Kitchen Toto (1987). A moving drama about coming of age amid the racial tensions in Kenya in the 1950s at the time of the Mau Mau uprising. A twelve-year-old black child is placed with a white family as a "kitchen toto," or houseboy, and befriends the eleven-year-old son of the white policeman.

The Year of Living Dangerously (1983). In Indonesia in 1965, the democratically elected government of President Sukarno was overthrown by General Suharto, who accused him of being pro-communist. A young Australian journalist (Mel Gibson) is witness to these events; his guide to the harsh realities of Indonesia is Billy Kwan (Linda Hunt in an Oscar-winning role). This excellent film was banned in Indonesia until 2000.

Battle of Algiers (1966). Fictionalized account of the struggle for Algerian independence, shot in a black-and-white documentary style and featuring many veterans of that struggle as actors. As the war grinds on, there are few heroes and many atrocities on both sides. In French with English subtitles.

CHAPTER 40
A WORLD WITHOUT BORDERS

INTRODUCTION

Globalization is the unifying concept of this last chapter. The image of a world without borders suggests a world in which economies, technologies, ideas, and cultures are all interconnected. Through mass media, mass production, and mass transportation, the world has become smaller and more integrated. For many societies this process has significantly improved standards of living. In other societies the results have been more mixed. Aspects of the process of globalization include:

- Global institutions. The world is increasingly shaped by multinational agencies and organizations. Global corporations operate apart from the restrictions imposed by any one government or legal system. Nongovernmental organizations (NGOs) try to address international problems without binding themselves to the policies of any single country.

- Global economy. Since World War II, the industrial nations have tried to eliminate barriers to free trade, such as protective tariffs and import duties. Many nations have formed trade associations, such as the EU, NAFTA, and ASEAN, which grant special trading privileges to member states. Free trade favors those states with the cheapest manufactured goods and often undermines indigenous handicrafts.

- Global culture. The products of the global economy have come to dominate consumer tastes all over the world. Consumers increasingly define themselves with reference to brand names and current fashions. The global culture is enhanced through the instant access of telecommunications and the Internet.

- Global migrations. The global economy seeks out the cheapest labor and resources, and as a result, millions of workers have relocated to new industrial centers seeking opportunities. Problems of rapid urbanization and environmental degradation often result. Some migrants have been the unwilling victims of trafficking and even slavery.

- Global inequities. The global economy favors nations with capital and highly developed economies. Those nations that are economically dependent find it difficult to break out of that role, although the Little Tigers of Asia demonstrate that this is possible. New technologies create a "computer divide" between the wealthy and the poorer nations.

- Resistance to globalization. Such dramatic changes have met with resistance from many quarters. Many cultures perceive a threat to their traditions and values. Islamic countries in particular have resisted the sexualized images of Western pop culture.

I. The global economy

   A. Economic globalization

      1. Global economy evident after collapse of communism

         a) Expanding trade, foreign investments, privatization of industry

         b) Free trade: free of state-imposed restrictions

      2. General Agreement on Tariffs and Trade (GATT)

         a) Formed in 1947 as vehicle to promote free trade

         b) In 1994, 123 GATT members created Word Trade Organization (WTO)

         c) Dramatic growth in world trade, 1966–1990

      3. Global corporations are symbols of the new economy

         a) Multinational businesses operate apart from laws and restrictions of any one nation

         b) Seek cheapest labor and resources; prefer lax environmental laws

         c) Pay less in taxes in developed world than formerly

   B. Economic growth in Asia

      1. Japan's "economic miracle"

         a) Postwar Japan had few resources, no overseas empire

         b) Benefited from U.S. aid, investments, and protection

         c) Japan pursued export-oriented growth supported by low wages

         d) Began with labor-intensive exports, textiles, iron, and steel

         e) Reinvested profits in capital-intensive and technology-intensive production

         f) Rapid growth, 1960s–1980s; suffered recession in 1990s

      2. The Little Tigers: Hong Kong, Singapore, South Korea, and Taiwan

         a) Followed Japanese model of export-driven industry; rapid growth in 1980s

         b) By 1990s highly competitive; joined by Indonesia, Thailand, and Malaysia

      3. The rise of China since the death of Mao Zedong

         a) Late 1970s opened China to foreign investment and technology

         b) Gradual shift from planned communist economy to market economy

         c) Offered vast, cheap labor and huge domestic markets

         d) China joined WTO in 2001

      4. Perils of the new economy: vulnerable to global forces

         a) Investors withdrew support from Thailand in 1997

         b) Ripple effect: contraction of other Asian economies

C. Trading blocs

   1. The European Union

      a) Begun in 1957 with six nations, now includes fifteen

      b) A common market, free trade, free travel within the Union

      c) Eleven members adopted a common currency, the Euro, in 1999

      d) Expectations of a European political union eventually

   2. Organization of Petroleum Exporting Countries (OPEC)

      a) Cartel established in 1960 to raise global oil prices

      b) After Arab-Israeli war of 1973, OPEC placed embargo on oil to United States, Israel's ally

      c) Price of oil quadrupled from 1973 to 1975, triggered global recession

      d) Overproduction and dissension among members diminished influence, 1990s

   3. Regional trade associations formed to establish free-trade zones for member states

      a) Association of Southeast Asian Nations (ASEAN) in 1967, five members

      b) North American Free Trade Agreement (NAFTA) in 1993: United States, Canada, Mexico

   4. Critiques of globalization

      a) To supporters, global economy efficient, best path to global prosperity

      b) To critics, widens gap between rich and poor, destroys environment, threatens local and traditional crafts and economies

II. Cross-cultural exchanges and global communication

   A. Global Barbie

      1. Western consumerism becoming a global phenomenon

      2. Sara versus Barbie in Iran

         a) Barbie seen as a threat to Islamic values, symbol of cultural imperialism

         b) Iranian dolls, Sara and her brother Dara (an Islamic cleric), are modest alternatives

      3. Barbie in Japan

         a) Image of Barbie unsettling, Mattel created a younger doll for Japanese market

         b) Whereas Iranians reject image of Barbie, Japanese adjust Barbie to their aesthetic

   B. Consumption and cultural interaction

      1. Global culture of consumption

         a) Satisfies wants and desires rather than needs or necessities

         b) Homogenization of global culture: blue jeans, Coca-Cola, McDonalds

      c)   Western icons often replace local businesses and indigenous cultures

      d)   Brand names also identify local products, for example, Swiss Rolex, Perrier, Armani

  2. Pan-American culture competes with United States

      a)   Eva Perón (Evita) and Ché have become pop icons in Argentina and beyond

      b)   Latin American societies blended foreign and indigenous cultural practices

C. The age of access

  1. Globalization minimizes social, economic, and political isolation

  2. Preeminence of English language

      a)   Critics: mass media become a vehicle of cultural imperialism

      b)   Internet is an information colony, with English hegemony

      c)   China attempts a firewall to control Internet information

  3. Adaptations of technology in authoritarian states

      a)   Zaire television showed dictator Mobutu Sese Seko walking on clouds

      b)   Vietnam and Iraq limit access to foreign servers on Internet

III. Global problems

A. Population pressures and environmental degradation

  1. Dramatic population increases in twentieth century

      a)   Population increased from 500 million in 1650 to 2.5 billion in 1950

      b)   Asia and Africa experienced population explosion after WWII

      c)   5.5 billion people in 1994; perhaps 11.6 billion people in 2200

      d)   So far, food production has kept pace with population growth

      e)   Fertility rates have been falling for past twenty years

  2. The planet's carrying capacity: how many people can the earth support?

      a)   Scientists and citizens concerned about physical limits of the earth

      b)   Club of Rome issued "The Limits to Growth" in 1972

      c)   Dire predictions not borne out by facts: prices have fallen, food has increased

  3. Environmental impact

      a)   Urbanization and agricultural expansion threaten biodiversity

      b)   Gas emissions, coal burning contribute to global warming

      c)   In 1997 at Kyoto, 159 states met to cut carbon dioxide emissions, U.S. opts out

  4. Population control: a highly politicized issue

      a)   Some developing nations charge racism when urged to limit population

      b)   UN agencies have aided many countries with family-planning programs

     c) China's one-child policy has significantly reduced growth rate

     d) Other cultures still favor larger families, for example, India

B. Economic inequities and labor servitude

  1. Causes of poverty

     a) Inequities in resources and income separate rich and poor societies

     b) Attendant problems: malnutrition, environmental degradation

     c) Legacy of colonialism: economic dependence

  2. Labor servitude increasing

     a) Slavery abolished worldwide by 1960s

     b) Millions still forced into bonded labor

     c) Child-labor servitude common in south and southeast Asia

  3. Trafficking of persons across international boundaries widespread

     a) Victims, mostly girls and women, lured with promises of work

     b) Often in sex industry; hugely profitable though criminal

C. Global diseases

  1. Many epidemics now under control

     a) Last major pandemic (1918–1919): flu epidemic that killed twenty to forty million

     b) Smallpox and diptheria eradicated

  2. HIV/AIDS identified in 1981 in San Francisco

     a) In 2000, 36.1 million people living with HIV/AIDS worldwide, 21.8 million in Africa

     b) Kills adults in prime; many children in Africa orphaned

     c) Threatens social and economic basis of African societies

     d) Many cannot afford treatment

D. Global terrorism

  1. The weapon of those out of power, of anticolonial and revolutionary movements

  2. Difficult to define terrorism

     a) Deliberate violence against civilians to advance political or ideological cause

     b) Rarely successful; often discredits potentially worthy causes

  3. 11 September 2001 focused international attention on terrorism

     a) Coordinated attack on World Trade Tower and Pentagon

     b) Source identified as Islamic militant Osama bin Laden and al-Qaeda network

     c) Angered by U.S. presence in Saudi Arabia; proclaimed *jihad,* holy war

4. Islamic State of Afghanistan was established 1996 by Taliban

   a) Imposed strict Islamic law: regulated dress, entertainment, media

   b) Women barred from education, work, health services

   c) November 2001, U.S. forces invaded Afghanistan, drove out Taliban, al-Qaeda

   d) Bush Doctrine of Deterrence: in March 2003 U.S. invaded Iraq

   e) Saddam Hussein captured in December 2003

E. Coping with global problems: international organizations

   1. Many global problems cannot be solved by national governments

   2. Nongovernmental organizations (NGOs)

      a) Red Cross, an international humanitarian agency, founded 1864

      b) Greenpeace, an environmental organization, founded in 1970

   3. The United Nations, founded in 1945 "to maintain international peace and security"

      a) Not successful at preventing wars, for example, Iran-Iraq war

      b) Cannot legislate, but has influence in international community

      c) More successful in health and educational goals: eradication of smallpox, decrease in child mortality, increase in female literacy

   4. Human rights: an ancient concept, gaining wider acceptance

      a) Nuremberg trials of Nazis established concept of "crimes against humanity"

      b) UN Universal Declaration of Human Rights: forbids slavery, torture, discrimination

      c) NGOs such as Amnesty International and Human Rights Watch

IV. Crossing boundaries

A. Women's traditions and feminist challenges

   1. Feminism and equal rights

      a) Status of women changed dramatically after WWII in industrialized states

      b) Women demanded full equality with men, access to education and employment

      c) Birth control enables women to control their bodies and avoid "biological destiny"

      d) U.S. Civil Rights Act of 1964 forbids discrimination on basis of race or sex

   2. Gender equality in China

      a) Communist states often improved women's legal status

      b) Despite legal reforms, China's women have not yet gained true equality

      c) One-child policy encourages infanticide or abandonment of baby girls

   3. Domesticity and abuse restricting rights of women in developing world

a) Women in Arab and Muslim societies twice as likely as men to be illiterate

b) Most Indian women illiterate (75 percent in 1980s) and confined at home

c) "Dowry deaths" common in India; burning of wives in Pakistan

4. Women leaders in south Asia

a) Effective political leaders: Indira Gandhi (India) and Benazir Bhutto (Pakistan)

b) Chandrika Bandaranaike Kumaratunga became president of Sri Lanka, 1994

c) Democratic activist Aung Sang Suu Kyi received Nobel Peace Prize in 1991 when under house arrest in Myanmar

d) UN launched a Decade for Women program in 1975

B. Migration

1. Internal migration: tremendous flow from rural to urban settings

a) Part of process of industrialization; in Western societies, 75 percent of population is urban

b) Urbanization a difficult transition for rural people

c) Crowded in slums (barrios) at the edge of cities; strain urban services

2. External migration: fleeing war, persecution, seeking opportunities

a) Thirteen million "guest workers" migrated to western Europe since 1960

b) Ten million migrants (mostly Mexican) migrated to United States since 1960

c) In oil-producing countries, foreigners make up half of working population

d) About 130 million people currently live outside their countries of citizenship

3. Migrant communities within host societies

a) Migrants enrich societies in many ways, but also spark hostility and conflict

b) Fears that migrants will undermine national identity, compete for jobs

c) Anti-immigrant movements (xenophobia) lead to violence and racial tension

C. Cross-cultural travelers

1. Mass tourism possible with more leisure and faster travel

a) First travel agencies: Thomas Cook and Karl Baedeker in nineteenth century

b) In 1800s, tourism fashionable for rich Europeans; adopted by working people later

c) By the twentieth century, leisure travel another form of consumption

d) After WWII, packaged tours took millions of tourists across the world

2. Effects of mass tourism

a) Now travel and tourism is the largest single industry on the planet

b) Low-paying jobs; profits go mostly to developed world

    c)   Tourism exposes cultural variations and diversity of local traditions

    d)   Tourism leads to revival and transformation of indigenous cultural traditions

IDENTIFICATION: PEOPLE

What is the contribution of each of the following individuals to world history? Identification should include answers to the questions *who, what, where, when, how,* and *why is this person important?*

Rachel Carson

Osama bin Laden

Aung Sang Suu Kyi

IDENTIFICATION: TERMS/CONCEPTS

State in your own words what each of the following means and why it is significant to a study of world history. (Terms with an asterisk are defined in the glossary.)

Globalization*

Free trade

General Agreement on Tariffs and Trade (GATT)*

World Trade Organization (WTO)*

Little Tigers

European Union (EU)

Organization of Petroleum Exporting Countries (OPEC)*

Association of Southeast Asian Nations (ASEAN)*

North American Free Trade Agreement (NAFTA)*

HIV/AIDS

Al-Qaeda

Taliban*

Red Cross

Greenpeace*

Nuremberg Trials

STUDY QUESTIONS

1. What are some of the characteristics of global corporations? What are the advantages and disadvantages of corporations that can operate without any national regulation?

2. What factors account for the postwar Japanese "economic miracle"? What factors led to a recession in Japan in the 1990s?

3. The Little Tigers of Asia have been able to escape the cycle of economic colonialism that has haunted so many former colonies. What factors account for this reversal?

4. What factors led to the oil embargo of 1973–1975? What were the results?

5. Discuss the concept of consumption as a form of self-expression. Give some specific examples from your own experience.

6. Summarize the critique of global consumerism using Barbie, Sara, and Licca to illustrate your answer.

7. What are the challenges of combating HIV/AIDS in Africa? What has been the impact on African societies?

8. What events led to the invasion of Afghanistan by the United States and the Northern Alliance in 2001?

9. What are some of the significant nongovernmental organizations (NGOs) operating in the world since WWII? What causes do these groups address?

10. What have been the principal causes of mass migration since World War II? What are some of the challenges presented by these migrations to host countries?

INQUIRY QUESTIONS

1. Why has it been so difficult to define terrorism? In what ways might modern terrorism be considered an aspect of globalization?

2. What have been the significant successes and disappointments of the United Nations since its founding in 1945? Why has the UN been more effective in addressing issues of health and human rights than in maintaining international peace and security?

3. Compare the goals of Western feminists with the goals of women in Asia and Muslim countries. To what extent does culture shape the goals of feminist leaders?

STUDENT QUIZ

1. The purpose of the General Agreement on Tariffs and Trade (GATT) was to
   a. funnel U.S. economic aid to NATO allies.
   b. attract emerging economies into trade alliances with the United States.
   c. eliminate barriers to free trade.
   d. regulate currency rates.
   e. set fair labor standards for the industrialized nations.

2. Which of the following is *not* a characteristic of modern global corporations?
   a. Global corporations seek out the cheapest labor and raw materials.
   b. Global corporations have helped provide more money for social services and welfare programs.
   c. Global corporations prefer locations with few, if any, environmental laws.
   d. Global corporations favor unrestricted free trade.
   e. Global corporations scatter operations all over the world.

3. Which of the following was *not* a factor in the Japanese postwar "economic miracle"?
   a. Massive aid from the United States enabled Japan to rebuild quickly after the war.
   b. Japanese products were not barred from the U.S. market.
   c. Restrictions imposed on the Japanese defense spending enabled them to channel much of their GNP into economic development.
   d. Abundant reserves of oil and gas fueled postwar industrialization.
   e. Cheap labor costs and a compliant workforce made Japanese industry very competitive.

4. Which of the following is not one of Asia's Little Tigers?
   a. Hong Kong
   b. Singapore
   c. South Korea
   d. Taiwan
   e. Vietnam

5. All of the following have contributed to the dramatic growth of the Chinese economy since the late 1970s *except*
   a. more efficient long-term economic forecasting by the Communist Party leadership.
   b. opening China to foreign investment and foreign technology.
   c. opening Chinese domestic markets to foreign imports.
   d. vast reserves of cheap labor.
   e. All of the above contributed to the growth of the Chinese economy.

6. In the 1970s OPEC demonstrated that
   a. the only way to defeat Israel was for all Arab states to work together.
   b. an alliance in control of a valuable resource could exert control over the global economy.
   c. Western powers could no longer dominate the Suez Canal.
   d. overproduction of petroleum products can cause a slump in global prices.
   e. all of the above.

7. One objective that the EU, ASEAN, and NAFTA all share in common is a commitment to
    a. human rights and environmental regulations.
    b. democratic governments.
    c. removing political barriers between member states.
    d. removing barriers to trade between member states.
    e. All of the above are common objectives to these associations.

8. Which of the following is *not* a good example of the Americanization of global culture?
    a. Barbie
    b. Coca-Cola
    c. McDonalds
    d. Rolex watches
    e. Pepsi

9. Which of the following statements is *not* true of modern global consumption?
    a. Consumption becomes a means of self-expression as well as a source of personal identity.
    b. Modern consumption is shaped by wants and desires rather than by needs or necessities.
    c. Global consumption is entirely one way: the tastes of the United States are imposed on the rest of the world.
    d. Where products scarcely vary from one another, consumers are encouraged to make purchases based on brand names.
    e. Global consumerism threatens local and indigenous cultures.

10. One significant result of the electronic information age is that
    a. English has become the primary language of global communications.
    b. social and political isolation has been vastly reduced.
    c. politically repressive regimes such as China are trying to control the Internet.
    d. the gulf between the technological haves and have-nots has widened.
    e. all of the above.

11. Between 2000 and 2050 the population is expected to continue growing in all of the following world regions *except*
    a. Africa.
    b. Asia.
    c. Europe.
    d. North America.
    e. Latin America.

12. The author of *Silent Spring* was
    a. Daw Aung San Suu Kyi.
    b. Benazir Bhuto.
    c. Betty Friedan.
    d. Simone de Beauvoir.
    e. Rachel Carson.

13. Global warming refers to
    a. natural variations in the global climate over time.
    b. the rise in global temperatures caused by atmospheric pollution such as the emissions of cars and factories.
    c. the risk of a nuclear war when the planet is politically "hot."
    d. the increase in temperature caused by volcanic activity on the ocean floors.
    e. none of the above.

14. The AIDS epidemic in sub-Saharan Africa means that
    a. millions of children have been orphaned.
    b. life expectancy is expected to drop from 59 to 45 years.
    c. the most productive members of African society have been struck down with the disease.
    d. limited resources have been exhausted trying to cope with the epidemic.
    e. all of the above.

15. Which of the following statements is *not* true of modern terrorism?
    a. Modern terrorists routinely employ violence against civilian targets.
    b. Modern terrorists use sophisticated modern weapons and technologies.
    c. Modern terrorists are not confined to any one state and operate effectively across borders.
    d. Modern terrorists have been largely successful in achieving their political objectives.
    e. All of the above statements about terrorism are true.

16. The perceived grievances of al-Qaeda against the United States and its allies include all of the following *except*
    a. U.S. support of the Israeli occupation of Palestinian lands.
    b. the presence of American troops in the holy land of Saudi Arabia.
    c. U.S. failure to support the *mujahideen* in their war against the Soviet Union.
    d. U.S. sanctions against Iraq.
    e. All of the above are grievances of al-Qaeda.

17. Which of the following would *not* be a good example of an NGO?
    a. Amnesty International
    b. Greenpeace
    c. Human Rights Watch
    d. the Red Cross
    e. the United Nations

18. The goals of feminism in industrialized nations after WWII include all the following *except*
    a. women's suffrage.
    b. equal pay for equal work.
    c. access to birth control and abortion.
    d. legal equality.
    e. All of the above are postwar goals of feminism.

19. As a result of China's one-child policy,
    a. the population of China has stabilized.
    b. a significant number of girl babies are missing.
    c. women have achieved full gender equity in China.
    d. lingering Confucian values have finally been rooted out.
    e. all of the above.

20. In spite of cultural prejudices against women in Asia, women have emerged as political
    leaders in all of the following countries *except*
    a. China.
    b. India.
    c. Myanmar (Burma).
    d. Pakistan.
    e. Sri Lanka.

MATCHING

Modern global agencies present an "alphabet soup" of acronyms, often difficult to remember. Try
to identify these acronyms. In the margin on the right, indicate what the letters stand for.

A.	EU	E.	ASEAN
B.	OPEC	F.	UN
C.	NAFTA	G.	NGO
D.	GATT	H.	WTO

1. ___ An alliance of oil-producing states for the purpose of regulating supply and prices.

2. ___ An economic alliance that includes most of the countries of Europe.

3. ___ An economic alliance of Canada, Mexico, and the United States.

4. ___ An economic alliance comprised of the industrializing nations of southeast Asia.

5. ___ Originally a union of noncommunist nations for the purpose of promoting free trade and
economic growth.

6. ___ An international agency that is not affiliated with any nation or government.

7. ___ An international body intended to resolve trade disputes with the power to enforce its
decisions.

8. ___ An international body with multiple missions: peace, security, health, education, and
human rights.

SEQUENCING

Place the following clusters of events in chronological order. Consider carefully how one event leads to another, and try to determine the internal logic of each sequence.

A.

_____ For a third time, Israel defeats an alliance of Arab states.

_____ Oil prices quadruple, triggering a global recession.

_____ With aid from the United States, Israel builds a powerful army and air force.

_____ Overproduction of oil creates a glut on global markets; oil prices drop again.

_____ OPEC imposes an embargo on oil exported to the United States.

B.

_____ Fighting continues among rival Afghan factions until the Taliban gains control and proclaims Afghanistan an Islamist state.

_____ A Soviet-backed coup establishes a socialist regime in Afghanistan.

_____ Following the September 11 attacks on the United States, the Northern Alliance and American forces crush the Taliban. The future of Afghanistan remains uncertain.

_____ Conservative Afghan Muslims react strongly against rapid social changes of the new regime and rebel.

_____ With support from abroad (including the United States), the Islamic *mujahideen* conduct a long and ultimately successful guerilla war against the Soviets.

_____ Soviet troops invade to regain control.

QUOTATIONS

For each of the following quotes, identify the speaker, if known, or the point of view. What is the significance of each passage?

1. "Suddenly we were seeing the West for the first time, the forbidden Berlin we had only seen on TV or heard about from friends. When we came home at dawn, I felt free for the first time in my life. I had never been happier."

2. "Barbie is an American woman who never wants to get pregnant and have babies. She never wants to look old, and this contradicts our culture. . . . Barbie is like a Trojan Horse. Inside it, it carries Western cultural influences, such as makeup and indecent clothes. Once it enters our society, it dumps these influences on our children."

3. "There's no question about it: the Internet is an information colony. From the moment you go online, you're confronted with English hegemony. It's not merely a matter of making the Net convenient for users in non-English-speaking countries. People have to face the fact that English speakers are not the whole world. What's the big deal about them, anyway? Our ideal is to create an exclusively Chinese-language network. It will be a Net that has Chinese characteristics, one that is an information superhighway for the masses."

4. "There once was a town in the heart of America where all life seemed to live in harmony with its surroundings. . . . Then a strange blight crept over the area and everything began to change . . . mysterious maladies swept the flocks of chickens, the cattle and sheep sickened and died. Everywhere was a shadow of death. The farmers spoke of much illness among their families. . . . There was as strange stillness. The birds, for example—where had they gone? . . . On the farms the hens brooded, but no chicks hatched. The farmers complained that they were unable to raise any pigs—the litters were small and the young survived only a few days. The apple trees were coming into bloom but no bees droned among the blossoms, so there was not pollination and there would be no fruit. The roadsides, once so attractive, were now lined with brown and withered vegetation as though swept by fire. . . . This town does not actually exist, but it might easily have a thousand counterparts in America or elsewhere in the world . . . every one of these disasters has actually happened somewhere. . . . A grim specter has crept upon us almost unnoticed, and this imagined tragedy may easily become a stark reality we all shall know."

5. "Women hold up half the sky."

MAP EXERCISES

1. Consider the states that are currently members of the European Union (Table 40.1, page 1137 in the textbook). Which western European nations have not yet joined the EU? What might be the advantages of not joining? What are the advantages of joining?

2. Thirteen additional nations are currently candidates to join the European Union, most of them from the former Soviet bloc. What might be the challenges of integrating these former communist economies into the long-time capitalist economies of western Europe?

3. Redraw the map of the world so that the size of each continent is roughly proportional to the number of people currently living with HIV/AIDS (see Map 40.2, page 1150).

4. Redraw the map of the world so that the size of each continent is roughly proportional to the current population (see Table 40.1, page 1143).

5. Consider the population data for major world regions (Table 40.2, page 1161). Calculate the percentage increase projected for each region between 2000 and 2050. Which world region is expected to experience the highest rate of increase? What impact might this increase have on the economy of that region? Which world region is expected to have the lowest rate of increase? What would be the economic impact of slow-growing (or declining) population?

Kandahar (2001). An Afghan woman returns to her homeland many years after fleeing to the west. She must reach the city of Kandahar in time to prevent her sister from committing suicide. Powerful images of life under the Taliban, a life often absurd yet at times also surprisingly beautiful. In both English and Pashtun.

East Is East (2000). About the hardships and rewards for the large family of a Pakistani father and a British mother living in Manchester, England, in 1971. Features both social conflicts and generational conflicts. Poignant and often funny.

Double Happiness (1995). The daughter of Chinese immigrants living in Canada struggles to fulfill the expectations of her traditional parents while at the same time pursuing her own dream of becoming an actress.

Mississippi Marsala (1992). About the pain and dislocation of migrants in a new land. An Indian family is expelled from Uganda in 1972 by dictator Idi Amin (because "Africa is for Africans") and resettles in Mississippi, where they must rebuild their lives. The plot features a romance between the daughter and a local black man (Denzel Washington).

El Norte (1984). Heartbreaking story of a brother and sister who flee the upheaval of Guatemala for the land of opportunity to the north (el norte). Shows the hardships of illegal immigrants. In Spanish with subtitles.

ANSWER KEY

CHAPTER 23: ANSWERS

STUDENT QUIZ

1. c	8. e	15. d
2. a	9. c	16. e
2. c	10. b	17. c
2. d	11. d	18. e
2. b	12. c	19. a
2. b	13. e	20. d
2. a	14. d	21. a

MATCHING

1. F	6. H
2. A	7. E
3. D	8. C
4. J	9. G
5. B	10. I

SEQUENCING

A. 2, 4, 1, 5, 3
B. 4, 2, 5, 1, 3

QUOTATIONS

1. Christopher Columbus's first impressions of the peoples he met in the Caribbean islands, in which he views the inhabitants of these islands as prospective converts to Christianity.

1. Afonso D'Alboquerque's account of the Battle of Hormuz in which he illustrates the effectiveness of the Portuguese artillery in a sea battle of early modern times.

CHAPTER 24: ANSWERS

STUDENT QUIZ

1. a	9. b	17. e
2. e	10. e	18. a
3. d	11. e	19. b
4. d	12. c	20. e
5. b	13. e	21. e
6. a	14. b	22. a
7. d	15. c	23. b
7. c	16. c	

MATCHING

1. D	7. J
1. F	8. I
1. H	9. B
1. G	10. L
1. E	11. C
6. K	12. A

SEQUENCING

A. 3, 1, 4, 2
A. 3, 2, 1, 4

QUOTATIONS

1. Martin Luther, responding to imperial authorities when they demanded that he recant his views.

1. Voltaire's battle cry against the Roman Catholic Church, which he considered an agent of oppression.

1. Louis XIV, "the sun king," who epitomized absolute monarchy, remarking on the immense power he held as a monarch who ruled by divine right.

1. Adam Smith propounding his belief about capitalism, that society as a whole benefits when individuals pursue their own economic interests.

CHAPTER 25: ANSWERS

STUDENT QUIZ

1. d	8. d	15. d
2. e	9. a	16. b
3. a	10. c	17. d
3. c	11. a	18. d
3. b	12. a	19. b
3. b	13. d	20. e
3. b	14. c	

MATCHING

1. D	7. J
2. E	8. H
3. C	9. F
4. A	10. K
5. B	11. G
6. L	12. I

A. 5, 3, 4, 2, 1
B. 3, 1, 5, 2, 4

QUOTATIONS

1. Aztec first impressions of Spanish forces; reveals Motecuzoma's fear of Spanish weapons in particular.

1. From James Cook's log; a description of his reception in Hawai`i; shows lack of metallurgy.

1. The Treaty of Tordesillas, 1494, which divided the unconquered world east and west between Spain and Portugal, a miscalculation that led to the Portuguese claim to Brazil.

1. Evasive response by a colonial viceroy to orders from the Spanish king, evidence that viceroys often acted on their own.

1. Account of the first year at Jamestown, where 90 percent of the colonists died from inadequate provisions.

1. Cortes to Motecuzoma, demanding Aztec gold.

CHAPTER 26: ANSWERS

STUDENT QUIZ

1. e	8. c	15. d
2. d	9. e	16. a
3. d	10. d	17. a
3. b	11. d	18. b
3. a	12. c	19. d
3. a	13. e	20. c
3. c	14. c	

MATCHING

1. J	6. B
1. D	7. H
1. E	8. A
1. G	9. F
1. C	10. I

SEQUENCING

A. 4, 1, 2, 3
A. 4, 3, 2, 5, 1
A. 3, 5, 4, 1, 2

QUOTATIONS

1. King Afonso I describing the disruption to his own society caused by Portuguese slave traders.

1. Olaudah Equiano describing the horrors of the middle passage.

CHAPTER 27: ANSWERS

STUDENT QUIZ

1. d	8. a	15. a
2. c	9. a	16. e
3. b	10. b	17. c
4. c	11. c	18. b
5. e	12. a	19. a
6. c	13. b	20. d
7. b	14. e	

MATCHING

1. H	6. D
2. E	7. I
3. A	8. G
4. C	9. F
5. B	10. J

SEQUENCING

A. 4, 2, 1, 3
B. 2, 3, 1, 5, 4
C. 3, 4, 2, 1

QUOTATIONS

1. From the "Closed Country Edict" of the Tokugawa shogunate (1635), which effectively sealed Japan off from any outside influences.

1. A letter from the Chinese emperor Qianlong to King George III of England in 1793 in which the emperor insisted on limited and carefully regulated outside trade.

1. A Western observer (actually the Jesuit missionary Matteo Ricci) describing the Confucian examination system and its impact on Chinese thought and learning.

1. Fabian Fucan of Japan, once a Christian convert, now denouncing the Jesuit missionaries as subversive.

CHAPTER 28: ANSWERS

STUDENT QUIZ

1. c	8. a	15. c
2. e	9. b	16. d
3. d	10. d	17. c
3. b	11. b	18. b
3. a	12. d	19. a
3. c	13. e	20. e
3. c	14. c	

MATCHING

1. G	7. C
2. E	8. L
3. H	9. J
4. B	10. K
5. D	11. A
6. F	12. I

SEQUENCING

A. 4, 3, 1, 5, 2
B. 3, 1, 4, 2

QUOTATIONS

1. Description of the *ghazi,* Muslim religious warriors who helped the Ottoman Turks defeat the Christian Byzantines.

1. Title claimed by Mehmed the Conqueror, Ottoman sultan, after he seized Constantinople and ended the Byzantine empire. The "two lands" are Europe and Asia; the "two seas" are the Black Sea and the Mediterranean Sea.

1. European diplomat Ghislain de Busbecq describing the hardiness of the Ottoman troops.

1. Babur, founder of the Mughal dynasty in India, describing his men's initial dislike of India compared to their central Asia homeland.

1. The Mughal emperor Akbar inviting various religious leaders to an interfaith dialogue.

CHAPTER 29: ANSWERS

STUDENT QUIZ

1. c	8. b	15. d
1. c	9. b	16. a
1. d	10. d	17. a
1. e	11. c	18. b
1. b	12. b	19. e
1. d	13. a	20. b
1. a	14. e	21. c

MATCHING

1 L	7. A
2. H	8. J
3. C	9. I
4. G	10. K
5. B	11. F
6. E	12. D

SEQUENCING

A. 3, 6, 4, 2, 1, 5
B. 2, 4, 3, 5, 1
C. 3, 5, 1, 4, 6, 2

QUOTATIONS

1. Otto von Bismarck setting Germany on a course that favors nationalism over political freedom.

1. Olympe de Gouges, "The Declaration of the Rights of Woman and the Female Citizen." This statement extends Locke's concept of natural rights to women as well as men.

1. Simón Bolívar expressing his bitterness at the dissolution of Gran Colombia.

1. Slogan of the National Assembly, the ideals embodied in the first constitution of the French Revolution.

1. The Declaration of Independence, written by Thomas Jefferson in 1776. Expresses the ideals of natural rights and contractual government laid out by John Locke almost a century before.

1. Slogan of American colonial resistance to British economic policies, before the revolution. Shows the relative narrow goals of the conflict: representative government and economic autonomy.

CHAPTER 30: ANSWERS

STUDENT QUIZ

1. b	8. e	15. c
2. b	9. b	16. c
2. e	10. d	17. a
2. c	11. a	18. e
2. d	12. c	19. e
2. a	13. a	20. e
2. d	14. e	

MATCHING

1. H	7. D
2. K	8. B
3. G	9. A
4. C	10. L
5. F	11. I
6. E	12. J

SEQUENCING

A. Two possible answers: 1, 3, 4, 2 more accurately describes the sequence in Britain and Europe. However, in the United States the use of interchangeable parts preceded the factory system, so the correct sequence would be 1, 2, 4, 3.

B. 2, 1, 3, 4

QUOTATIONS

1. A female coal drawer (Betty Harris) testifying before Parliament in 1842 about the conditions for women in the coal mines.

1. Thomas Malthus in "An Essay on the Principle of Population" in 1793 asserting that the human population will never catch up to the food supply; therefore, periodic famine is inevitable.

1. Argument that a woman's true place is in the home: here, Mrs. John Sandford in *Woman in Her Social and Domestic Character,* 1833.

1. Karl Marx and Friedrich Engels from *The Communist Manifesto* (1848). Marx and Engels argued that the class struggles engendered by industrialization would intensify, erupt into violence, and eventually lead to a more just, socialist society.

CHAPTER 31: ANSWERS

STUDENT QUIZ

1. e	8. a	15. d
2. c	9. c	16. b
2. d	10. e	17. b
2. d	11. d	18. a
2. b	12. c	19. e
2. c	13. e	20. a
2. a	14. a	

MATCHING

1. F	7. C
2. L	8. E
3. J	9. G
4. H	10. B
5. A	11. I
6. K	12. D

SEQUENCING

A. 2, 5, 1, 4, 3
B. 3, 2, 4, 1
C. 5, 2, 1, 4, 3

QUOTATIONS

1. Abraham Lincoln in 1858 while running for the Senate. This "house divided" speech and others given at the same time made Lincoln a national figure in the antislavery movement and led to his election in 1860.

1. "Declaration of Sentiments" from the Seneca Falls Convention of 1848. The document went on to demand full citizenship for women, including the right to vote.

1. The Emancipation Proclamation issued by President Lincoln January 1863. Note that Lincoln did not yet free all slaves, since five slave states were fighting with the Union. Full emancipation for all slaves followed with the Thirteenth Amendment to the Constitution in 1865.

1. An expression of the intentions of *La Reforma* made by a liberal politician, Ponciano Arriaga in 1856–57. This description describes the inequity of Mexican land distribution for a whole century following independence.

1. The United States Congress in 1892 justifying the continued exclusion of Chinese immigrants.

CHAPTER 32: ANSWERS

<u>STUDENT QUIZ</u>

1. b	8. b	15. b
2. e	9. e	16. c
3. a	10. d	17. a
4. c	11. a	18. a
5. c	12. e	19. b
6. d	13. b	20. d
7. a	14. e	

<u>MATCHING</u>

1. K	7. J
2. D	8. G
3. E	9. A
4. B	10. F
5. I	11. L
6. C	12. H

<u>SEQUENCING</u>

A. 1, 5, 2, 6, 4, 3, 7
B. 1, 6, 2, 5, 3, 4, 7
C. 1, 3, 5, 6, 4, 2, 7
D. 1, 4, 6, 5, 3, 2, 7

<u>QUOTATIONS</u>

1. Slogan of the Self-Strengthening Movement of nineteenth-century China, an effort to graft European science and technology onto traditional Confucian values.

1. From the Ottoman Constitution of 1908, the liberal political agenda of the Young Turks. Modeled after many Western constitutions, this document granted full civil rights and responsibilities to all ethnic and religious minorities within the empire.

1. Tsar Alexander II explaining to the Russian nobles the necessity of emancipating the serfs.

1. Commissioner Lin Zexu appealing to British Queen Victoria to stop the flow of opium into China, 1839. The letter was never delivered, the opium traffic continued, and Chinese efforts to stop it led to a disastrous war.

1. From the letter delivered by Commodore Matthew Perry to Japan in 1853. It was addressed to the Japanese emperor from the president of the United States, Millard Fillmore.

CHAPTER 33: ANSWERS

STUDENT QUIZ

1. e	9. a	17. c
1. d	10. b	18. e
1. b	11. e	19. c
1. a	12. e	20. b
1. c	13. d	21. a
1. e	14. a	22. e
1. e	15. d	23. e
1. d	16. e	24. a

MATCHING

1. F	7. J
2. D	8. K
3. A	9. H
4. I	10. L
5. B	11. C
6. E	12. G

SEQUENCING

A. 3, 4, 2, 5, 1, 6
B. 2, 4, 3, 1
C. 4, 2, 6, 1, 3, 5

QUOTATIONS

1. The Monroe Doctrine, issued by U.S. president James Monroe in 1823, stating that the U.S. government would not permit any future colonization in the New World. Later, the Monroe Doctrine became a rationalization for direct U.S. intervention in Latin America.

1. This could be any European imperialist asserting his cultural superiority. It happens to be Cecil Rhodes speaking specifically of British expansion into southern Africa in the 1870s.

1. The views of a social Darwinist, in this case the British philosopher Herbert Spencer. Social Darwinists argued that humanity as a whole benefited through the competitive struggle for survival and so nothing should be done to help the "weakest."

1. From "The White Man's Burden" by Rudyard Kipling in 1899. The poem was addressed to the American people shortly after the Spanish-American War. This passage refers to the thankless work of laboring abroad for the benefit of ungrateful colonial peoples.

1. Frederick Lugard justifies the British model of indirect rule in Africa.

CHAPTER 34: ANSWERS

<u>STUDENT QUIZ</u>

1. d	9. b	17. b
2. e	10. c	18. e
3. e	11. b	19. b
4. c	12. d	20. e
5. b	13. d	
6. d	14. a	
7. a	15. c	
8. a	16. d	

<u>MATCHING</u>

1. C	7. J
2. A	8. I
3. K	9. F
4. B	10. G
5. D	11. E
6. H	

<u>SEQUENCING</u>

A. 6, 2, 5, 4, 7, 1, 3, 8
B. 6, 3, 7, 1, 4, 2, 5
C. 3, 2, 5, 1, 6, 4

<u>QUOTATIONS</u>

1. U.S. president Woodrow Wilson asking Congress on 17 April for a formal declaration of war against Germany in response to submarine attacks on American vessels.

2. Slogan of the Bolshevik Party early in the revolution. Addresses three of the primary concerns of the Russian people: withdrawal from the war, an equitable distribution of land, and affordable food.

3. From the Treaty of Versailles of 1919, the terms imposed on Germany. In these passages, Germany was forced to accept full responsibility for the war and to agree to pay unspecified reparations to the Allies, terms that crippled the postwar German economy.

4. The first of Wilson's Fourteen Points and the U.S. proposal for a peace settlement after the war. Wilson recognized that the system of secret alliances had led to the war, but he was unable to persuade the other Allied leaders to endorse his program.

5. V. I. Lenin in his 1918 treatise on Bolshevik political theory, *State and Revolution,* arguing that capitalist democracy is inherently unequal and must be broken by the proletariat.

6. "Dulce et Decorum Est" by a young British poet and soldier, Wilfred Owen, who tried to demythologize the war with powerful images of the suffering of soldiers.

CHAPTER 35: ANSWERS

1. c	11. e
2. e	12. c
3. d	13. d
4. e	14. e
5. d	15. a
6. a	16. b
7. e	17. d
8. d	18. c
9. c	19. e
10. e	20. b

MATCHING

1. E	5. D
2. C	6. F
3. H	7. G
4. B	8. A

SEQUENCING

A. 2, 6, 4, 1, 3, 5
B. 2, 4, 1, 5, 3
C. 5, 4, 2, 1, 3

QUOTATIONS

1. An excerpt from John Steinbeck's novel of the depression, *The Grapes of Wrath,* which describes the mounting frustration and rage of unemployed Americans toward government and those in power.

2. Adolf Hitler presents his theory of racial purity in *Mein Kampf,* 1924.

3. Joseph Stalin, 1927, justifies the aggressive program of collectivization.

4. Mao Zedong on the peasant movement. Mao differed from Marx and Lenin in his belief that that revolution sprang from the rural peasantry.

CHAPTER 36: ANSWERS

<u>STUDENT QUIZ</u>

1. a	11. a
2. a	12. a
3. e	13. c
4. c	14. d
5. a	15. d
6. d	16. b
7. d	17. e
8. c	18. e
9. d	19. a
10. c	20. d

<u>MATCHING</u>

1. F	6. G
2. H	7. I
3. B	8. E
4. J	9. C
5. D	10. A

<u>SEQUENCING</u>

A. 5, 6, 2, 1, 3, 4
B. 3, 1, 6, 2, 4, 5

<u>QUOTATIONS</u>

1. Bal Gangadhar Tilak, from his address to the Indian National Congress, calling for a boycott of British goods and resistance to British rule.

2. A white settler in Kenya candidly expressing the view held by many colonial administrators.

3. Marcus Garvey, who championed a "Back to Africa" movement, calling for the creation of an autonomous black state.

CHAPTER 37: ANSWERS

WORLD WAR II ALIGNMENTS

NATION	ALLIED OR AXIS	LEADER DURING WWII
Britain	Allied	Winston Churchill
China	Occupied by Japan	Jiang Jieshi and Mao Zedong (resistance)
France	Occupied by Germany	Marshal Pétain headed puppet government
		Charles de Gaulle led French resistance
Germany	Axis	Adolf Hitler
Italy	Axis	Benito Mussolini
Japan	Axis	Minister Tojo Hideki, Emperor Hirohito
Soviet Union	Allied	Joseph Stalin
United States	Allied	Franklin D. Roosevelt, later Harry S. Truman

STUDENT QUIZ

1. d	8. d	15. c
2. c	9. c	16. d
3. b	10. d	17. a
4. e	11. b	18. b
5. d	12. b	19. a
6. b	13. e	20. c
7. c	14. e	21. d

SEQUENCING

A. 3, 2, 5, 1, 4
B. 2, 4, 1, 5, 3
C. 5, 3, 1, 2, 4

QUOTATIONS

1. Adolf Hitler exulting that with Japan on their side the Axis powers would win the war.

2. The Truman Doctrine of President Harry S. Truman in 1947 stating that the United States would supply military aid to any nation fighting against a communist takeover.

3. Winston Churchill, March 1946, describing the Soviet Union's control of all of eastern Europe within a year of the end of the war.

4. Joint statement issued by Adolf Hitler and British prime minister Neville Chamberlain after the Munich Conference in September 1938, whereby Britain agreed to Germany's demand to take the Sudetenland from Czechoslovakia. This policy of appeasement only convinced Hitler that the British lacked the will to fight.

5. Agreement by Churchill, Roosevelt, and Stalin at the Yalta Conference, February 1945, to hold democratic elections in all the territories liberated from the Axis powers. Of course, no such elections were held in the states controlled by the Soviet Union.

6. Heinrich Himmler, in an address to SS generals, justifying the mass murder of Jews.

CHAPTER 38: ANSWERS

STUDENT QUIZ

1. c	8. d	15. b
2. c	9. e	16. d
3. e	10. e	17. d
4. e	11. a	18. e
5. b	12. d	19. a
6. a	13. d	20. e
7. b	14. e	

MATCHING

1. C	7. E
2. D	8. K
3. F	9. H
4. L	10. I
5. B	11. A
6. J	12. G

SEQUENCING

A. 3, 5, 4, 1, 2
B. 3, 2, 1, 5, 4
C. 4, 5, 2, 1, 3
D. 2, 1, 4, 6, 3, 5

QUOTATIONS

1. Fidel Castro, in 1961, a few months after the failed Bay of Pigs invasion, publicly announcing his commitment to communism.

2. Nikita Khrushchev, in his 1961 "Report to the Communist Party Congress," discussing the shortcomings of the capitalist system.

CHAPTER 39: ANSWERS

<u>STUDENT QUIZ</u>

1. b	8. e	15. b
2. d	9. b	16. d
3. c	10. c	17. d
4. c	11. e	18. b
5. e	12. d	19. c
6. a	13. a	20. e
7. b	14. e	

<u>MATCHING</u>

1. L	8. N
2. F	9. H
3. K	10. G
4. M	11. I
5. B	12. A
6. D	13. E
7. J	14. C

<u>SEQUENCING</u>

A. 2, 6, 1, 4, 3, 5
B. 5, 2, 1, 3, 4
C. 4, 1, 3, 5, 2 (or possibly 4, 1, 2, 5, 3)

<u>QUOTATIONS</u>

1. Mohandas Gandhi expressing his philosophy of forgiveness and nonviolence several days before his assassination in 1948.

2. Leader of independent Ghana, Kwame Nkrumah, arguing for African unity and neutrality in the cold war in 1961. His dream of a united Africa has not yet materialized.

3. India's first president, Jawaharlal Nehru, articulating the position of nonalignment as an honorable alternative to cold war alliances at the Bandung Conference in Indonesia in 1955.

4. The Balfour Declaration, 1917: statement issued by British foreign secretary Balfour in support of the concept of a Jewish homeland in Palestine, the basis for Zionist claims before and after World War II.

5. In a speech to the Muslim League in 1940, Muhammad Ali Jinnah, leader of India's Muslims, during the first half of the twentieth century, formulating some of the reasons why Muslims deserved and already constituted their own nation.

6. Nelson Mandela, leader of the African National Congress at his trial in 1963 shortly before he was jailed. He was released in 1990 and became the first black president of South Africa in 1994.

CHAPTER 40: ANSWERS

<u>STUDENT QUIZ</u>

1. c	8. d	15. d
2. b	9. c	16. c
3. d	10. e	17. e
4. e	11. c	18. a
5. a	12. e	19. b
6. b	13. b	20. a
7. d	14. e	

<u>MATCHING</u>

1. B: Organization of Petroleum Exporting Countries
2. A: European Union
3. C: North American Free Trade Agreement
4. E: Association of Southeast Asian Nations
5. D: General Agreement on Tariffs and Trade
6. G: nongovernmental organization
7. H: World Trade Organization
8. F: United Nations

<u>SEQUENCING</u>

A. 2, 4, 1, 5, 3
B. 5, 1, 6, 2, 4, 3

<u>QUOTATIONS</u>

1. Kristina Matschat, an East German, on her disbelief and happiness when the Berlin Wall fell.

2. Majid Chaderis, director of Iran's Institute for the Intellectual Development of Children and Young Adults, on the cultural gulf between Islamic Iran and the West, and on the unwanted cultural influence and even dominance of the West.

3. Xia Hong, a manager for an Internet access provider in Shanghai, lamenting the dominance of the English language on the Internet.

4. Scientist Rachel Carson in *Silent Spring,* warning about environmental dangers of the modern world.

5. Mao Zedong, acknowledging the importance of women's roles in a statement reflective of the communist dedication to women's rights and gender equality.